Authoritarianism in an Age of Demo

Far from sweeping the globe uniformly, the third wave of democratization" left burgeoning republics and resilient dictatorships in its wake. Applying more than a year of original fieldwork in Egypt, Iran, Malaysia, and the Philippines, Jason Brownlee shows that the mixed record of recent democratization is best deciphered through a historical and institutional approach to authoritarian rule. Exposing the internal organizations that structure elite conflict, Brownlee demonstrates why the critical soft-liners needed for democratic transitions have been dormant in Egypt and Malaysia but outspoken in Iran and the Philippines. When regimes maintain coalitions through ruling parties, democratization becomes an uphill battle against fortified incumbents. Systematic cross-regional comparison shows how the Egyptian and Malaysian regimes have become nearly impregnable through party-based coalitions. Meanwhile, the Islamic Republic has seen open elite factionalism and the rise of a viable, although unsuccessful, reform movement. More hopefully, the downfall of Ferdinand Marcos in the Philippines demonstrates why an institutionally weak regime is vulnerable to opponents pushing for change forcefully rather than hesitantly, as Iran's reform movement did. Party institutions long predate the third wave and promise to far outlast its passing. By establishing how ruling parties originated and why they impede change, Brownlee illuminates the problem of contemporary authoritarianism and informs the promotion of durable democracy.

Jason Brownlee is Assistant Professor of Government at the University of Texas at Austin. Prior to arriving at the University of Texas, he was a postdoctoral Fellow at Stanford University's Center on Democracy, Development, and the Rule of Law. Professor Brownlee's research addresses domestic and international processes of democratization. His work has appeared in *Comparative Politics*, *Studies in Comparative International Development*, and the *Journal of Democracy*.

Authoritarianism in an Age of Democratization

JASON BROWNLEE

University of Texas, Austin

CAMBRIDGE UNIVERSITY PRESS
Cambridge, New York, Melbourne, Madrid, Cape Town, Singapore, São Paulo

Cambridge University Press
32 Avenue of the Americas, New York, NY 10013-2473, USA

www.cambridge.org
Information on this title: www.cambridge.org/9780521869515

First published 2007

Printed in the United States of America

A catalog record for this publication is available from the British Library.

Library of Congress Cataloging in Publication Data

Brownlee, Jason, 1974–
Authoritarianism in an age of democratization / Jason Brownlee.
  p. cm.
Includes bibliographical references and index.
ISBN-13: 978-0-521-86951-5 (hardback)
ISBN-13: 978-0-521-68966-3 (pbk.)
  1. Authoritarianism. 2. Democratization. I. Title.
JC480.B76 2007
320.53–dc22   2006029809

ISBN 978-0-521-86951-5 hardback
ISBN 978-0-521-68966-3 paperback

To my parents,
Mac and Becky Brownlee

The nobles are to be considered in two different manners; that is, they are either to be ruled so as to make them entirely dependent on your fortunes, or else not. Those that are thus bound to you and are not rapacious, must be honored and loved.... But when they are not bound to you of set purpose and for ambitious ends, it is a sign that they think more of themselves than of you; and from such men the prince must guard himself and look upon them as secret enemies, who will help to ruin him when in adversity...

— Niccolò Machiavelli, The Prince, Chapter IX

Almost everywhere, the trend after independence has been in one of two directions: toward a one-party state with consequent stability (if the resulting single party grouped the major elements) or toward a breakdown of the party system with consequent instability...

— Immanuel Wallerstein, Africa: The Politics of Independence

Contents

List of Figures and Tables

Figures

Tables

Abbreviations and Acronyms

ACC	Association of Combatant Clerics
AF	Alternative Front
ASU	Arab Socialist Union
COMELEC	Commission on Elections
DAP	Democratic Action Party
DPI	Database of Political Institutions
IAEA	International Atomic Energy Agency
IIPF	Islamic Iran Participation Front
IMF	International Monetary Fund
IMP	Independence of Malaya Party
IRC	Islamic Revolutionary Council
IRP	Islamic Republican Party
KBL	Kilusang Bagong Lipunan [New Society Movement]
LABAN	Lakas ñg Bayan [Power of the People] Movement
Lakas-NUCD	Lakas ñg Sambayanan [Strength of People's Power] – National Union of Christian Democrats
LP	Liberal Party
LR	Liberation Rally
MB	Muslim Brotherhood
MCA	Malaya Chinese Association
MCP	Malayan Communist Party
MIC	Malayan Indian Congress
MP	Member of Parliament
Namfrel	National Citizens Movement for Free Elections
NDP	National Democratic Party
NEP	New Economic Policy

NF	National Front
NOC	National Operations Council
NP	Nacionalista Party
NPA	National People's Army
NPUP	National Progressive Unionist Party
PAS	Parti Islam Se-Malaysia [Islamic Party of Malaysia]
PDP	Philippine Democratic Party
PRM	Parti Rakyat Malaysia [People's Party of Malaysia]
RAM	Reform the Armed Forces Movement
RCC	Revolutionary Command Council
SCC	Society of Combatant Clergy
UMNO	United Malays National Organization
Unido	United Democratic Nationalist Organization

Acknowledgments

Many colleagues and friends in the United States and abroad supported me as I researched and wrote this book. Quite a few of them pushed me to explore much more intellectual terrain than I had planned, from elections to parties to social conflict. Although I remain fully responsible for the argument made here, as well as whatever errors linger, I gratefully acknowledge the role these persons played in making this book much more than it otherwise would have been.

My first thanks go to the members of my Ph.D. committee in Princeton University's Department of Politics. Atul Kohli's patient counsel played a critical role in the evolution of my ideas. At key points, he steered me back on course when my efforts would otherwise have gone astray. Nancy Bermeo supported my work with generous praise and incisive comments, boosting my enthusiasm while illuminating new challenges. Deborah Yashar helped me clarify fuzzy claims and inchoate ideas. Finally, Bob Vitalis graciously agreed to join the committee as an outside, and scrupulous, reader. He has taught me how to strengthen my work while enjoying it all the more.

Beyond recognizing this immediate circle of advisors, I thank three close colleagues who responded to rough drafts with sharp suggestions. Dan Slater welcomed me to "travel" beyond the Middle East and guided me into the region he knows so well. Moreover, he graciously commented on the entire manuscript, suggesting numerous improvements that I endeavored to make. David Waldner relentlessly pushed me to expand the theory's scope, a charge I assumed with some reluctance but reflect on with deep gratitude. Completing this auxiliary committee is Ben Smith, who helped me think about what makes autocracy work (and why we should study that more).

The list of individuals who have commented on or otherwise aided this project is at least twice as long as I am able to include here. I express my sincere thanks to Kamran Aghaie, Lisa Anderson, Michele Penner Angrist, Aslı Bâli, Will Barndt, Eva Bellin, Marc Berenson, Cathy Boone, Bill Case, Gladstone Cuarteros, Larry Diamond, Yoav Di-Capua, Tyler Dickovick, Kent Eaton, Charles Franklin, Barbara Geddes, John Gershman, Ellis Goldberg, Fred Greenstein, Jeff Herbst, Steve Heydemann, Amaney Jamal, Maye Kassem, Charlie Kurzman, Steve Levitsky, Evan Lieberman, John Londregan, Ellen Lust-Okar, Jim Mahoney, Eric McDaniel, Patrick McDonald, Nagla Mostafa, Pete Moore, Negin Nabavi, Marina Ottaway, Marsha Pripstein-Posusney, Elliot Ratzman, Liz Rosenberg, Nil Satana, Andreas Schedler, Oliver Schlumberger, Philippe Schmitter, Samer Shehata, Amy Shuster, Richard Snyder, Jeannie Sowers, Josh Stacher, Kathryn Stoner-Weiss, Andrew Tabler, Julie Taylor, Josh Tucker, Lucan Way, and Carrie Rosefsky Wickham. Matt Johnson and Laura Sylvester ably assisted me during the final stage of research and revisions. Two anonymous reviewers at Cambridge University Press provided insightful comments on the manuscript. I am especially grateful to Arang Keshavarzian and Erik Kuhonta, colleagues from Princeton, whose early observations helped me discern the ways institutions shaped behavior.

Institutions are not only the core of this book's thesis, they were the prerequisite for its production. In addition to the individuals named here, several organizations enabled the public presentation and execution of my research. My deep thanks go to the Comparative Politics Research Seminar at Princeton University, the Woodrow Wilson Scholars Program, the Society for Comparative Research, the European University Institute, the American Political Science Association, the Middle East Studies Association, and the Institute for Qualitative Research Methods, whose inaugural training camp had a formative impact on my research design. Financial support was provided by Princeton University, Princeton's Center for the Study of Religion, the MacArthur Foundation, the American Research Center in Egypt, the American Institute of Iranian Studies, the Association of Princeton Graduate Alumni, the Princeton Institute for International and Regional Studies, and the Fulbright Foundation. In addition, the Center on Democracy, Development, and the Rule of Law at Stanford University generously supported a year of research and rewriting. A stellar production team at Cambridge University Press has allowed me to consolidate the work begun under these institutions and realize the confidence earlier colleagues placed in the project. I feel incredibly fortunate to have experienced Lew Bateman's deft editorial direction and the craftsmanship of copy editors Ruth Homrighaus and Laura Lawrie.

While completing research abroad, I incurred countless debts to individuals and institutions, who selflessly shared their knowledge and time. Among the many who facilitated my work are Saad Eddin Ibrahaim and the Ibn Khaldun Center for Development, Mustafa Kemal Al-Sayid and the Center for the Study of Developing Countries at Cairo University, Pedram Saeed and the Parliamentary Research Center in Tehran, and Fazil Irwan at the Institute of Strategic and International Studies Malaysia. Special credit goes to Joel Rocamora and his gracious staff at the Institute for Popular Democracy in Manila, whose generosity and attention enabled a whirlwind tour interviewing the Philippine political elite.

I send heartfelt thanks to Larry David, Darren Star, and Joss Whedon, whose projects pleasantly distracted me from my own.

I am grateful to Joan Asseff for her cheer and encouragement as I completed this book during the past year.

Finally, my deepest love and gratitude go to my parents, Mac and Becky Brownlee. Beyond innumerable amounts of moral and logistical support, they were my closest advisors as I chose this subject and took it forward. I dedicate this book to them.

Introduction

Authoritarianism in an Age of Democratization

In the last quarter of the twentieth century, democratically elected governments replaced authoritarian regimes at an astounding rate. From the end of the Portuguese dictatorship in 1974 to the Mexican opposition's victory in 2000, more than five dozen democracies were established or restored in Europe, Latin America, Asia, and Africa (Huntington 1991: 14–15; Diamond 1999: 25). Among the most inspiring stories of this so-called third wave of democratization was the 1986 overthrow of President Ferdinand Marcos in the Philippines: Filipinos flooded the streets of Manila to end Marcos's regime. Their accomplishment seemed to promise that peaceful opposition could transform repressive regimes into representative ones.

When the people of the Philippines again took to the streets exactly twenty years later, however, their actions were the bellwether of a more troubling trend. On 24 February 2006, Philippine president Gloria Macapagal Arroyo declared a state of emergency, closed opposition newspapers, and began detaining alleged conspirators. It was not Arroyo's first encounter with coup plots or mass demonstrations: These were common occurrences in the raucous post-Marcos era. Political instability had plagued the country's last autocrat, and it continued to plague his elected successors.

If twenty years of "People Power" had failed to consolidate democracy in the Philippines, the political trends were considerably bleaker elsewhere. Five time zones away from the Philippines, Egyptian president Hosni Mubarak appeared to have evaded the travails dogging Arroyo. Nearly a year earlier, the long-ruling Mubarak had garnered international and domestic acclaim for allowing opposition candidates to participate in the upcoming contest for the presidency. By the day of the Philippine protests in February 2006, Mubarak had begun his "elected" fifth six-year term in office, whereas the second-place finisher was serving a five-year prison sentence for his activities in the opposition. If Philippine democratization bestowed an ambiguous legacy, the contours of Egyptian authoritarianism were all too stark: Thirty years of political liberalization, including the latest sheen of presidential campaigning, had neither dislodged incumbent elites nor empowered their opponents. Although Filipinos had ousted one dictator and labored to bolster their troubled democracy, Egyptian activists struggled in vain to curtail authoritarianism.

In light of events in the Philippines and Egypt, it is clear that the third wave left both burgeoning republics and durable dictatorships in its wake. Thirty years after the third wave began, the foundations of democracy remained unsteady in many countries, and in others they were utterly absent. The persistence of regimes such as Egypt's under Mubarak has confounded the expectation that authoritarianism was merely a transitional phase before democracy, proving instead that under certain conditions autocracies can last. This stark lesson is not new, but it is novel in the context of trends in political science scholarship. As democracy flourished in unexpected territory, political scientists forecast the downfall of many remaining autocrats. But the well-studied epoch of the third wave was only part of the story. The remainder is a tale of authoritarianism in an age of democratization.

This tale – the story of the embattled Arroyo and the emboldened Mubarak writ large – is the subject of this book's investigation. What forces set these two countries on such disparate paths? What factors distinguish the debility of Marcos's regime and subsequent administrations from the surfeit of authority enjoyed by Mubarak and his predecessors? The basic answer of this book is that institutional differences separate unstable regimes from durable dictatorships. The organizations structuring elite relations and decision making determine whether an autocrat's coalition will fragment, thereby opening space for the opposition, or cohere, excluding rival movements in the process. As the book's first epigraph from Machiavelli implies, undemocratic regimes are not inherently fragile; they weaken when their leaders drive dissatisfied elites into the opposition's ranks. Preventing this from happening entails more than the individual authority of an especially charismatic, willful, or ruthless dictator: It requires organizations, most commonly political parties, that dominate national affairs and regulate elite conflict. Such "ruling parties" generate political power for the members of a dictator's coalition. They thereby bind together self-interested leaders and ensure continued allegiance. The process is self-reinforcing in two respects: When factions of opportunistic leaders are bound together institutionally, the ruling party provides collective benefits for the coalition's members and draws them centripetally, as it were, to eschew the opposition. And the opposition, denied insider allies, remains weak and marginal to national decision making. Its exclusion compounds advantages already enjoyed by regime elites and magnifies the benefits to insiders of working through the ruling party. Deflecting a democratic tide, ruling parties have been the root cause of regime persistence in much of Africa, the Middle East, and Asia.

Four Cases, Two Trends

To show how the emergence of democracy and the persistence of dictatorship have hinged on parties, this book draws on original research from Egypt, Iran, Malaysia, and the Philippines. The cases provide valuable variation along an array of potential explanations for why autocratic regimes fared so differently at holding onto power during the same period, roughly the final quarter of the twentieth century. My approach is explicitly comparative: I look at similarities and contrasts across cases, drawing conclusions based on the links and gaps between putative causes and outcomes of interest. The cases represent the mixed yield of the third wave of democratization, a period during which some dictators suddenly lost power, whereas their peers elsewhere retained it.

One indicator of the variance in political contestation between the cases is each regime's performance in elections they held and attempted to control. Not all authoritarian regimes permit such elections, but most do, and the practice became increasingly common in the 1980s and 1990s. Results in these "limited elections," manipulated as they are to the advantage of incumbents, act as a barometer of a regime's control over the political arena and the opposition's capacity to contest that dominance. Each of this book's four selected regimes held limited multiparty (or, in the case of Iran, multifactional) elections during the third-wave era. On their own, these elections neither catapulted the opposition into office nor insulated rulers from challenge. In two cases (Egypt, Malaysia), the opposition consistently failed to make electoral gains against the regime, while the other pair of regimes (Iran, the Philippines) proved more susceptible to their opponents' campaigns.

The Egyptian regime currently led by President Mohammed Hosni Mubarak (r. 1981–present) is one of the oldest authoritarian regimes in the developing world. Inaugurated in 1952 by a military coup that overthrew the country's monarchy, it has been run since then by a small circle of officers and apparatchiks. From 1954 to 1976, party politics was limited to a single organization connected to the president. From 1976 onward, presidents Anwar Sadat (r. 1970–1981) and Mubarak have overseen a period of "guided multipartyism" in which they allowed a total of eight parliamentary elections by 2005. The elections have been overtly autocratic in their process and results: Throughout this period, the ruling party has maintained a supermajority (a two-thirds majority) of seats in the People's Assembly (Majlis al-Sh'ab). Thus, a pluralist veneer has not kept the Egyptian regime from dominating multiparty elections in the same way that it lorded over the single-party polls of a prior period. At best, opposition groups have managed periodically to win approximately a quarter of seats in parliament, but they have never disrupted the hegemony of the ruling political organization established after the 1952 coup. Durable authoritarianism, not democratization, has characterized Egyptian politics for the past half-century.

On the eastern edge of the Middle East, the Islamic Republic of Iran has experienced the kind of open elite conflicts that Egyptian rulers have managed to suppress or mend. Although the Egyptian leadership remains cohesive, Iran's political elite has been rent into competing factions, one of which openly advocates the regime's democratization. This internal contest was not evident in the brutal aftermath of the 1979 revolution, when ascendant religious leaders quashed attempts by rival clerics and lay politicians to codify popular sovereignty in the nascent regime. But a short while later, clergy close to the Ayatollah Ruhollah Khomeini (r. 1979–1989) began feuding among themselves. After a brief attempt at operating through a common party, elite factions publicly competed against one another in elections for the country's parliament and presidency. Khomeini's successor, Leader Ali Khamenei (r. 1989–present), failed to insulate himself from opposition, and in the 1990s a well-supported and influential alliance of center-right and left-wing elites collaborated against him and won election. This movement for democratic reform controlled the elected portion of Iran's government for four years, providing an opportunity for political change unparalleled in other autocratic regimes of the Middle East. Underestimating the intransigence of their adversaries, the reformists ultimately squandered this chance at transforming Iran. But as their movement suffered defeat and Khamenei's faction reasserted control, political authority in the Islamic Republic remained weak and contested, vulnerable to the turbulence of elite conflict that Egypt has so consistently evaded.

In Southeast Asia, the experiences of Malaysia and the Philippines mirror the Egyptian-Iranian contrast between elite unity and uncompetitive elections on the one hand and elite discord and contested elections on the other. A third as populous as Egypt and twice as prosperous, the economic dynamo of Malaysia bears striking political similarity to the Middle East's largest state. For more than fifty years, Malaysia has been ruled by a single party, one that has proven invincible in the stilted contest of electoral politics. Given Malaysia's advanced socioeconomic development, its durability as a Southeast Asian autocracy is especially intriguing. In the context of rapid economic growth over the past three decades, Malaysia's ruling party has never lost the supermajority commanded by its parliamentary coalition. This trend of electoral dominance began long before the third wave, in experimental polls held by the British colonial administration. Since Malaysia gained statehood in 1957, the United Malays National Organization (UMNO) has trumped its opponents in no fewer than eleven national parliamentary elections. Consequently, the country's premier has always come from UMNO. Between 1981 and 2003, the redoubtable Mahathir Mohamad filled this post, ruling longer than any of his predecessors and nearly coterminously with Mubarak in Egypt. Both men blocked their opponents from power during the very period of world history in which autocrats around the globe seemed to be flailing.

In this dubious achievement, Mahathir's regime far surpassed the brittle autocracy of Ferdinand Marcos (r. 1972–1986) in the neighboring Philippines, which has not experienced the prolonged dominance of a sole party since gaining its independence from the United States in 1946. The archipelago nation of ninety million (more populous than Iran or Egypt) has been plagued by weak parties. Consequently, the pattern of elections is essentially the inverse of trends in Egypt and Malaysia. Power oscillates between parties, and politicians are constantly realigning themselves to pursue opportunities for advancement. The prevalence of elite factionalism in the Philippines implies a basic similarity with politics in Iran: Rulers in both countries have a difficult time accumulating and exercising authority. As one leader rises, his or her ascent seems to push other prominent figures into the opposition. Marcos reintroduced multiparty elections under restrictive conditions in 1978 and was ousted from power within two electoral cycles. His defeat by People Power matches (and indeed helped to create) the archetypal narrative of third-wave democratization: An increasingly unpopular ruler used elections as a ploy to sustain his power and inadvertently catalyzed his own defeat. Yet when we place the Marcos regime in the historical context of earlier Philippine politics and in a comparative perspective with Egypt, Iran, and Malaysia, we can see why that story is incomplete. It was not elections that toppled Marcos but, rather, the underlying volatility of political power in the absence of party institutions, an instability that had plagued presidents of the Philippines before and would trouble those who came after him.

Figure 0.1 depicts the varied electoral performance of regimes in Egypt, Iran, Malaysia, and the Philippines since their founding. The graph provides the share of parliament won by the regime's principal party or faction through elections. For the sake of comprehensiveness, this figure includes the Philippines' period of unsteady democratic rule before Marcos declared martial law in 1972. These data do not reflect consistently free and fair electoral outcomes. Rather, they indicate the regime's relative capacity to manipulate results and marginalize its opponents. In this respect, the Philippine regimes – both democratic (1935–1972) and autocratic (1972–1986) – have been weak compared to those of Egypt and Malaysia. With one exception (the 1969 polls that UMNO froze), these countries' presidents and premiers have consistently prevented the opposition from gaining a substantial hold in the legislature. Iran's regime, like the Philippine regime, has proven less capable of blocking the opposition in its postrevolutionary history.

What Autocrats' Elections Are and Are Not

By the end of the twentieth century, most authoritarian regimes practiced some form of "political liberalization," a broad concept that denotes the lifting of earlier restrictions on individual expression and opposition organization (O'Donnell and Schmitter 1986: 7). Yet in many cases, liberalization has not brought democratization: Regimes have permitted opposition movements to contest elections but have stopped short of rotating power or allowing fair elections that would have risked their secure tenure in office. Indeed, given the strong continuities of this period, it might be more accurate to call the third wave a period of plebiscitarian politics, in which liberalization measures backfired on some rulers but did not threaten others, than to consider it a period of democratization.

Scholars have long disagreed about the import of limited elections. Observing authoritarian regimes two centuries apart, Alexis de Tocqueville and Aleksandr Gelman reached contradictory conclusions about the dangers autocrats face when tinkering with political reform. De Tocqueville saw regime concessions as destabilizing: "[E]xperience teaches us that, generally speaking, the most perilous moment for a bad government

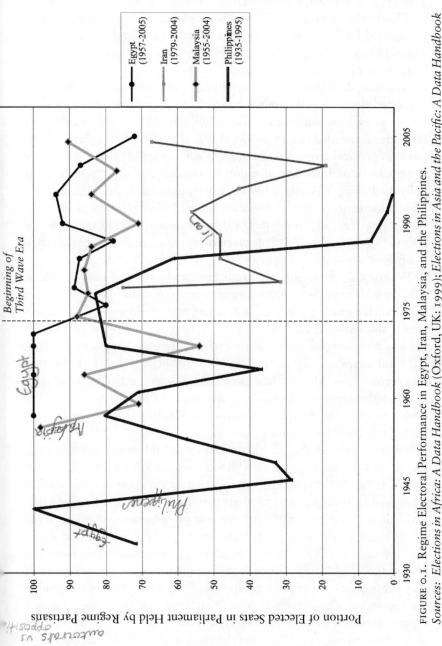

FIGURE O.I. Regime Electoral Performance in Egypt, Iran, Malaysia, and the Philippines.
Sources: Elections in Africa: A Data Handbook (Oxford, UK: 2001); *Elections in Asia and the Pacific: A Data Handbook* (Oxford, UK: 1999), and recent media reports. See individual chapters for citations on the 2000 and 2005 Egyptian elections, the 2004 Iranian elections, and the 2004 Malaysian elections.

is one when it seeks to mend its ways," he declared (Tocqueville 1955: 176–177). In contrast, Gelman thought political openings allowed incumbent leaders to deceive and distract their opponents. "Liberalization is an unclenched fist," he said, "but the hand is the same and at any moment it could be clenched again into a fist" (Brzezinski 1989: 45–46, quoted in Shin 1994: 142–143).

Following de Tocqueville, many scholars have seen inclusion by means of limited elections as a path to change. In their landmark study of transitions away from authoritarianism, Guillermo O'Donnell and Philippe Schmitter contended that post–World War II autocrats "can justify themselves in political terms only as transitional powers" (1986: 15) and saw a slippery slope from liberalization to democratization: "[O]nce some individual and collective rights have been granted, it becomes increasingly difficult to justify withholding others," they claimed (1986: 10). Along the same lines, Giuseppe DiPalma wrote that "dictatorships do not endure" (1990: 33), and Adam Przeworski reasoned that "liberalization is inherently unstable" (1991: 58).

Yet given the enduring and nontransitional nature of many autocracies, these claims overstate the danger elections pose to rulers. Malaysian premier Mahathir's 5–0 record of winning parliamentary elections is less memorable than Marcos's 3–1 record seeking the Philippine presidency, but it is no less significant. Contrary to the intuition that elections destabilize autocracies, many parties like Mahathir's UMNO survive elections on a regular basis. Most of these polls are not single-party affairs but races in which the opposition can participate, sometimes with great verve. The longevity of ruling parties in this context challenges the Tocquevillian perspective on liberalization.

If elections are not the "death of dictatorship" (Huntington 1991: 174), are they instead the autocrat's livelihood? Gelman's description of liberalization as "an unclenched fist" echoes in works that have not only framed elections as a common feature of authoritarianism but even posited that manipulated elections may reinforce and prolong autocratic rule (Linz 1975: 236; Hermet 1978: 14; Joseph 1997: 375; Chehabi and Linz 1998: 18; Remmer 1999: 349; Przeworski 2001: 15–16). Elections, in this view, are not the lid of Pandora's box, unleashing a torrent of political change, they are a safety valve for regulating societal discontent and confining the opposition. The durable authoritarian regimes of Egypt and Malaysia support this view of elections as mechanisms of control. But the opposition's electoral success in Iran and the Philippines signify that opposition activists may turn a regime's pressure valve into a spingboard for entering government.

The shift to authoritarianism with multiparty elections, then, does not represent an unwitting step toward full democratization, but neither do manipulated elections automatically protect rulers by reducing international pressure and corralling the opposition. Autocrats' elections, I maintain, are best viewed as one of the later stages in a long political process that may lead either to durable authoritarianism or to opportunities for democratization. When elections deal surprise defeats to autocrats, they culminate opposition groups' efforts to break the regime's dominance. In this sense, election results in authoritarian contexts tend to ratify rather than redistribute the power that competing groups wield.

Manipulated elections do not signify change in themselves, but they do provide a visible indicator of political competition, even as they call for deeper inquiry into the sources of such contestation. Despite being held under conditions that are neither free nor fair, elections under authoritarian regimes provide information about rulers, their critics, and the support competing factions command in the wider population. From Peru to Ukraine, electoral defeats for dictators have become what military withdrawals were in the 1980s: a signal that power has shifted from self-appointed leaders to popularly supported movements. Figure 0.1 confirms that there is nothing inherently competitive about elections in nondemocratic regimes, but surprise victories by Marcos's challengers and Iran's reform movement show that oppositionists can make headway in elections. The "stunning defeats" of incumbents are a sign to look closely at prior events and the hidden arena of a regime's internal politics (Huntington 1991: 178). Because autocrats' elections entail public clashes between opposing political factions, they provide a useful lens for gauging the distribution of power between a regime's coalition and its foes, even when they are corrupted by fraud and interference. When opposition candidates win elections, they demonstrate a capacity for surmounting the imposed constraints on political activity. Such victories may then provide leverage for effecting foundational changes in the allocation and use of national authority. Viewed from another angle, elections provide information about autocrats' control over the influential elites who support them in the electoral subterfuge that allows them to win. The electoral victories of dictators – premised as they are on collaboration against the opposition – evince elite cohesion and internal political stability, whereas electoral losses are the aftershocks of coalitional fissures.

In sum, then, elections under authoritarianism tend to reveal political trends rather than propel them. This interpretation differs from conventional democratization approaches as well as more simplistic, popular treatments of elections.[1] Viewing elections as symptoms, not causes, of regime change or regime durability directs attention further back in the chain of explanation to the nerve center of authoritarianism: the ruling organization and the coalition it houses.

Ruling Parties and Regime Persistence

Political institutions govern the interactions of individuals and groups. They set out the "rules of the game" (North 1990: 3). In developing countries, these rules are engrained within organizations that comprise a certain set of members. Thus, some bodies, such as political parties, may be both institutions and organizations (Knight 1992: 3). The study of institutions enables us to make sense of how political actors behave and how effective they are at achieving their goals. Without taking institutions into account, we are left to observe major events without the contextual reference points of what motivates the actors involved and what determined their success. Institutions are especially vital in the study of regime change and continuity, when actors engage in a high-stakes conflict to restructure the political system.

By looking at institutions, we can understand the political constraints and inducements that shape behavior and outcomes, such as election results under autocratic regimes. It is natural to imagine democratization movements, as well as dictatorships, as driven by the most prominent leaders involved. Political change thus appears as an archetypal clash between heroes and villains – the Corazon Aquinos challenging the Ferdinand Marcoses of the developing world. But although leadership on both sides plays an important role in determining when and how regimes may reform, rulers and opposition activists operate in a context that predates their entry into politics (Marx 2004 [1852]: 15). Prior history, organizational networks, economic resources, and ideology are among countless variables that influence whether, how, and how effectively actors will push for change or seek to prevent it. Although political leaders stand at the forefront of politics, these less visible factors constantly shape the choices they face and the outcomes they bring about. Recognizing such structural

---

[1] Journalists' accounts often portray elections – or even the announcement of upcoming elections – as momentous events. The *New York Times*, for example, gave front-page coverage in its national edition to Mubarak's 26 February 2005 announcement that contested presidential elections would be held later that year – the very polls that doomed opposition leader Ayman Nour by virtue of his second-place finish to the guaranteed winner, Mubarak.

influences, democratization scholars have increasingly sought to integrate them into accounts of human agency and choice (e.g., O'Donnell and Schmitter 1986; Remmer 1991; Snyder 1992; Haggard and Kaufman 1995; Bratton and van de Walle 1997; Mahoney and Snyder 1999). This book continues in that vein by examining the relationship of political parties and political leaders to the maintenance and decline of authoritarian rule. In developing a theory that ties ruling parties to regime persistence, I explicitly build on earlier work on formal institutions and the subsequent efforts of "new institutionalists" (e.g., March and Olsen 1984; Evans, Rueschemeyer, and Skocpol 1985; Thelen 1999).

Political scientists have long recognized the importance of political institutions, particularly parties. Memorably, Samuel Huntington wrote that "he controls the future who organizes its politics" (1968: 461). More permanent than mere factions, parties are organizations that bring together often differently interested members to seek influence over government (Duverger 1954 [1951]: 1–2; Sartori 1976: 27; Ware 1996: 4–5). Parties are heterogeneous and may pursue different ends and adopt different means. The party's agenda may not be idealistic or even programmatic in the sense of a fixed political platform rooted in a particular philosophical stance. Indeed, parties are comprised of self-interested actors who may behave quite capriciously. Sartori reminds us: "[P]arty members are not altruists, and the existence of parties by no means eliminates selfish and unscrupulous motivations. The power-seeking drives of politicians remain constant. What varies is the processing and the constraints that are brought to bear on such drives" (1976: 25).

The party's operations channel its members to work together over a substantial period of time rather than individually in pursuit of immediate gains. These constraints contrast dramatically with the open rivalries from which parties are often born. In the United States, the exigencies of electoral politics drove leaders to form parties as they wooed voters (Huntington 1968: 131). In the developing world, parties also were a means of gathering popular support in the pursuit of power through elections or mass demonstrations during and after colonialism (Zolberg 1966: 15).

Unlike in the United States, where power has historically been shared by two parties, in developing states one dominant party organization has often succeeded in monopolizing power. Immanuel Wallerstein's observation (quoted in the second epigraph) about the tendency toward either stable single-party regimes or unstable regimes without parties applies across most of the developing world, not just in postcolonial Africa, where he noticed this trend (1961: 95–96). For decades, leaders in countries as diverse as Kenya, Mexico, the Soviet Union, and Taiwan have dominated national political life through parties. Their peers in regimes such as those of Egypt and Malaysia continue to rule.

To understand how parties bring political stability to authoritarian regimes, we must theorize the relationship of the party to the leaders it holds together. Even when a single figure occupies the helm of a regime, autocrats do not rule completely alone: They depend on coalitions of elites. Elites are national-level agenda setters, figures who wield regular and substantial influence over a country's political system (Burton, Gunther and Higley 1992a: 8). They are insiders with privileged access to the rulers and the state. In contrast, opposition figures may command national prestige, but their relationship to the administration of national politics is more distant: Elites are the "ins," whereas opposition figures are the "outs." Although the line between elite and opposition may blur as the ruler co-opts activists or ejects long-time loyalists, the distinction remains salient to understanding the everyday conduct of politics under authoritarianism.

Although elites are political insiders, they do not act autonomously. On the contrary, their very influence as agenda setters depends on the broader constituencies they lead. Whereas elites bring their own voice, resources, and skills to a coalition, their larger importance is connected to the support they command among broad groups whose members share their background, ideology, or interests. Because elites are linked to their constituents, societal support empowers elites at the same time that it constrains them. The positions they take may cause conflict with leaders who have different outlooks: A business owner who wants to rationalize the bureaucracy may clash with a lifelong state bureaucrat speaking for thousands in the civil service, for example.

It is at this point – the nexus of elite interaction – that parties exert a critical influence on elite behavior. In a context where elite differences appear irresolvable, parties mediate conflict and facilitate mutually acceptable solutions. They do so by generating political influence that reduces individual insecurity and assuages fears of prolonged disadvantage. As the top organization of national power, ruling parties provide a political arena that is linked to but distinct from its leaders' social constituencies. They create a structure for collective agenda setting, lengthening the time horizon on which leaders weigh gains and losses. Elites can envision their party bringing them medium- and long-term gains despite immediate setbacks; moreover, their overriding priority is to maintain a place in the decision-making process. A precipitous exit could threaten their elite status, costing them vital influence in the regime's development. Ruling parties thus resolve conflicts in a positive-sum fashion, so that no single faction suffers permanent defeat by another. Even where a party's methods of promotion depend on personal ties more than individual merit, the party nonetheless regulates the pursuit of individual ambition within a set of comprehensible rules. Personnel may fluctuate rapidly during a party's formative years, but over time the institution acquires a structure that remains relatively constant from day to day. In this context, careers seem less threatened by the disputes of a given day. The party thereby generates incentives for long-term loyalty. When policy interests collide, leaders perceive the opportunity for the gradual reconciliation of otherwise competing factions. They can anticipate long-term gain through short-term concessions. Rival factions benefit jointly rather than profiting at the expense of one another. The consequence for authoritarianism is long-term cohesion among the ruler's most influential members and the maintenance of political stability.

Conceiving of ruling parties and political coalitions in this way embeds elite behavior in the institutional context where preferences are formed and decisions made. Once we understand the role of ruling parties in sustaining coalitions of seemingly disparate elites, it is easy to see how the absence of such an organization can facilitate, but not determine, regime change and democratization. When parties have declined or disappeared, intraelite conflicts escalate, and leaders polarize into competing factions. Driven by pragmatism as much as principle, careerist figures then defect from the regime and ally with the opposition: Former regime supporters become reluctant reformists. Now filling the classic role of active and public soft-liners, such defectors enable potent counteralliances against the regime. The realignment of previous supporters of authoritarianism with the opposition presents a structural opportunity for democratization. At that point, the strategies and decisions of the antiregime coalition powerfully affect whether the regime will stand or fall.

Accounts of elections or protest movements thereby describe the climax of a longer drama, one in which institutional variations shape the opening acts. Because institutional factors vary so clearly across the two pairs of cases studied in this work, the comparison of Egypt and Malaysia to Iran and the Philippines vividly captures the effect of ruling parties on a regime's power. Egypt and Malaysia's leaders maintained ruling parties and sturdy coalitions that consistently marginalized the opposition. The National Democratic Party (NDP) in Egypt and UMNO in Malaysia brought elite cohesion within the regime and electoral control in the public arena. Ruling party institutions took unlike countries down kindred paths of durable authoritarianism. On the alternative path trod by Iran and the Philippines, elite rivalries were not contained within a party and instead escalated into open factionalism. Disgruntled elites allied with the opposition and competed fiercely at the polls; elite defectors dealt electoral defeats to the regime's candidates. From that point, oppositionists could push for regime change, an option pursued successfully by Philippine activists but eschewed by Iranian reformists, who feared a second revolution. A structural opportunity for democratization thus yielded very different outcomes based on the strategies of reform-minded activists in the opposition. The absence of ruling parties was necessary but insufficient for a breakdown of authoritarianism.

Although at first brush this set of cases may seem an eclectic group, the historical and institutional narratives I develop in this book demonstrate the utility of treating seemingly disparate cases in a common framework. By pairing cases from two different regions, this comparison highlights a political logic that single-country monographs might leave unexposed (Karl 1997: 22; Bunce 2003: 191; Huber 2003: 5). Dissimilarities in political-economic and historical factors and in international relations allow this study to take seriously an array of alternative accounts (Skocpol 1979: 42; Waldner 1999: 12–15). It is in light of such competing arguments – and not just in spite of them – that the explanatory strength of institutional analysis becomes strikingly apparent: Ruling parties in Egypt and Malaysia have structured very different kinds of conflicts toward very similar outcomes. Amid diversity in culture, history, and economics, political commonalities elucidate general patterns. Regionally bounded explanations (for example, the influence of large Muslim majorities in the Middle East or of more advanced socioeconomic development in Southeast Asia) have a hard time accounting for these cross-regional trends. Nor can they explain intraregional differences. Divergent outcomes occurred within the same regions, whereas similarities spanned both regions. These contrasts point us toward a political, institutional explanation that accounts for cross-regional commonalities and intraregional variations.

The chapters that follow draw on fifteen months of fieldwork gathering primary materials and conducting interviews with political elites in Egypt, Iran, Malaysia, and the Philippines. Keeping in mind the needs of a general audience as well as comparative specialists, I have organized the case materials around the theoretical argument: Rather than provide country-specific case chapters, the book follows the causal narrative.

Chapter 1 sets the theory of ruling parties and regime persistence in the global context of recent democratization and authoritarianism. The book's subsequent chapters then trace shared causal paths in the two pairs of cases from the period of regime formation through recent regime outcomes. Chapters 2 and 3 cover the earlier portions of the story, exploring the origins of parties during regime formation in the four cases and then moving from the initial institutional products of regime formation to the intermediate legacies of party maintenance or deactivation. The final three empirical chapters then show why variations in party institutions wrought dramatically different consequences during the third wave of democratization: Chapter 4 analyzes how ruling parties in Egypt and Malaysia sustained coalitions and insulated incumbents as leaders confronted new policy issues. The fifth chapter examines why Khamenei's regime in Iran suffered elite defections and electoral defeats at the same time that Mubarak's party enjoyed unrivaled dominance. Challengers to Marcos in the Philippines are treated in Chapter 6. Finally, the conclusion ties together the preceding materials by drawing a set of general lessons on democratization and authoritarianism. It exploits the advantages of a cross-regional paired comparison to engage a variety of alternative explanations and address why a focus on ruling parties most adequately accounts for the observed variation in regime outcomes. Its final section considers the prospects of moving from durable authoritarianism to durable democracy.

I

The Political Origins of Durable Authoritarianism

The end of authoritarianism has long been forecast but has yet to come (Pye 1990). In the 1990s, it was hoped that the wave of democratic change would continue unabated. Autocrats, it appeared, were trapped between political bankruptcy, on one side, and precarious liberalization, on the other. Those who excluded the public from national politics had no legitimating ideology and could only defend themselves as provisional stewards of the nation (O'Donnell and Schmitter 1986: 15). If they sought to prolong their rule indefinitely, they had to resort to elections and other democratic procedures, thereby adopting the mantle of republicanism even as they eschewed its fundamentals (Fukuyama 1989; Zakaria 1997). Anecdotally, both premises found dramatic support. After regime-initiated elections in the Philippines (1986), Chile (1988), Poland (1989), and Nicaragua (1990) ended in opposition victories, Huntington remarked that "liberalized authoritarianism is not a stable equilibrium; the halfway house does not stand" (1991: 174–175).

But elsewhere, the "halfway house" had become a fortress – not a way station but a way of life. By 2001, five dozen regimes blended liberalization with repression and signified the durability of authoritarianism during a period that had augured global democracy. As autocratic incumbents learned to garb themselves in elections and thereby entrenched themselves further, the trend toward electoral democracy slowed. From 1987 to 1996, the world witnessed a gain of fifty-two electoral democracies (from 66 to 118). Over the next nine years, the rate of democratization slowed considerably, netting only four electoral democracies (Freedom House 2006). This leveling off signaled that many regimes were not as brittle as their forebears. The holdouts confounded theories of political liberalization by feigning pluralism while monopolizing power.

Whereas such authoritarian regimes attracted new labels that highlighted their electoral features, the underlying causes of their resilience drew less attention. This chapter explores the problem of durable authoritarianism and elucidates why many autocracies survived the third wave. It builds on three prior literatures (social structural approaches, transitions theories, and the hybrid regimes subfield) to provide an institutionalist theory of regime change and stability.

Comparative politics scholars clearly "thrive on political change," especially the instauration of democracy after years of dictatorship (Bermeo 1990: 359). But in order to explain regime change, we must take stock of regime continuity as well. The first part of this chapter revisits the dialogue between voluntarist and structural approaches by retrospectively testing the explanatory power of several early social structural accounts, which relied on slow-changing socioeconomic variables and were subsequently criticized for minimizing the role of individual agency and leadership. This discussion suggests the usefulness of studying these social structural variables for understanding the third wave of democratization and its undercurrents. It points to the need to gauge social and political inertia during the 1990s and early 2000s, when "hybrid regimes" swept up the study of comparative democratization. Accordingly, the chapter's second part questions the explanatory utility of hybrid regimes and evaluates whether the dictator's latest clothes – limited elections and other plebiscitary ruses – have fundamentally altered the way authoritarian regimes function or fail. The chapter's final section explains why ruling parties sustain authoritarianism and where such parties originate. Elites are tied to social constituencies and embedded in political organizations. An account of ruling party politics brings these variables together, integrating the prevailing approaches to regime change in a general institutional theory of authoritarianism and opportunities for democratization.

The Ongoing Role of Structural Variables

The collapse of a dictatorship seems a sign of the supremacy of the human will. Jubilant masses flood the streets, statues fall, and parliaments reawaken with new faces. At that moment, the "inhuman" forces of social structure and political organization appear peripheral to the action at best. Yet, in another sense, the victory of dissidents and activists is but the final act of a longer drama. To examine only this moment is to overlook the historical background that preceded and culminated in regime change.[1] If a scholar divorces such an episode from its antecedents, he will be unable to explain why a regime fell and why similar regimes elsewhere did not. Therefore, a comparative analytic lens must be able to zoom out from present events to capture the historical context in which human action occurs.

In one of the first broad attempts to gauge the prospects for democratization, Seymour Martin Lipset proposed that regimes can be divided into three categories: durable democracies, durable dictatorships, and unstable regimes (Lipset 1959: 74). These categories anticipated Huntington's later distinction between "form of government" and "degree of government" (Huntington 1968: 1), eschewing the subsequent tendency to conflate the two variables (Shin 1994: 151). Lipset's regime types have remained useful for identifying trends in regime change and continuity for decades (Huntington 1984, Waldner 2002a).

Leading social scientists of the 1960s and 1970s saw democratization as a gradual, arduous process. Democracy, they argued, would depend on certain social and economic preconditions (Lipset 1959), hinge on the development of a robust middle class that disrupted aristocratic authority by force (Moore 1966), or involve the gradual expansion of the franchise by an unthreatened set of elites (Dahl 1971). Even Dankwart Rustow, who challenged the idea that there are economic or cultural prerequisites for democracy, still held that national populations would need to share a common identity and have an agreed-on territory before a democratic government could be securely installed (Rustow 1970). Structural theorists agreed that democratization would not be easily achieved by many of the newly independent countries of the postcolonial world.

Subsequent events have validated this perspective to a rarely recognized degree. Political events largely supported the initial expectations of structural theorists that democratization would be rare and slow in much of the

---

[1] The comments of an anti-Milosevic activist in Serbia are arguably as applicable to social scientists as to journalists: "One problem with world media is that they are only, you know, recording the final act – half a million people in the streets getting inside a parliament on the television, and boom, they lost it, it's finished. That was not that way. The non-violent struggle in Serbia lasted for 10 years, and we had so many successes and failures in this struggle." *Source:* "Revolution on Ice," *On the Media*, 24 March 2006, http://www.onthemedia.org/transcripts/2006/3/24/03. Accessed: 10 Febuary 2007.

developing world. Indeed, many of the changes that occurred took place in governments that structural theorists had deemed "unstable regimes" that bridged the gap between durable democracies and durable dictatorships – the very realm where such upheaval was anticipated. Nearly half of the cases of third-wave democratization conformed to earlier expectations. And of the great many countries deemed unlikely to democratize, fewer than two dozen had broken free of dictatorships by 1991.

To resist the temptations of presentism and evaluate a robust version of structural theories, however, we must consider what evidence would disprove the logic of Lipset and his contemporaries. Structural theorists maintained that regime change would be rare and that countries' governments would tend to remain in the same category over time (durable democracy, durable dictatorship, or unstable regime) rather than shift dramatically from one category to another. Consequently, two trends would undermine structural theories: Many regimes making a lasting shift from democracy to dictatorship or many regimes making a lasting shift from dictatorship to democracy.

In successive columns, Table 1.1 lists the early front-runners of democratization – regimes deemed to be democratic or approaching democracy by Lipset (1959), Rustow (1967), Huntington (1968), and Dahl (1971) – against the sum product through the third wave (Huntington 1991).[2] The overlap of early assessments and subsequent outcomes in twenty of twenty-two cases strongly supports the long-term development of democratic regimes, as anticipated by the collected scholars. If a comparativist had used the collection of regimes coded democratic by 1971 and predicted that these cases would be democratic twenty years later, she would have been right 91 percent of the time. (If we expand the time horizon ten years, thereby encompassing Mexico's democratization in 2000, predictive accuracy increases to 95 percent.) Most of these countries were not "durable" democracies, for many experienced substantial interims of authoritarian rule, yet neither were they durable dictatorships.

The composite list in Table 1.1 includes twenty of the developing world democracies Huntington identified in *The Third Wave*.[3] But it

---

[2] The cases are Lipset's "democracies and unstable dictatorships" in Latin America, plus the African and Asian countries that had the "best prospects" for democracy (1959: 74, 101); Rustow's "contemporary democratic systems" (1967: 290); Huntington's two-party and multiparty systems (1968: 421); and Dahl's polyarchies and near-polyarchies (1971: 248).

[3] For the sake of consistency, I have retained Dahl and Huntington's questionable coding of Malaysia as "democratic." Whether included in the data or not, the continuity of the

TABLE 1.1. *Social Structural Forecasts of Democracy and Recent Outcomes*

Lipset (1959)	Rustow (1967)	Huntington (1968)	Dahl (1971)	Huntington (1991)
Argentina		Argentina		Argentina
Brazil		Brazil		Brazil
Chile	Chile	Chile	Chile	Chile
Colombia	Colombia	Colombia	Colombia	Colombia
Costa Rica	Costa Rica		Costa Rica	Costa Rica
			Dominican Republic	Dominican Republic
	Greece			Greece
		Honduras		Honduras
	India			India
Israel	Israel	Israel	Israel	Israel
		Jamaica	Jamaica	Jamaica
Japan	Japan		Japan	Japan
Lebanon			Lebanon	
			Malaysia	Malaysia
Mexico	Mexico			
		Peru		Peru
Philippines	Philippines	Philippines	Philippines	Philippines
	Sri Lanka	Sri Lanka		Sri Lanka
			Trinidad and Tobago	Trinidad and Tobago
Turkey			Turkey	Turkey
Uruguay	Uruguay	Uruguay	Uruguay	Uruguay
		Venezuela	Venezuela	Venezuela
12 countries	11 countries	12 countries	14 countries	20 countries

also misses twenty-two unanticipated democratizers: Bolivia, Botswana, Bulgaria, Czechoslovakia, East Germany, El Salvador, Ecuador, Gambia, Guatemala, Hungary, Malta, Mongolia, Namibia, Nicaragua, Pakistan, Panama, Poland, Portugal, Romania, Senegal, South Korea, and Spain. Changes that entailed a shift from long-lived dictatorships to thriving democracies – as in Portugal and Poland, among others – dramatically overrode the expectations of earlier theorists. These cases reveal the bias in these structural approaches toward *overestimating* the durability of authoritarianism, which clears the structural theorists of the earlier charge

UMNO-led government throughout the period in question supports the structuralists' assumption about the rarity of dramatic change.

that they underestimated the problem of democratic breakdown (Linz 1978). Examples of regime change from durable dictatorship to durable democracy are harder to find than cases in which autocracy endured. Developments confirmed the structural theorists' expectation that nondemocratic rule would continue to encompass much of the developing world. In 1991, the people in ninety-two countries continued to live under authoritarian rule (Diamond 1999: 25). Structural theorists' predictions for the continued absence of democracy proved correct in most of these cases.

Far from refuting the original political development scholars, then, recent history has gone a long way toward validating many of their assumptions and expectations. Most of the countries that scholars such as Dahl and Lipset judged democratic have fared well over the last decades. Meanwhile, most of the countries that drew their skepticism have continued to grapple with autocratic governments. Events that appeared contingent and unique when viewed over a limited time span seem more explicable if considered over a span of decades. When the regime fluctuations of the 1970s and 1980s are set amid longer trends, we see that theories of slowly achieved social and political transformation captured as much as they missed. Despite initial forecasts of far-reaching and deep transformations during the third wave, many regimes remained highly structured by prior experiences and conditions. Structural theories can play an important role in examining these complex developments. The strong correlation between recent outcomes and early regime types does not mean that history is destiny or that prior democratic experience causes later democratization. It does suggest, however, that the preference of transitions scholars for micro-level accounts over macro-level approaches may have more to do with their tendency to frame historical events over a short period than with the exhaustion of prior theories. The resilience of authority structures for both the strongest democratic prospects of the 1960s and the regimes deemed to be likely autocratic holdouts reinforces the need for a balanced and careful integration of structure and agency.

Great strides toward democracy have been made in the past fifty years by many regimes, but in their shift from authoritarian rule to democratic practices, quite a few of them have displayed substantial continuity with their prior political experiences. Such regimes stand testament to Joseph Schumpeter's contention that "social structures, types, and attitudes are coins that do not readily melt" (1947: 12). Military regimes in Latin

America withdrew from power, providing a second chance for democracy to grow in a number of countries with previously weak but substantial records in representative government. The fall of dictatorships in the Eastern Bloc and the collapse of the Soviet Union brought both democratization (in those states closest to continental Europe) and authoritarian relapse (in Russia and Central Asia) (Kitschelt 1999). With few exceptions, Middle Eastern regimes have not experienced marked change (Brownlee 2002a: 485). China's dictatorship has persisted, as has India's democracy. Although democratic states have been inaugurated across much of South and East Asia (in Bangladesh, Thailand, Indonesia, the Philippines, and South Korea, for example), autocracy continues elsewhere (in Pakistan, Myanmar, Cambodia, Malaysia, Singapore, and North Korea), and today fewer than half the regimes of Asia are electoral democracies (Diamond 2002: 31). Nor is the record in Africa much brighter. Ten years after sub-Saharan Africa's liberalization experiences began, half of those countries experiencing "flawed" or "democratic" transitions are still not electoral democracies, and in all but one of the rest transitions to democracy were either "blocked or precluded" (Bratton and Van de Walle 1997: 286–287; Freedom House 2004: 725–726).

Early structural theories, premised on the assumptions of social continuity and inertia, merit a prominent position in understanding this spectrum of development. They and subsequent transitions approaches shared the view that democratic outcomes in Latin America and Southern Europe were possible in the immediate future. Structural research had elaborated the local background conditions, such as levels of literacy and economic opportunity, that boded well for the instauration (or resurrection) of a democratic system. Later, the action-oriented approach to democratization of transitions scholars suited the political context to which it was applied: Rulers and oppositionists had reached a form of parity in which decisions mattered greatly for tipping the political order into the hands of the people. Discerning how and why similar opportunities emerge in other countries is a valuable area for research and one subject of this book. The choices made by the leaders of future transitions will be best informed by an accurate portrayal of the slow-moving historical and rapidly changing agent-activated components of democratization.

Once we recognize that both macro- and micro-level explanations are invaluable for illuminating when and why regimes become vulnerable to human agency, the question then becomes *when* each of these two different approaches should be employed. In that regard, the explanatory strength of each may be illustrated in an analogy from earth sciences.[4] Slow and momentous, structural changes resemble "tectonic shifts," observable only over long stretches of history. During the course of these shifts, regimes are still subject to sometimes seismic tremors and quakes. Actor-focused approaches to democratization capture these sudden fluctuations at the surface. Social structures and political institutions help account for the subterranean stability or volatility that explains the quakes' occurrence or absence.

Keeping the imagery of plate tectonics in mind, it is easy to reconcile the rivalrous research programs of transitions scholars and their forerunners. Structural theories capture the variation between broad and generally long-lasting regime categories – between durable democracies, durable dictatorships, and unstable regimes. Barrington Moore Jr.'s *Social Origins of Dictatorship and Democracy*, for example, accounted for the emergence of durable dictatorships, such as those of Russia and China, and durable democracies, such as those of the United States and United Kingdom (Moore 1966). Voluntarist theories account for shifts between these types or within them, as in the tempestuous regimes that suffered autocratic interregnums during the 1970s. The prime example of this approach is O'Donnell and Schmitter's *Transitions from Authoritarian Rule* project, which explicitly examined "rapidly changing situations, where [the] very parameters of political action are in flux" (O'Donnell and Schmitter 1986: 4). In short, structural explanations help explain which regimes are most likely to be durable – that is, better protected from opposition challenges – and which are more likely to be weak, unstable, and otherwise exposed to change. When political arrangements are uncertain, agential accounts become particularly valuable. To the extent that structural variables separate the relatively constant and certain from the comparatively vulnerable and contested, they illuminate the comparativist's subject.

Several scholars have taken an approach to merging structural and voluntarist approaches similar to my own. Most specifically, the framework

---

[4] My example here comes from the work of Paul Pierson, who has lucidly categorized causal arguments by the time span of processes and outcomes (Pierson 2003: 179). Pierson uses meteorological examples to clarify these differences: some causal processes may build up quickly and deliver their effects rapidly, like tornadoes; other phenomena, akin to global warming, may be the result of a more gradual accumulation of causal factors, and they may release their effects over a long period of time, as well.

I have outlined is anticipated by Arthur Stinchcombe's language of "revolutionary situations": "[A] sociological theory of revolution ought not expect to be able to tell who will win in a revolutionary situation, but to tell that there will be a fight with unlimited means, a fight not conducted under defined norms for deciding political battles. Explaining who won, and why, is primarily a problem of military science, not of social science" (1965: 170). Stinchcombe's notion of extraordinary periods in which political conflicts supercede conventional constraints is echoed in a variety of later works on regime change. Atul Kohli's "crisis of governance," Deborah Yashar's "democratizing moments," and Lucan Way's "pluralism by default" all denote the same basic phenomenon: An opening in which the fundamental parameters of public life are uncommonly contested and vulnerable to change by the actors involved (Kohli 1990: 400; Yashar 1997: 17; Way 2002: 141). I call these periods "opportunities for democratization."[5] Such opportunities do not presuppose that change will occur. Indeed, the aforementioned examples include many instances of continuity: India's democracy survived its "crisis," Guatemala lapsed back into authoritarianism despite its "democratizing moment," and "pluralism by default" has not ruptured Belarus's dictatorship. Yet these opportunities for democratization – these structural openings – do not occur in more consolidated, more durable regimes. Where they do occur, they evince the potential for transformation that characterized Lipset's "unstable regimes."

It follows from this discussion that integrated democratization theories carry a dual responsibility. First, they must account for the presence or absence of opportunities for democratization. Then, they must answer the transition scholar's question of how rulers and their challengers fare during such moments. In developing and defending such a theory, comparativists must assess which social, economic, and political structures

---

[5] "Opportunities for democratization" are a subset of the broader notion of "critical junctures" (Collier and Collier 1991: 27; Mahoney and Snyder 1998: 18–19). For a recent application, consult Mahoney (2002). Earlier work by Juan Linz, in which he ties the concept to Max Weber's work and quotes British physicist Sir James Jeans, largely anticipates and elucidates the basic logic of critical junctures: "The course of a railway train is uniquely prescribed for it at most points of its journey by the rails on which it runs. Here and there, however, it comes to a junction at which alternative courses are open to it, and it may be turned on to one or the other by the quite negligible expenditure of energy involved in moving the points" (1978 100, fn. 8). In the cases examined here, it is not simply human "energy" or choices but the contested *conclusion* of *competing choices* that sets the two pairs of regimes on widely divergent courses.

are most determinative in distinguishing broadly between durable and vulnerable regimes.

A Brand New Authoritarianism?

Although the initial literature on transitions from authoritarianism may have overestimated the role of human agency in the downfall of dictatorships, subsequent works – including some by the Transitions project's original leaders – explicitly blended structure and agency (Schmitter and Karl 1991; Haggard and Kaufman 1992; Linz and Stepan 1996; Collier 1999; Kitschelt 1999). Occasionally, such works explained both regime change and regime persistence (Snyder 1992; Bratton and van de Walle 1997; Yashar 1999). Thus, by the late 1990s, the field of comparative democratization was budding with integrative, general approaches that crossed regions. To a great extent, however, subsequent scholars have not forged ahead on this path with the same close attention to causal mechanisms and historical processes. Case study research has instead moved toward classifying "hybrid regimes," authoritarian systems that display features of democracy such as elections and parliaments. As a flurry of new typologies outpaces the development and confirmation of explanations, these new authoritarian subtypes risk becoming an intellectual cul-de-sac.

Ten years after Huntington's *Third Wave*, comparativists flocked to explain the resilience of dictatorships in democratic garb, and with good reason. Whereas dozens of autocratic regimes have lost power since the 1970s, others have survived, even thrived, in the same era. For Huntington, the third wave of democratization encompassed thirty-five countries that had earlier been under authoritarian rule. By 2001, a far greater number had adopted the ruse of party competition without meaningfully ceding power to their competitors. Marking a trend of plebisctarianism without democratization, from 1975 to 2000 forty-four states introduced limited multiparty elections under conditions of continued autocracy. Authoritarianism with elections is today the modal form of autocracy, more than twice as common as fully closed, exclusionary authoritarianism without any pretext of pluralism (Table 1.2). A third of the developing world's governments permit constrained pluralistic competition but prevent the regular rotation of elites (Schumpeter 1947: 269).

Although Larry Diamond has recognized that "hybrid regimes...are not new," scholars have generally treated these nondemocratic systems

TABLE 1.2. *Political Regimes in the Developing World (circa 2001)*

World Regions/ Regime Types	Liberal Democracy	Electoral Democracy	Electoral Authoritarian	Closed Authoritarian	Sum
Eastern Europe	11	3	5	0	19
Central Asia & the Caucasus	0	0	7	1	8
Latin America & Caribbean	17	11	4	1	33
North Africa & the Middle East	1	0	10	8	19
Sub-Saharan Africa	5	10	26	7	48
South, Southeast, & East Asia	2	8	6	8	24
World	**36**	**32**	**58**	**25**	**151**

Source: Schedler (2002: 47)

as if they are a novel phenomenon warranting new labels (2002: 23).[6] Regimes that hold elections in manipulated conditions are said to be in a "gray zone" between exclusionary autocracy and liberal democracy (Carothers 2002). In the vein of an earlier literature on "democracy with adjectives" (Collier and Levitsky 1997), comparativists have turned out numerous studies of authoritarianism with adjectives, including "semi-authoritarianism" (Ottaway and Olcott 1999), "electoral authoritarianism" (Schedler 2001), and "competitive authoritarianism" (Levitsky and Way 2002). Authoritarian regimes that provide limited opportunities for the opposition to contest political power are not transitioning to democracy, these scholars argue, but they may under certain conditions be vulnerable to domestic campaigns for change through the same venues of inclusion they have fostered (Schedler 2002: 38; Levitsky and Way 2002: 54–55). Regardless of what name it goes by, this notion of authoritarianism with moderate competition is substantively equivalent to Juan Linz's much earlier definition of authoritarianism: "Authoritarian regimes are political systems with limited, not responsible, political pluralism ... without intensive nor extensive political mobilization ... and in which a leader (or occasionally a small group) exercises power within formally ill-defined limits but actually quite predictable ones" (1964: 297).

[6] The seminal works on hybrid regimes are Zakaria (1997), Carothers (2002), Diamond (2002), Levitsky and Way (2002), Schedler (2002), and Ottaway (2003).

The advent of the category of hybrid regimes may have marked the long-needed recognition of the "actually quite predictable" limits in which many autocracies operate, boundaries that can be quite durable.[7]

The fresh branding of old regimes does not necessarily illuminate the goings-on of the world's autocracies or explain why so many still stand. Indeed, as scholars devise new names for authoritarian hybridity, they may needlessly confuse scholarly discourse and fragment knowledge (Armony and Schami 2005: 126; Snyder 2006: 227). There is still much we do not know. Have elections changed the substance of authoritarian rule, making autocracies less or more stable? Although authoritarian regimes have changed their visage, have their internal politics been altered through the adoption of pseudodemocratic procedures, or are limited elections simply a new feature that may merit study but does not warrant new regime typologies?

Whereas the hybrid regimes literature has concentrated on what occurs outside today's regimes, prior institutionalist works have analyzed the internal politics of authoritarianism. The study of the interaction between political institutions and political agents provides a solid tradition from which to approach contemporary authoritarianism. For well more than two decades, the "new institutionalism" has sought to improve on earlier behavioralism, with its tendency to strip away the political and social context of human action, and on the "old institutionalism" that treated formal rules as determinative.[8] Political institutions link past social, economic, and historical processes to the decisions and movements of today. As the "ligatures fastening...large-scale processes to each other," institutions have proven incisive for explaining regime change and stability (Katznelson 1997: 103). Therefore, they offer a suitable bridge for connecting the influence of socioeconomic variables to the influence of particular actors and groups.

---

[7] Linz also recognized a less stable condition of authoritarianism: the "authoritarian situation" he observed under Brazil's military regime (1973: 235). This apt diagnosis conforms with the earlier discussion of "unstable regimes." Brazil's gradual and meaningful liberalization became an archetype for theorizing the relative brevity of military regimes as compared to personalistic and party regimes.

[8] James March and Jonah Olsen coined the term the "new institutionalism" in a 1984 article and imbued the area with an intellectual coherence for political scientists. Since then, numerous scholars have self-consciously identified themselves as working in this field. The literature is vast, including such works as Evans, Rueschemeyer and Skocpol (1985), Knight (1992), Thelen (1992), Haggard and Kaufman (1995), and many monographs since.

Institutionalist analysis has been especially fruitful in the field of comparative democratization. Stephan Haggard and Robert Kaufman closely studied the role of political parties in enabling regimes to conduct economic reform while avoiding political instability (1995: 291). Examining a very different set of cases, Michael Bratton and Nicolas van de Walle pointed to the prevalence of personalistic rule in sub-Saharan Africa and the ways in which such patrimonial regimes were vulnerable to mass protest (1997: 83). A further advance came with Barbara Geddes's systematic study of authoritarian breakdown, which demonstrated robust relationships between particular forms of nondemocratic rule and the likelihood of regime collapse (1999a; 1999b). Usefully distilling decades of secondary literature, Geddes's tripartite typology of military, personal, and single-party regimes exposed general patterns amid the turmoil and torpor of postcolonial development. Military regimes tended to have the shortest duration (average length of rule: 8.5 years), because when professional soldiers' regimes were threatened, they could preserve the integrity of the armed forces by withdrawing from power and returning to the barracks. In contrast, single-party leaders, who depended on political dominance for career advancement, were least likely to relinquish power (average longevity: 22.7 years). Personalistic leaders lasted longer than military ones but not as long as single-party rulers (average lifespan: 15.0 years) (Geddes 1999a: 37).[9]

By treating the institutions of authoritarianism as independent variables rather than derivations of underlying social cleavages, Geddes's variables were one step less distal than the theories of Lipset and Moore from recent regime outcomes. Her theory, along with those of the forebears whose works she synthesized, also provided a framework in which to situate transitions from authoritarian rule previously thought to be contingent. Given the recent trends in global democratization and authoritarianism, such an approach is warranted and needed. Institutional

---

[9] Geddes places a few especially resilient regimes (Egypt, Suharto's Indonesia, Stroessner's Paraguay) in "a doubly hybrid Personal/Military/Single-Party category" (1999b: 22). This coding decision raises one of the more serious problems about Geddes's project: that duration may be driving the regime classifications rather than the other way around. The longer a regime survives, the longer it provides the coder with observable "data" of different regime traits. Because Geddes generally codes regimes with one type for the full duration, the data miss the nuances of intra-authoritarian change, particularly the way leaders may change the regime's institutional profile over time. These problems necessitate closer examination of regime development and the genetic causes of variations in authoritarianism, a principal task of this project.

variables offer lenses for discerning general patterns against the empirical glare of seemingly serendipitous events. Distinguishing between more personalistic regimes and more institutionalized regimes, for example, goes a long way toward explaining some of the most salient trends of the third wave and its undercurrents. Six out of O'Donnell and Schmitter's eight cases of change were transitions from military rule, the least durable form of authoritarian regime in the developing world. Thus, Geddes's tripartite regime typology may remain useful for explaining democratization and authoritarian durability even as autocracy seems to be taking new forms.

To determine whether authoritarianism with elections warrants its own category or whether conventional institutional variables remain sufficiently robust that new regime categories are extraneous, I statistically tested the impact of limited elections, along with nonelectoral institutional variables and a conventional set of control variables (economic, regional, age), on the durability of 135 authoritarian regimes during the period 1975–2000. To measure whether or not the regime held multiparty elections, I drew on the World Bank Database of Political Indicators and constructed a dummy variable that takes the value of 1 in the presence of limited multiparty elections (Beck et al. 2001).[10] For information on regime types and duration, I used Geddes's dataset and added eleven monarchies (Bahrain, Egypt, Ethiopia, Jordan, Kuwait, Morocco, Nepal, Oman, Qatar, Saudi Arabia, and United Arab Emirates) and nine

---

[10] It is common to use Polity or Freedom House data to track the political opening of an authoritarian regime (Munck and Verkuilen 2002; Mainwaring and Perez-Linan 2003). Such studies reveal gradual political changes but do not capture discrete changes within regimes, such as shifts from single- or no-party regimes to multiparty regimes. Accordingly, their measures do not match well with the theory being evaluated: that political openings weaken dictatorships. The Database of Political Institutions provides more traction on this problem because it better disaggregates theorized causes – the array of political institutions – from outcomes that may be conflated with levels of political and civic freedom. The database covers the period 1975 to 2000 and includes a seven-point scale of legislative and executive electoral competitiveness: 1 = no legislature, 2 = unelected legislature/executive, 3 = Elected legislature/executive, one candidate/post, 4 = one party, multiple candidates, 5 = multiple parties are legal but only one party won seats, 6 = multiple parties did win seats but the largest party received more than 75 percent of the seats, 7 = largest party got less than 75 percent (Keefer 2002: 10). The DPI's independent data on multipartyism cut across Geddes's regime types and are not endogenous to the outcomes of breakdown or continuity. Regime years that measured 1–4 in the DPI index were coded as not having multiparty elections. Those that received a score of 5–7 were coded as holding multiparty elections.

post-Soviet states for which economic data were available (Armenia, Azerbaijan, Belarus, Georgia, Kazakhstan, Russia, Tajikistan, Ukraine, and Uzbekistan). There are three main regime types (military, personalist, single-party) as well as the monarchy regime type and a series of mixed types (military-personal, single-party hybrids, and regimes that blend elements of military, personal, and single-party rule). Effects of regime types are measured against the omitted category of personalist regimes. Data on GDP/capita and economic growth come from the Penn World Tables 6.1 (2000) and gauge the effects of development on regime outcomes. Regional dummies and a set of age variables test the impact of geopolitical neighborhood and longevity. The dependent variable is the breakdown of a regime in a given year, measured by a dummy variable that takes the value of 1 when breakdown occurs. Thus, statistically significant positive coefficients mean less stability while negative coefficients indicate greater resilience.

Table 1.3 gives the results of three successive tests.[11] Model 1 omitted the regime types variables and tests the effect of limited elections on regime breakdown alongside the standard set of controls. Although the coefficient for limited elections was positive, pointing in the direction of Huntington's notion of unstable equilibrium, it was not statistically significant. Model 2 removed elections and reintroduced the regime types. Both the military and single-party regime types proved statistically significant, reconfirming that military regimes tend to be less stable than personalist regimes whereas single-party regimes are substantially more stable. Finally, Model 3 tested whether elections are significantly related to breakdown when all the other variables are included. The coefficient of the limited elections variable remained positive and statistically insignificant.

The results show that the institutions of authoritarian rule are more influential than the presence or absence of elections. Geddes's regime types remained a valid explanatory frame, even during a period in which political trends seemed to change. Specifically, "single-party regimes" remained the most robust type regardless of whether multiparty elections were introduced. Multiparty elections, the main characteristic of the new hybrid regimes, had no statistically significant effect. Party institutions bolstered the endurance of *both* liberalized and unliberalized authoritarian

---

[11] In addition to conducting these logit regressions I performed pairwise correlation tests on the elections and regime breakdown variable. There was no significant correlation between the two variables. Military and single-party regimes were each significantly correlated with the dependent variable.

TABLE 1.3. *Logit Regression of Elections, Regime Types, and Regime Breakdown (1975–2000)*

Dependent Variable = End of Regime	Model 1 (Elections)	Model 2 (Regime Types)	Model 3 (Elections and Regime Types)
Limited elections	.0573		.186
	(.278)		(.295)
Regime types			
Military		1.353**	1.357**
		(.422)	(.421)
Military-personalist		.578	.608
		(.442)	(.444)
Single-party hybrid w/personalist/military		−.049	−.013
		(.443)	(.446)
Single party		−1.290**	−1.278**
		(.446)	(.444)
Military-personalist-single party		−.933	−.990
		(.840)	(.844)
Monarchy		−.450	−.383
		(1.072)	(1.076)
Economic variables			
Per capita GDP$_{ln}$	−.422*	−.379*	−.414*
	(.180)	(.190)	(.198)
Lagged GDP growth	−2.638*	−2.916*	−2.897*
	(1.182)	(1.266)	(1.27)
Regional variables			
Asia	−.206	−.278	−.290
	(.897)	(.986)	(.985)
Central America	.499	−.008	−.0352
	(.962)	(1.029)	(1.029)
Central/Eastern Europe	.308	.138	.199
	(1.054)	(1.100)	(1.102)
Middle East-NorthAfrica	−1.367	−1.592	−1.650
	(1.077)	(1.359)	(1.363)
South America	.759	−.0613	−.0133
	(.966)	(1.052)	(1.055)
Sub-Saharan Africa	−.622	−.611	−.589
	(.921)	(1.013)	(1.012)
Duration variables			
Age of regime	.003	.059	.0524
	(.077)	(.078)	(.079)
Age^2	−.0003	−.0008	−.0006
	(.003)	(.003)	(.003)
Age^3	.000005	.000008	.000006
	(.00003)	(.00003)	(.00003)
Constant	.668	−.2397	−.034
	(1.721)	(1.902)	(1.929)
N =	1299	1299	1299
Log Likelihood	−272.34452	−257.82332	−257.62781
% Correctly predicted	94.3	94.3	94.3

$*p < .05$; $**p < .01$; cell entries are logistic regression coefficients; standard errors in parentheses

regimes.[12] These results point to the secondary role of elections as symptoms, not causes, of regime change. Less institutionalized regimes may lose control of elections, but elections in themselves are not the trigger of that loss.

These findings refute Huntington's "halfway house" thesis that liberalized authoritarianism is untenable. Elections provide an arena for political contestation, but they are not an independent causal factor. Functioning as they are intended, rigged ballot boxes offer domestic and international benefits to autocrats. It is the unintended capacity of elections to remove incumbents from office that makes so-called electoral authoritarian regimes vulnerable to societal protest. The test of elections and political duration reaffirms the significance of political institutions even as it directs our attention to explaining this link between ruling parties and regime persistence.

Failure to maintain elite alliances prompts defections and instability. Hence, the public manifestation of political dissent triggered by an election is the aftermath of prior discord among the regime's leaders. If the regime's core has not splintered, however, liberalization will not be accompanied by high levels of contestation; an inclusionary gesture such as multiparty elections will simply allow opposition movements one further venue in which to face a cohesive elite. The asymmetry of power between these groups will persist, and incumbents will remain entrenched. It follows that the consequences of limited multiparty politics depend on the institutions for restraining elite conflict. Regimes without the party institutions for managing their coalitions are vulnerable to being destabilized by elections, whereas those that rule through parties can reap prolonged dominance over their rivals.

Party Institutions and Authoritarian Rule

Parties are the foundation of political stability today, much as they were during the initial postcolonial period (Zolberg 1966; Huntington 1968). Through parties, autocratic rulers draw on the support of a cohesive coalition while suppressing advocates of representative governance. The effects of these sturdy coalitions are apparent in some of the longest-lived nondemocratic systems, including those of Egypt (1952–present), Malaysia

---

[12] Variables measuring economic performance were also significant, pointing again to the need to incorporate socioeconomic development in causal narratives of regime change and continuity.

(1957–present), Mexico (1929–2000), Kenya (1963–2002), Singapore (1965–present), and Syria (1970–present). Ruling parties – national organizations with mass membership and a sustainable decision-making structure – bridle elite ambitions and bind together otherwise fractious coalitions.[13] Anchored in an institutional setting that generates political power and long-term security, rival opportunists cooperate. The resulting cohesion within the regime enables control over elections and other points of contact with opposition movements. Where parties have not been maintained, competition for political power arises: Factions collide rather than collude, and losers ally with the opposition in new countercoalitions.

This theory provides a complete explanation for the varying regime outcomes of developing countries and extends from the initial period of regime formation through recent political events. My account of divergent political trajectories evolves against the backdrop of certain characteristics shared by the four selected cases and common in a much broader range of states. Placed in relief against these shared circumstances, the contrasts of party development and regime outcomes become all the more stark and intriguing.

The first shared condition is the phase of regime formation, in which political actors struggle to define the boundaries and bases of the national political community. This is a period of indeterminacy and open-ended conflict, during which competing groups set down the rules of the game. In cases of rapid, dramatic change, as when regime change is the result of a revolution or coup, the period of regime formation may be as brief as two years, as it was in Egypt (1952–1954) and Iran (1979–1981). In situations of negotiated national independence and gradual colonial withdrawal, it may last more than a decade (Malaya, 1946–1957) or decades (the Philippines, 1899–1946). Because regime formation provokes social conflict between different groups in society, it is also a period of institution building: As leaders seek to gain power, they build organizations through which they may mobilize and channel their supporters (Huntington 1968: 417). In all of the present cases, regime formation entailed party formation, although the viability of these organizations varied in critical ways.

---

[13] I use the term "ruling party," rather than another label, to distinguish predominant organizations like the NDP and UMNO from more exclusionary and more competitive party systems. On one side stand genuinely *single*-party regimes (such as Communist Cuba) that permit no alternative parties. On the other are *dominant* party democracies (India under the Congress Party, Japan under the Liberal Democratic Party), in which opposition parties are not regularly disadvantaged through illegal and extralegal electoral manipulation (Pempel 1990).

Those variations mark the first contrast needing explanation: Why did some regimes develop ruling parties, whereas others operated with weak parties and even dissolved those organizations within a short time?

The second shared condition of the four cases is their adoption of limited elections in which opposition parties could compete against the ruling elite, albeit at a substantial disadvantage. By 1980, all four regimes had held at least one parliamentary election with multiple contestants. In the context of rulers' democratic ruse, differences in opposition performance provide the second contrast that merits explanation: Why did some elections become unexpected vehicles for opposition success and the activation of new alliances for regime change? The answer to this question is nested in the legacies of the first inquiry: The divergence in institutional development over the preceding years. The political antecedents of the third wave determined the vulnerability of regimes to opposition challenges and continue to structure the distribution of power between rulers and ruled.

By selecting only regimes that hold limited elections, I can limit my focus to the nonelectoral factors that vary across the cases; in other words, this project attempts to control for the electoral features of contemporary authoritarianism. Since approximately two dozen regimes do not hold elections at all, it is important to specify how the present comparison can help comparativists differentiate among such closed regimes (Snyder 2006: 224). Although this book does not analyze closed regimes like those of Saudi Arabia or Myanmar, the present institutional theory can inform a future exploration of these regimes and their ilk. Notably, the statistical test of authoritarian breakdown indicates that the longevity of closed authoritarian regimes is conditioned by the organization of power, just as it is in more inclusionary autocracies. Regardless of their lack of elections, these regimes appear just as susceptible to coalitional tensions as the authoritarian regimes of Iran and the Philippines. Even more important, the causal mechanisms that maintain the Egyptian and Malaysian regimes are sufficiently general that they may well apply to closed regimes. Even when such regimes lack ruling parties, they may benefit from other institutions that mediate among elites, inculcate loyalty, and deter defection. Indeed, studies of the Saudi monarchy or the Burmese junta point to the role of ties that structure elite behavior in ways similar to the pattern in Egypt and Malaysia (Herb 1999: 3–4; International Crisis Group 2000: 4, 7). Therefore, the present theory may be generalized and tested beyond the implicit scope of the present four cases.

Having posited the contextual similarities of Egypt, Iran, Malaysia, and the Philippines, I can now detail the theory of ruling parties and durable authoritarianism as it extends from regime formation to recent regime outcomes. Three factors explain the process from regime creation to continuity or collapse: *Early elite conflict* accounts for the origins of party institutions. These *party institutions* then determine the durability of authoritarianism. Finally, in a situation of institutional decline and elite defections, the level of *political confrontation* influences whether democratization will follow. As I have noted earlier, my aim is to explain large differences in the stability and fragility of current regimes. Hence, the goal is to account for broad variations between durable authoritarianism and opportunities for democratization. Where opportunities for democratization emerge, the proximate analyses of transitions studies account for who wins and why. In this theory, there are two basic causal paths, each of which passes through three periods: Regime formation, institutional legacies, and regime outcomes. Figure 1.1 diagrams these divergent paths.

Early Regime Formation: The Origins of Ruling Parties

The years during which political regimes first emerge are formative for subsequent regime durability or instability. Early conflicts set the stage on which subsequent political actors engage one another, laying down the governing parameters within which future political movements operate.[14] During such periods, ruling parties have historically emerged as a consequence of would-be rulers' desire to mobilize mass support and elites' desire for the security that accompanies the triumph of one faction over others. Party institutions are the tools that rival political forces use to compete. When leaders co-opt or suppress elite rivals while containing or marginalizing alternate political movements with a popular base, they build ruling parties that house robust coalitions. In contrast, when

---

[14] Moments of regime formation are, like opportunities for democratization, critical junctures. At the same time, this approach heeds the concerns that critical juncture frameworks risk being applied in an ad hoc manner. When each comparativist determines a new critical juncture for his or her particular case, it is difficult to adjudicate between competing arguments or accumulate knowledge across projects (Geddes 2003: 140–141). The specification of regime formation episodes as critical junctures matches our knowledge about the emergence of new systems of political authority as formative events. Rather than implying a sui generis empirical claim about specific cases, the argument relies on our ontological understanding of the relative fluidity of state and regime creation.

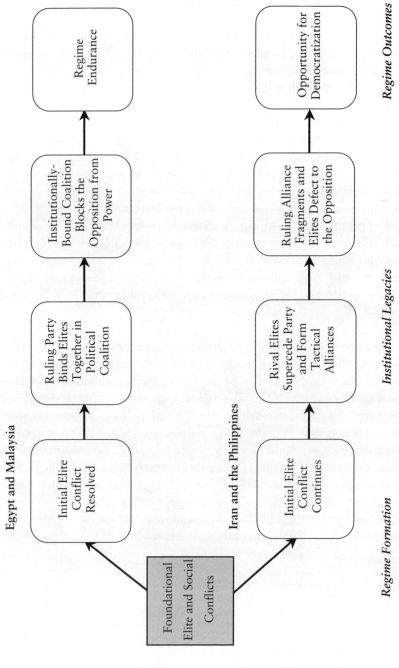

Egypt and Malaysia

| Initial Elite Conflict Resolved | → | Ruling Party Binds Elites Together in Political Coalition | → | Institutionally-Bound Coalition Blocks the Opposition from Power | → | Regime Endurance |

Iran and the Philippines

| Initial Elite Conflict Continues | → | Rival Elites Supercede Party and Form Tactical Alliances | → | Ruling Alliance Fragments and Elites Defect to the Opposition | → | Opportunity for Democratization |

Foundational Elite and Social Conflicts

Regime Formation   *Institutional Legacies*   *Regime Outcomes*

FIGURE 1.1. Ruling Parties and Durable Authoritarianism.

leadership rivalries persist and challenger movements maintain broad social support, the parties that emerge are weak organizations, containing deep divisions that subsequently cause their complete dissolution.

Whether elites decisively resolve their core conflicts during the period of regime formation, then, determines if a ruling party emerges and binds together a cohesive multifactional coalition. The institutional legacy of the regime formation period subsequently ensures further stability for those leaders with ruling parties or unmediated elite factionalism for those with weak parties. In the latter instance, rulers may subsequently deactivate existing party institutions for fear that rivals will take hold of them. They then narrow their coalitions along strict ideological or personal lines, marginalizing other figures in the ruling cadre. Such actions have the unintended consequence of hastening the outcome they are meant to prevent: Rulers who seek to consolidate their authority instead disperse it. In the other case, in which ruling parties hold the elite together and provide mechanisms for long-term political security, leaders can resolve differences that would otherwise have escalated.

As the architecture of contemporary politics, institutions link early outcomes with recent developments. The conflicts and conditions surrounding party creation play a significant role in determining whether parties sustain coalitions in a self-reinforcing cycle of elite cohesion or disintegrate as disputes intensify. Because of the political logic detailed above, however, they do not determine institutional continuity indefinitely. Parties create a political context in which disputes transcend the immediate problem of allocating resources; they extend influence horizontally and temporally. In addition, they are useful in resolving newly emerging problems such as generational change, shifts in the national economy, and domestic or international pressures. But when institutions weaken, actors may attempt to reshape the parameters of political life. In these moments of uncertainty, the leadership and decisions of previously excluded groups acquire significance (Krasner 1984: 240).

Medium-Term Institutional Legacies: Ruling Parties and Elite Behavior

Once a regime has been formed, the act of governing raises new challenges and prompts leaders to broaden their initial clique. In this task, the party brings new elites into the ruling class and joins otherwise disparate figures. Developed to meet the exigencies of regime formation, parties in which elite conflicts have been resolved soon acquire a second use: They curb leaders' ambitions and bind together political coalitions.

Ruling parties regulate intrinsic conflicts among competing, ambitious elites (Aldrich 1995: 22).[15] Typically, the most successful of these individuals hold posts in the cabinet, military, or domestic repressive agencies. Whatever the post to which they aspire, power seekers vie with one another for a finite number of top-level positions. Parties adjudicate among the contestants in this race for advancement, assuring those who are not successful today that they will have opportunities in the future. A similar dynamic links power holders – those who have achieved key positions and wield some influence over the government's course – to parties.

Although speaking on behalf of their own interests, elites also represent (implicitly if not juridically) the country's diverse social constituencies. The social bases of political power sometimes put leaders at loggerheads, as the nonelites who support them may want very different things. Those figures who participate in national-level agenda setting tend to do so because they wield certain influence in society. Elites may command a substantial popular base, the loyalty of civil servants, economic clout in the business sector, technocratic expertise, or something else. In any of these situations, elite status is a two-way street: Leaders' choices are constrained by the very constituencies or backgrounds that imbue them with influence (Migdal 1988: 22–23). This does not mean political power is merely derivative of social background, as once they take a seat at the regime's table, elites acquire tools for responding to and influencing the groups that helped them reach that position. It does mean, though, that disagreement and conflict are constant features of authoritarian rule. Elites' broader ties influence where they stand on issues and when they clash with one another.

When elites disagree, the party regulates these disputes and enables solutions that might otherwise prove elusive among rivalrous leaders left to their own devices. At this point, parties "promote the achievement of collective choices" – solutions that transcend factional advantage and benefit all participants (Aldrich 1995: 23). Thus, beyond managing competition *for* power, parties restrain the conflicts of actors *in* power. The centripetal pull ruling parties exert on elite behavior is not a direct by-product of preexisting preferences (Geddes 1999b: 11). After all, the elites

---

[15] Parties were earlier treated as "essential agencies of mobilization" (Lipset and Rokkan 1967: 4) and "transmission belts between the population at large and the governmental structure" (Kirchheimer 1966: 177), but constituents may be mobilized and their opinions transmitted without parties. Rather than simply conveying societal concerns, ruling parties manage competing interests and reconcile the elites who articulate such demands.

of any given regime draw on a variety of social constituencies and have disparate individual ambitions. Rather, it is the effect of an institutional setting in which organizational loyalty is the product of self-interest. Leaders' actions are shaped not only by their material interests and vocational backgrounds but also by the political process by which immediate concerns become long-term considerations.

By offering a sustainable system for members to settle disputes and exert influence, ruling parties generate and maintain a cohesive leadership cadre. So long as the organization manages its members' ambitions, individual pursuits can be the root of continued allegiance. Decision making occurs in a context where the maintenance of national-level agenda setting is a constant priority (Waldner 1999: 29). In such a forum, even rival projects pushed by leaders with conflicting constituencies (for example, capitalists favoring privatization against civil servants tied to bloated state bureaucracies) may be accommodated. The institutional realm thereby extends the time horizons – the temporal perspective over which costs and benefits are weighed – of those involved. It also provides a common project of collective, if contentious, leadership that stands apart from the excluded opposition movements that advocate the fundamental redistribution of power.

When parties harness elites together, they provide collective security, a sense among power holders that their immediate and long-term interests are best served by remaining within the party organization. This collective security depends on leaders' binding themselves together in an arrangement that generally precludes certain actions, mainly the permanent exclusion or elimination of fellow party leaders (Ikenberry 2001: 4). The party's members understand that no faction will indefinitely trump the others, and thus the organization's decisions will, over time, reflect its composition (Ikenberry 2001: 6; Schickler 2001: 26). The "binding commitments" of a ruling party's elite help to ensure the regime's long-term dominance by reducing the threat of elite defection (Ikenberry 2001: 10). Elite cohesion then redounds to the benefit of the regime's rulers, lengthening the time span over which they may exercise their acquired influence and thus enhancing the party's capacity to mollify today's discontent with the prospect of fresh achievements tomorrow. Once politicians begin experiencing the collective benefits brought by a party, they are likely to support its continued operations.

Because ruling parties deliver increasing "returns to power" through the reinforcing cycle of elite privilege and political dominance, it seems sensible for leaders who benefit from parties to maintain them (Ikenberry

2001: 41). Why then do some leaders get rid of parties? Why do leaders with political organizations actually abandon those organizations rather than build them up as lasting bulwarks against the opposition? This enigma is important, because the presence or absence of ruling parties often separates regimes that are susceptible to opposition challenges from their nearly impregnable counterparts. The explanation for why leaders dismantle parties depends on the very same logic as the explanation for why they maintain them: Elites behave opportunistically in response to the political context that surrounds them, especially the level of immediate threats to their position (Waldner 1999: 29, 33). The early defeat of elite rivals creates an initial security on which leaders may build their own parties and incorporate new members. But the irresolution of foundational conflicts deprives elites of that reassurance. Instead of producing an organization that initially coheres around one predominant faction and gradually expands to include others, the party remains a site of internecine struggle. Far from acting to regulate elite ambitions, the party is overwhelmed by them. In reaction to perceived threats from rivals within the organization, leaders then opt to disband the party. This bid for power may produce the desired effect of marginalizing rival political actors, yet it also narrows decision making around the ruler and threatens to siphon influence from other leaders.

Regime Outcomes: Ruling Parties and Durable Authoritarianism

Opposition campaigns for regime change depend on the public presence of elite defectors. Discussions of "soft-liners," those political elites who reach out to moderate opposition movements, tend to leave open the question of what factors distinguish elite defection from reaffiliation (O'Donnell and Schmitter 1986: 19; Przeworski 1986: 56). Because the political decisions of elites exceed the collection of individual interests, elite behavior – including the choice to ally with the opposition – must be embedded within ruling parties (Heydemann 1999: 211). When parties hold the ruling coalition together, such influential partners tend not to emerge, opting instead to continue supporting a system that provides them influence over the national agenda. In the context of weakening parties and widening elite rifts, however, regime supporters realign. Driven by pragmatism as much as by principle, they back the opposition and pursue their interests by challenging the status quo. At such moments, the political contest for power is less constrained by existing institutions and more vulnerable to the efforts of societal activists. This marks the key distinction between durable authoritarianism and contested regimes in which opportunities for democratization emerge.

The institutional context of elite conflict strongly influences whether elites will seek allies outside the ruling clique and whether they will partner with the opposition. Just as parties enable lasting political coalitions, their absence brings the opposite. If rulers dismantle the party to insulate their closest confederates, fears of exclusion proliferate. Distance breeds distrust. No mechanisms exist to mediate interfactional conflict, and debates escalate into battles for political life or death. The lack of a party to regulate elite interaction heightens the allure of working from the outside. Previous defenders of the system campaign for reform rather than waste away in a hierarchy that offers no opportunity for success. Defectors expose internal conflicts to public view and may participate in a counteralliance of long-time activists and recently estranged regimists. As intraelite rivalry feeds into interfactional competition, the regime becomes susceptible to previously suppressed opponents.

Institutional decline yields an opening for redrawing the parameters of political authority and even restructuring the system from dictatorship to democracy. These are the opportunities for democratization mentioned earlier. With the national polity thrown into open conflict, the confrontation of different elite groups and mass movements determines whether the system will resettle in an authoritarian or democratic form and which factions will be in control. In this context of exceptional uncertainty, the strategies of participants can strongly influence national political changes. Regime transformation hinges on the readiness of moderate oppositionists to forcefully advocate the establishment of popular sovereignty and representative government. Although party institutionalization accounts for the presence or absence of opportunities for democratization, whether activists take advantage of such opportunities depends on the stance and strength of the groups involved.

Parties protect leaders from many politically lethal threats, especially the risk of coalition fragmentation, but they do not convey immortality to a regime. After decades of power, regimes may exhibit the traits of elite disunity that are endemic to less institutionalized systems. Elite conflicts have periodically dealt the killing stroke to long-lived party regimes. When parties – often decades old – suffer from organizational decay, mechanisms of reward and sanction weaken. Loss of privileges alienates party members and inclines regime supporters toward the opposition (Kalyvas 1999: 337; Herbst 2001: 361; Solinger 2001: 37). Valerie Bunce posits that the seeds of the Soviet Union's collapse were planted decades before 1991; suffused into the makeup of the socialist state, they subsequently engendered divisive competition. Yet she also notes that the nature of Soviet-era institutions cannot account for the timing of the fall (Bunce 1999, 141–142). Hence, these party regimes might have collapsed earlier, but they could also have lasted longer. When the Communist Party and Mexico's Institutional Revolutionary Party lost power after ruling for nearly three-quarters of a century, they epitomized the durability, not the fragility, of party regimes. Recognizing that party institutions are robust but not invulnerable, the task is to understand why they sustain elite solidarity for as long as they do and what repercussions their weakening has for political coalitions. It is easy to conceive of scholars' someday writing, in terms similar to Bunce's, that the NDP and UMNO's regimes were "fated to end" (Bunce 1999: 142). Analysts of that transformation may discern democracy's portents in the episodes discussed later. The question remains, however, how soon they will be penning such retrospectives.

Conclusion

Explaining why many regimes continue to cling to power requires that we comprehend not just the third wave but also its undercurrents. For this task, structural variables that seemed antiquated may prove surprisingly useful, particularly if they are integrated with the study of political action through institutions. This book's institutional approach to regime outcomes is premised on the notion that ruling parties underpin durable authoritarianism by providing a political setting for mediating elite disputes and preventing elite defections to the opposition. The principal ingredient for sustaining broad leadership coalitions is national-level agenda-setting influence, through which otherwise clashing factions may be reconciled.

Elections are the autocrat's latest fashion, but regime endurance continues to depend on what takes place inside the ruler's coalition. That arena is the focus of the following chapters, which investigate where ruling parties come from and why variations in the institutions of authoritarian rule in four states have produced different outcomes during an era of democratization. Ruling parties enable durable authoritarianism – robust nondemocratic rule in which opportunities for regime collapse are structurally precluded by the maintenance of elite cohesion and incumbent dominance over alternative social movements. When leaders lack the requisite party mechanisms for managing their coalitions, they breed discontent inside the regime. Their alliances fragment, producing elite defections, electoral defeats, and destabilization. Previously isolated opposition movements can partner with former regime loyalists while mobilizing their constituencies against the regime. The following chapters present this narrative as it unfolded in Egypt, Iran, Malaysia, and the Philippines, beginning with each regime's formative conflicts.

2

The Inception of Ruling Parties

In contrast to the institutionalist narratives of later chapters, this chapter highlights the more open-ended contests that accompanied the scramble to shape emerging political systems. During the fluid and uncertain period of regime formation, early victories held the potential to channel society's course for generations. Drawing rarely repeated public attention and engagement through street demonstrations, national elections, or campaigns of violent repression, leaders vied for control and struggled to cast emerging states in ways favorable to their own ambitions. The outcomes of these elite battles – specifically, whether one faction triumphed or its opponents retained a presence in the regime – were embodied within the organizations of national leadership and agenda setting: political parties.

The historical accounts contained here are integral to a full understanding of how the legacies of the past are imbricated with the politics of the present: In short, the early interplay of key political actors yielded the institutional legacies that would structure national politics. These accounts of regime formation are intended to enrich current analyses of party building that focus largely on social conflict while paying less attention to the contested interaction of ambitious elites (Smith 2005: 422). Leaders in Egypt, Iran, Malaysia, and the Philippines created parties as a way of challenging their strongest rivals, whether foreign occupiers, violent radical movements, or mainstream political competitors. In Egypt and Malaysia, this broad struggle climaxed within the ascendant elite's own ranks as certain leaders defeated peers who promoted more open political systems. This resolution of elite conflict solidified the initial agenda of the ruling party and demarcated the coalitions that subsequently led each country for decades. In comparison, parties in Iran and the Philippines displayed much less cohesion and stability from the outset. Ridden from the start by elite rivalries and unbridled competition, they proved defective in the area of conflict management. Ultimately, leaders in both parties opted to dispense with the organizations and rule directly, without an organization mediating between different factions.

Given the role Egypt and Malaysia's ruling parties later played in maintaining coalitions of different personal and political-economic factions, it may seem paradoxical that their formative phase entailed the forced congruity of elites and programs. This pattern reflects the differing challenges leaders face during periods of regime consolidation – when organizations are young and inchoate, if present at all – as opposed to subsequent conventional political episodes, during which they have an institutional apparatus at their disposal. When initially achieving power, would-be rulers must decisively defeat their rivals. Once in command, they are positioned to incorporate their critics through parties and other institutional channels that regulate politics. Rulers consolidate regimes by besting their competitors in periods of polarization and open conflict; they sustain those regimes through organizations and rules that ensure subsequent public confrontations are a rarity. Over time, ruling parties enable a coalitional diversity that would have hobbled them at their inception. This concept bears a semblance to Huntington's notion of the party as a "buckle which binds one social force to another" (1968: 405). The focus here, however, is on the leaders of disparate social constituencies and the way in which their long-term cooperation through the ruling party may be premised on the initial victory of a smaller and much less pluralist group of elites as the party comes into existence.

The argument that the resolution of elite conflict enabled ruling party regimes in Egypt and Malaysia that did not take root in Iran and the Philippines explains the causes of institutional variation, enabling a more holistic understanding of ruling parties' subsequent effects on national politics in developing countries. Table 2.1 provides an overview of this comparison, showing the main actors during regime formation in Egypt, Iran, Malaysia, and the Philippines and the effects of elite conflict on party development. The two sections that follow will describe periods of regime formation, first in Egypt and Malaysia and then in Iran and the Philippines, with an emphasis on how their ruling parties arose in these periods and the extent to which elite conflict was decided in favor of one faction or left unresolved.

TABLE 2.1. *Early Elite Conflict and Party Legacies*

Regime (*formative period*)	Initial Leadership Organization	Dominant Elite	Rival Elite	Elite Conflict Outcomes	Moderate Opposition (*outcome*)	Militant Opposition (*outcome*)	Party Legacies
Egypt (*1952–1954*)	Revolutionary Command Council	Nasser	Naguib	Naguib and supporters defeated and excluded from power.	Wafd, Muslim Brotherhood, other parties (*banned*)	N.A.	Liberation Rally established. Continues through successor ruling party organizations.
Iran (*1979–1981*)	Islamic Revolutionary Council	Khomeini, Beheshti	Bani-Sadr, leftist clerics	Bani-Sadr exiled. Intra-clergy debate over popular sovereignty continues.	Iran Freedom Movement, communists (*banned*)	Mojahedin-e-Khalq (*repressed*)	IRP defeats challengers but party leaders, citing internal rifts, dissolve it in 1987.
Malaysia (*1946–1957*)	United Malays National Organization	Tunku Abdul Rahman	Dato Onn	Onn leaves UMNO, which then promotes Malay-dominant multi-communalism.	Islamists, independents (*marginalized*)	Malaya Communist Party (*repressed*)	Through Alliance and National Front, UMNO commands political arena in post-independence period.
Philippines (*1899–1946*)	Nacionalista Party	Quezon	Osmeña, Roxas	No single dominant leader. Incessant competition for presidency.	Federal Party, Popular Front (*marginalized*)	N.A.	Nacionalista-Liberal Party duopoly. Rampant clientelism and party switching.

Pluralism Defeated: Ruling Party Foundations in Egypt and Malaysia

The durability of nondemocratic rule in Egypt and Malaysia throughout the late twentieth century conceals a contested lineage of mass politics and early elite conflict about each country's basic political structure. For nearly two years after the Egyptian monarchy was overthrown, soldiers debated their role in the country's future: Should they return to the barracks or actively guide national policy? In the decade-long run-up to independence, Malay leaders pondered how they would preserve their traditional privileges once British colonial rule ended. What would be the involvement of non-Malays in national politics? Could the country's substantial Chinese and Indian minorities enjoy political equality with Malays, or would they be granted second-class citizenship and participate in a subordinate role? In very distinct ways, these discussions about the political supremacy of Egypt's soldiers and the continued dominance of Malaya's ethnic majority defined each country's polity, the breadth and character of its ruling class, and the nature of elite-mass relations. Thus, the abortive opposition campaigns of the 1980s and 1990s must be set against a backdrop of earlier questions about the distribution of newly acquired power and the organizations that would sustain it over time. To the dismay of pluralistically inclined leaders, these concerns were answered by the victory of exclusionary elites who favored a narrow rulership and gave only minimal influence to broader movements.

As Egypt and Malaysia's regimes formed in the 1950s, leaders established parameters of political life that would endure into the next century. The uncertainty and promise of this period evoked broad engagement across social classes, communal groupings, and nongovernmental associations. The leaders who vied to set the political agenda were enmeshed in these mass constituencies and invoked their participation to press their case. The popular and fatherly Mohammed Naguib called on his civilian supporters in Egypt's capital, as well as his loyal confederates in the military, as he tried to thwart Gamal Abdel Nasser's grab for power. In Malaysia, Dato Onn Jaafar sought to galvanize a broad movement of Malays and non-Malays to block the ascent of UMNO in critical elections before independence. Ultimately, the battles in the streets of Cairo and the polls of Kuala Lumpur were ancillary to the core struggle between elites with different visions for their new countries. When Naguib and Onn lost their positions in the leadership's core, the organizations left in their wake were strengthened and emboldened through programmatic unity and elite conformity. The end of intraelite factionalism inaugurated ruling parties with an exclusionary agenda and cohesive coalition. Nasser and Abdul Rahman not only curtailed the democratic trends advocated by Naguib and Onn, they also established the infrastructure for durable authoritarianism.

No Return to the Barracks: Egypt, 1952–1954

Between the start of 1952 and the close of 1954, a military-led dictatorship arose and replaced Egypt's ailing monarchy. Six months after Egyptians across the country had clamored for independence, Gamal Abdel Nasser and the Free Officers overthrew the king, expropriated large landholders, and neutralized existing political parties. As Nasser and his cohort transformed from coup plotters to rulers of the new Egyptian republic, they developed a national party that would serve their regime for decades. At the outset, a dictatorship headed by a former colonel was far from the minds of most officers, and a majority of the coup executors viewed liberal democracy as the best mode of government for Egypt (Beattie 1994: 44). But the momentum of reform soon swept the Free Officers far beyond their original, self-assigned mandate, transforming their inner council from provision caretakers to perpetual rulers with a national political organization, the Liberation Rally. This organization took form while Nasser's cadre suppressed their most formidable critics, members of the military who advocated a rapid return to parliamentary government. When the new leaders defeated liberal-leaning figures within their own ranks, they erected the framework for autocratic rule.

At the time of the coup, military rule seemed an unlikely outcome for Egypt. The armed forces had been a peripheral participant in the political arena, which was dominated by conflict among British occupiers, Egypt's king, and the country's opposition parties. The British had ruled Egypt since 1882, although they expanded local leaders' control over domestic affairs after 1922 (Abdel-Malek 1968: 18). Under the 1923 constitution, they reserved the right to protect their interests and those of other foreign populations. Although Britain remained the de facto sovereign, Egypt's king ruled and headed the government. From 1936 through 1952, that monarch was Farouk, great-great-grandson of Muhammad Ali (r. 1805–1849), the founder of the modern Egyptian state. Farouk's penchant for indulgence and mismanagement eroded his popularity, and Egypt's loss to Israel in the 1948 war further discredited him (Herb 1999: 211–212). As Egyptians pressed the British for independence, they came to see Farouk as an obstacle to that campaign. Yet they also deemed most of the local political alternatives similarly corrupt and ineffectual.

Chief among the parliamentary opposition stood the Wafd ("delegation") Party. The Wafd had led the 1919 revolt against British rule and remained the traditional standard-bearer for Egyptian self-determination. Yet the party's nationalist stance weakened as its leadership increasingly protected the interests of the country's landed aristocracy (Ayubi 1995: 107). By the 1940s, the Wafd had become a virtual partner in a conservative alliance with the monarchy (Abdel-Malek 1968: 18–19). Despite its multiclass constituency and appeal in both urban and rural areas, Wafd leaders feared that sudden independence might threaten their property holdings and their dominance of the countryside. Emblemizing this conservatism, one prominent Wafd leader quipped to the U.S. ambassador a year before the coup: "I own 8000 feddans [approximately 8,000 acres]. Do you think I want Egypt to go Communist?" (Gordon 1992: 24). The Wafd was further constrained by the king's power to dismiss parliament at will. Despite winning every parliamentary election from 1923 through 1952, the Wafd actually governed for a total of only six years and ten months (Zaki 1995: 10). Hampered by its own interests, on the one hand, and the perennial intervention of the British and the king, on the other, the Wafd lost public support as the drive for independence intensified.

As parliamentary politics proved too feeble to wrest control from the British, more radical efforts gained momentum. Nearly six hundred Egyptian fighters died in acts of anticolonial resistance in December 1951 (Abdel-Malek 1968: 32). On 16 January, demonstrations began in Cairo, and similar protests sprouted up in other parts of the country. On 25 January, British soldiers attempted to quell unrest in the town of Ismailia, assaulting local police and killing more than fifty people (Vatikiotis 1991: 371–372). The next day, rioters in Cairo set fire to much of the city's business district (Gordon 1992: 27; Zaki 1995: 11). The army was deployed to restore order in the streets of the capital, and mass arrests soon followed. The prime minister declared the country to be in "a state of siege," and the government incarcerated thousands accused of aiding the guerilla attacks (Abdel-Malek 1968: 37). These draconian measures appeared effective, and the clashes of January 1952 did not recur in the subsequent months.

As Egypt pulled back from the brink of civil conflict and national politics remained tumultuous, a new set of actors stealthily approached the political arena. While control of the country's flimsy parliament changed hands three times in just six months, a covert network of proindependence military officers prepared to accomplish what the civilian opposition had failed to do for thirty years: Seize control from the British and the king and put Egypt's government in the hands of Egyptians (Abdel-Malek

1968: 37).[1] On the night of 22 July 1952, a group of junior military men led by Colonel Abdel Nasser who called themselves the Free Officers arrested upper-ranking royalist officers in Cairo, seized control of the national media communications centers, and closed the capital's roads and bridges. The following morning, Free Officers member Anwar Sadat announced the group's takeover and its commitment to the Egyptian people in a radio broadcast (Hamrush 1993: 123). The king, who was away in Alexandria, tried for several days to escape the officers' grasp, taking refuge in his palaces and imploring Britain for assistance. These efforts proved futile; on 26 July, he was forced to abdicate his throne and leave the country (Vatikiotis 1991: 378–379; Gordon 1992: 60). Egyptians poured into the streets to celebrate what the officers had accomplished (Hamrush 1993: 123). Meanwhile, the traditional opposition parties initially rallied to the Free Officers' cause, chagrined by the soldiers' effectiveness at toppling the monarchy but expecting that professional politicians would be the main beneficiaries (Vatikiotis 1991: 379).

The Free Officers had envisioned themselves as provisional stewards who would rout the constitutional monarchy's worst elements and thereby enable a government based on popular sovereignty to take hold. Yet success and popular adulation steadily emboldened the military leaders to become rulers, not just political custodians (Gordon 1992: 58). Nasser gradually came to perceive popularly elected government as an impediment to Egypt's development and reversed his initial plans of handing over power to one (Beattie 1994: 70). Thus, a mission of reform soon expanded to become a more radical enterprise bent on reconstituting the foundations of Egyptian society. Nasser assembled a portion of the Free Officers, along with a small number of officers uninvolved in the original coup, to create a fourteen-member Revolutionary Command Council (RCC) to administer the country (Beattie 1994: 85). The RCC's members then set out to remedy the country's ills as they perceived them, targeting the landholding aristocracy, political parties, and fellow officers who favored a return to civilian government. This last phase of intramilitary conflict was critical in erasing the idea that Nasser and his associates would serve in a transitional capacity, as intended at the coup's inception.

Nasser and his confederates realized that land reform would weaken the old landed elites, many of whom had supported the monarchy, and help the new regime garner support in the countryside through economic

---

[1] In fact, the most recent precedent dated to 1882, when Colonel Ahmad Orabi seized effective control of the Egyptian government until his removal by British forces, which had occupied the country (Vatikiotis 1991: 151–154, 379).

redistribution (Hudson 1977: 239). The RCC thus pushed through a limit on individual holdings of a maximum of 200 feddans (approximately 208 acres), overriding the concerted objections of prime minister Ali Mahir and an assembly of twenty-two large landholders, who preferred a less radical 1,000-feddan limit. Dismissing Mahir from his position and replacing him with RCC member General Muhammad Naguib on 8 September 1952, the RCC announced the land reform decree the following day (Gordon 1992: 67). Although the changes affected only 12 percent of the areas targeted, they disrupted the landed aristocracy's long-held security at the top of the Egyptian political hierarchy, decisively shifting power from the old class to the new leadership as "large landlords ceased to exist as a political force" (Richards and Waterbury 1996: 155).

Having subordinated Egypt's landed elite, Nasser's junta next targeted the political parties that had opposed the monarchy and still commanded a large following. Throughout its experiment with constitutional monarchy, Egyptians had enjoyed a lively, if often ineffectual, array of opposition parties. In a span of months, the RCC replaced this fractious multipartyism with single-party dominance. Their primary foe was the Wafd, the presumptive beneficiary of a return to elections. Land reform had shaken the Wafd's wealthy constituents in the countryside. Intergenerational cleavages and public disenchantment further weakened the organization's ability to contest the Free Officers' expanding control of the state (Gordon 1992: 23). The RCC also contended with parties that supported populist measures against the aristocracy. Striking against movements from across the political spectrum, it first placed party formation under the authority of the Ministry of Interior, limiting the ability of new parties to form (Hamrush 1993: 133; Beattie 1994: 78). The council then revoked the 1923 constitution on 10 December 1952, and its officers began taking positions in the state bureaucracy. On 17 January 1953, they announced the dissolution of all existing opposition parties and the beginning of a three-year transition period "to enable the establishment of healthy constitutional democratic government" (Hamrush 1993: 137–138). Only the Muslim Brotherhood (MB), whose ties with some of the Free Officers' members had begun more than a decade before the 1952 coup, was initially exempted (Beattie 1994: 48).

A week after it had deactivated Egypt's existing parties and six months after it had deposed the king, the RCC created a single channel for mass politics: The Liberation Rally (LR) (Hamrush 1993: 139). The Liberation Rally provided a national organization that could aggregate members of the disbanded opposition parties. Its platform was emblematic of its purpose of filling the political vacuum: Using broad language about equality

in domestic politics and independence in Egypt's foreign relations, the LR
sought to collect support from across traditional ideological lines (Beattie
1994: 80–81; Al-Bishri 1991: 148; Abdel-Malek 1968: 92). The institutional forebear of the Arab Socialist Union and the present-day National
Democratic Party, the Liberation Rally connected the nascent regime to
"villages and tribes, universities, trade unions, mosques, Coptic churches,
and Jewish synagogues" (Halpern 1963: 308–309).[2] Although it aggre-
gated the country's neutralized opposition forces, the Liberation Rally also
betrayed the RCC's drift from navigating a return to parliamentary rule
to consolidating power around Nasser and his fellow Free Officers. On
6 February 1953, Nasser became the LR's secretary-general (Abdel-Malek
1968: 92).

Nasser's bid for hegemony cleared its final obstacle in the spring of
1954, when he drowned out Mohammed Naguib's call for a return to
the barracks. During the RCC's first year in power, General Naguib had
served as the group's elder statesmen. His stature as a revered national
figure had helped dignify the RCC's inchoate administration during its
initial months (Beattie 1994: 68). He filled the prime minister's role following Ali Maher's dismissal in the fall of 1952. When the country was
formally declared a republic on 18 June 1953, Naguib became Egypt's first
president (Abdel-Malek 1968: 93). The presidency weakened Naguib's
influence within the officer corps by taking the armed forces out of his
command, but it also set him up as a front-runner for political power
in any shift to civilian rule (Beattie 1994: 90). Although Naguib had
been peripheral in the original coup, he was titled "Leader of the Revolution" in December 1953 (Abdel-Malek 1968: 91). Such prominent –
albeit largely ceremonial – positions and titles redounded to Naguib's
credit, and he often received public adoration for the RCC's policy initiatives (Dekmejian 1971: 25). Unlike the Free Officers, to which he did
not formally belong, Naguib was from a military family and had a more
conventional and stricter idea of the military's political role than that
espoused by some of his interventionist juniors (Vatikiotis 1991: 384).
Naguib advocated – and, by virtue of his popularity, would likely have
benefited from – a transition to fully elected government.

By the spring of 1954, Nasser's civilian foes were nearly completely
decimated. A September 1953 crackdown by the RCC had imprisoned

---

[2] The Muslim Brotherhood was conspicuously resistant to the Liberation Rally's pull.
Beattie traces part of Nasser's growing antagonism toward the MB to the Islamist group's
refusal to join the LR (Beattie 1994: 82–83).

thirty-four members of a provisional opposition alliance. Then, on 14 January 1954, the RCC dissolved the Muslim Brotherhood over Naguib's objection, thus ending the Islamist group's year-long grace period (Hamrush 1993: 146). Given the RCC's pervasive control over society, one can understand why the final opportunity for a mass challenge originated within the council itself. Although it had acted effectively to quell dissent, the RCC presided over an ambivalent and divided military from which the council's members differed in many ways. Although most of the RCC favored Nasser's autocratic direction, the larger officer corps did not, as Beattie argues: "[P]rima facie evidence pointed to the numerical superiority of prodemocratic officers. Weekly postcoup forums among artillery and cavalry officers gave evidence of strong prodemocracy sentiments" (1994: 85). Within the RCC, President Naguib became a forceful spokesman for popular sovereignty. But when he called for a quick transition to parliamentary government, nearly all of the other RCC officers balked (Ansari 1986: 83–84).

In response, Naguib tried to trump the RCC with his public status, in essence leveraging nominal power into political influence over the regime's direction. Isolated within the Revolutionary Command Council but beloved by most Egyptians, Naguib resigned on 24 February 1954, publicly challenging Nasser and the RCC to reinstate him. They refused. Demonstrators in Cairo and Alexandria filled the streets in protest (Hamrush 1993: 146). Thousands of Muslim Brotherhood supporters rallied for Naguib in the capital on 28 February (Beattie 1994: 94). Two hundred officers from the armored corps also pressed the issue, demanding Naguib's return to the premiership. Days later, Nasser complied but soon after arrested the officers who had made the case for Naguib's return to power (Gordon 1992: 129). The RCC next detained seventy-four oppositionists belonging to the Muslim Brotherhood and other banned parties, thereby undermining Naguib's civilian supporters as well. In response, Naguib called for their release and declared at a major press conference, "I do not want to be president of a republic that is not democratic and not parliamentary" (Hamrush 1993: 147–148). Discussion then returned to the confines of the council as Naguib called for a handover to an elected government by July of that year (Beattie 1994: 94).

Nasser and the RCC appeared to concede on 5 March, announcing elections for a Constituent Assembly in July and the end of martial law a month prior to the polls. The council also restored Naguib to his position as prime minister and RCC chairman, reversing his resignation (and Nasser's assumption of his posts) weeks earlier (Vatikiotis 1991: 385).

With his authority seemingly reinforced, Naguib struggled to tip the balance against Nasser in the following three weeks, yet gradually RCC leaders demonstrated to the remaining divisions of the military that their support within the armed forces exceeded what Naguib could muster (Gordon 1992: 128, 133). Sensing victory over the military's advocates of civilian rule, Nasser and his partisans turned their attention to the public.

Ostentatiously touting its self-abnegating course, the RCC resolved on 25 March that it would dissolve on 24 July and return Egypt to civilian control (Vatikiotis 1991: 385, Beattie 1994: 95). In addition, the council vowed to recognize political rights and lift the ban on independent political party organizations (Hamrush 1993: 150). Yet these promises were merely the instruments for dispatching Naguib's supporters and settling the debate over who would rule Egypt. The RCC's posture of political liberalization lured Nasser's adversaries out onto the streets of Cairo, where they would be vulnerable to physical assaults by the Liberation Rally. The day after the council's announcement, opposition parties, the lawyers' and journalists' syndicates, and university students rallied with the common goal of overcoming the RCC. Conspicuously absent from this alliance was the Muslim Brotherhood, which had reached an accord with Nasser during the prior month; hundreds of imprisoned MB members were freed, and the group's leaders began to eschew the newly emboldened opposition (Gordon 1992: 135, Beattie 1994: 96). As the opposition took to the streets, Nasser activated the Liberation Rally, portions of the armed service, and the transportation workers' union in a countermobilization effort that discredited the revival of parties as a return to the corrupt practices of the monarchy period (Hamrush 1993: 152). The fabricated crisis provided the pretext for freezing any movement toward democracy and broke the link between Naguib's faction in the military and their backers in society (Vatikiotis 1991: 386). Despite their determination, students, professionals, old party politicians, and other pro-Naguib demonstrators were outnumbered and overpowered; after the Brotherhood's defection, they lacked the mass support needed to repel the Liberation Rally's broad assemblage of labor unions and government workers (Dekmejian 1971: 30, Beattie 1994: 96).[3]

---

[3] While the Liberation Rally was originally formed to fill the void left by Nasser's dissolution of existing parties, it is worth noting that during the March 1954 crisis it played a pivotal role in proregime mobilization and established the working class as a bastion of regime support for years to come (Beattie 1994: 80, 98).

Competing rallies quickly gave way to bloody clashes, and prodemocracy forces were decimated by 28 March. By that point, the Liberation Rally had deployed "mob and police violence...cowing the opposition and compelling the [RCC] to answer the loud cries for it to retain leadership of the country" (Gordon 1992: 135). The next day, just four days after they had announced a political opening, the RCC leaders "heeded" the public's demand for them to remain in power, reestablishing censorship of the press and the ban on opposition party activities (Beattie 1994: 97). The council's about-face from liberalization to repression dashed any hopes for a return to parliamentary democracy (Hamrush 1993: 152). Naguib no longer had the influence to challenge his fellow officers. He continued to hold the office of president but had been ejected from the RCC (Abdel-Malek 1968: 95). Nasser assumed the effective executive post of prime minister on 7 April (Hamrush 1993: 152).

In the wake of the March 1954 crisis, the Muslim Brotherhood remained the only significant challenge to the RCC's monopolization of political power. Because of its connections to the RCC and its persistent popularity, the MB enjoyed an extended reprieve from the RCC's conventional tactics. Although the RCC had formally disbanded the Brotherhood in January 1954, the subsequent pact between Nasser and MB leaders evinced the RCC's desire not to antagonize MB activists or push them into a lasting alliance with other opposition elements (Beattie 1994: 91). For their part, the MB had largely declined formal cooperation with the traditional parties, most infamously in March 1954 (Hamrush 1993: 145). But in subsequent months, with the RCC's other critics swept away, the Brotherhood became increasingly isolated: Nasser discredited the group in the national media and forced its leaders into hiding. Struggling against this campaign of persecution, the Muslim Brotherhood fragmented, with one splinter group advocating violent confrontation with Nasser's regime (Beattie 1994: 99–100). In Alexandria on the evening of 24 October 1954, a member named Mahmoud Abdel Latif attempted and failed to assassinate Nasser, who was delivering a public address (Gordon 1992: 179, Beattie 1994: 100). The incident, which some have alleged was a regime-staged event, curtailed what little tolerance the regime still showed to the Muslim Brotherhood. The RCC immediately cracked down on the MB, arresting an estimated four to seven thousand of its members and forcing the organization underground (Abdel-Malek 1968: 96; Dekmejian 1971: 33). Naguib was also accused of involvement in the assassination plot. On 14 November 1954, he was removed from the presidency and placed under house arrest (Abdel-Malek 1968: 96).

By the end of 1954, less than thirty months after the original coup, Nasser and the remaining leaders of the RCC had solidified their control. In the process, they had forged an organization, the Liberation Rally, that outflanked the opposition and channeled mass support. Through a referendum and uncontested plebiscite in 1956, Egyptians approved a new constitution, which ended the transition period, and chose Nasser as president with an alleged 99.9 percent vote share (Hamrush 1993: 153). The 1956 constitution granted the president broad authority, allowing his decrees to carry the power of law. It also instituted the National Union, the organizational successor of the Liberation Rally, to which all Egyptians were to belong and which replaced all other alternative parties (Hamrush 1993: 155).

The Defeat of Nonethnic Politics: Malaya, 1946–1957

The protracted transition of British-ruled Malaya into the sovereign constitutional monarchy of Malaysia involved both mass mobilization among the country's ethnic (Malay) majority and the transfer of powers held by the peninsula's traditional rulers, the sultans, to a new political elite. Yet the activation of Malays as a political constituency accompanied the entrenchment of Malay dominance over the country's "nonnative" ethnic groups. The decade leading up to independence in 1957 saw the defeat of an alternative, nonethnic political party led – ironically enough – by the founder of the ultimate guardian of Malay privileges, the United Malays National Organization. Hemmed in by the sultans' resistance on one side and his Malay countrymen's fears on the other, Dato Onn tried unsuccessfully to broaden UMNO's program. Rebuffed, he then made a bid for a broad nonethnic party that would bring the mass of Malays, Chinese, and Indians together in a step toward popular democracy that would secure elected authority above Malay royalty. The failure of Onn's Independence of Malaya Party (IMP) ratified UMNO's supremacy in the emerging political order and assured the sultans an important, albeit largely symbolic, role embodying Malay traditions and the Malays' historical dominance.

What would become the modern state of Malaysia began as a collection of contiguous sultanates on the peninsula of Malaya. Not until the British established indirect rule in the late nineteenth century did these traditional kingdoms develop collective political coherence. Already using the "Straits Settlements" (Penang, Malacca, and Singapore) as trading posts on the busy route between India and China, British officials began to eye Malaya's mineral-rich central region. These designs led to the Pangkor Treaty of 1874, which brought British interests into the area, and the creation of the Federated Malay States (composed of Perak, Selangor, Pahang, and Negri Sembilan) in 1896 (Jomo 1986: 142–143). In the Federated Malay States, the traditional rulers retained authority in cultural matters and "nominal autonomy" overall, but they ceded executive power, including the power to collect taxes and regulate labor, to a central figure, the British-designated chief secretary (Jomo 1986: 160; Smith 1994: 86). Hence, rather than displace local leaders, who served as valuable intermediaries between colonial administrators and the population in the Federated Malay States, the British ruled indirectly via Malaya's sultans and the aristocracy surrounding them. In the peninsula's remaining states (Perlis, Kedah, Kelantan, and Terengannu in the north; Johor in the far south), British control was less invasive and less centralized. The Unfederated Malay States were administered by British "advisers" who deferred to the local sultan (Smith 1994: 6).

The eventual struggle to determine the form of Malaysia's postindependence regime occurred between at least four political interest groups that arose during Britain's prolonged intervention in Malaya and its construction of a national administrative apparatus. On one side were the British themselves, determined to maintain easy access to the peninsula's mineral riches and the rubber plantations cultivated under British auspices.[4] Often facilitating these plans were the sultans, who continued to relinquish power to British administrators until 1946, when they began to be seen as forsaking their Malay subjects. Leading the drive for a more forceful stance against the British were Anglophone Malay aristocrats, who had ascended through the ranks of the nascent civil service to assume administrative leadership positions (Yeo 1980: 319). These so-called administocrats feared British plans would cost them their traditional advantages over non-Malays (Jomo 1984: 245). Consequently, they rallied mass support in a broad political awakening of rural Malays. The subject of their concerns was the substantial nonnative (non-*bumiputra*, "sons of the soil") population: The Chinese and Indian immigrants who had fueled the growth of Malaya's colonial economy. The presence of millions of Chinese tin miners and small businessmen, as well as Indian rubber farmers, threatened a seismic shift in the peninsula's demography and a political earthquake in the event of a rapid British departure.

Although nationalist sentiment among Malays predated Japanese wartime rule (1941–1945) and the subsequent return of British forces,

---

[4] In the wake of World War II, Malaya had become "Britain's single most profitable colony...contributing more foreign exchange...than the rest of the empire" (Gomez and Jomo 1999: 10).

it was the Malayan Union proposal that sparked political awareness and mobilization among the mass of Malays (Means 1976: 53). The Malayan Union would have placed the nine states of Malaya, plus the Straits Settlements of Penang and Malacca, under full British jurisdiction while providing for a unitary government with equal citizenship rights for *bumiputras* and nonnatives (von Vorys 1975: 65; Means 1976: 52). In October 1945, Sir Harold MacMichael was delegated to proffer the union to the sultans, promoting it as a form of democracy with equality across ethnicities. The new system was designed both to appeal to wealthy Chinese elites and to undermine the peninsula's growing communist movement, which was also predominantly Chinese (Case 1996a: 74–75). Most critically, the union would effectively replace indirect rule through the sultans with a less cumbersome system of unmediated British control (Means 1976: 52). The sultans would retain their thrones but play a consultative part on the margins of government (Cheah 1988: 21). At the time that they received the proposal, most of the sultans were already politically weakened by their wartime collaboration with Japanese forces, a fact MacMichael was quick to exploit with threats of deposing the rulers (Smith 1994: 97). All nine sultans acceded to the odious Malayan Union, their only option if they hoped to preserve even the symbolic stature of their posts (von Vorys 1976: 66).

A public announcement of the Malayan Union agreement in January 1946 evoked their subjects' defiance. By threatening to level the political playing field among the country's ethnic groups while stripping the sultans of their remaining powers, the agreement managed to antagonize the vast majority of Malays (Smith 1994: 98). Far from reassuring the country's population, it intensified Malay fears that the British designs would impart a new sociopolitical hierarchy, with Chinese as the dominant class and the less educated Malay peasantry subordinate. A. J. Stockwell describes the reaction: "Both retired Malayan Civil Servants and active Malay leaders attacked an agreement which seemed to strip the Sultans of their sovereignty, end the autonomy of the States and abolish the privileged position of the Malay people.... By attempting – if unwittingly – to marry the idea of sovereignty with the actuality of power, the British raised those Malay grievances which had previously existed at the administrative level to the grander and more uncontrollable scale of constitutional conflict" (1977: 488).

Malays who had previously deferred to their monarchs now forcefully pressured the sultans and British administrators to protect their historic privileges. They held mass rallies and demonstrations across the country

(Means 1976: 53). Public protest crystallized in a political party founded to defeat the British plans. Gathering in Kuala Lumpur in early March, some two hundred Malay leaders announced, on behalf of "the whole Malay population . . . as represented by the United Malays National Organization, exercising the national will," that the union agreed on by the sultans was "null and void," and they declared their strong opposition to the plan (Ongkili 1985: 50). UMNO thus coalesced from forty-one Malay clubs and associations partnering to block the Malayan Union (Stockwell 1977: 491; Gomez and Jomo 1999: 11).

Opposition to the Malayan Union was spearheaded by Dato Onn Jaafar, a Malay aristocrat from the province of Johor, the historic heartland of Malay resistance to foreign rule. Onn was the adopted son of Johor's sultan and had benefited from education both in his homeland and abroad in England. Rapidly moving up the local bureaucracy, he was occasionally estranged from the royalty that had earlier promoted him. Yet Onn's efforts as a skilled administrator earned him the respect of the sultan's subjects in Johor. By leading the drive to create UMNO, Onn vaulted into the role of a national leader, broadening his appeal far beyond his home region (Stockwell 1977: 490–491).[5] On 1 April 1946, he delivered the coup de grâce to the Malayan Union, pressing the sultans to heed the Malay masses' vocal entreaties and abstain from the union's inauguration ceremony (Stockwell 1977: 494). In a single stroke, Onn pushed UMNO ahead of the traditional elite as the true representative of Malay concerns and the most critical interlocutor for British negotiators (Smith 1994: 99–100).

With the subsequent creation of the Federation of Malaya, British plans for political change surrendered to long-established social hierarchies. The system designated citizenship without nationality for the country's Chinese and Indians and imposed barriers to their political participation that Malays did not face (von Vorys 1975: 78–79). As a "coalition of communal leaders," the Federation of Malaya reinforced Malay dominance and confirmed Britain's failure to build citizenship around individual rights and nonethnic identities (von Vorys 1975: 80, 83).

This accord did not guarantee a smooth road to independence, however. By codifying Malay supremacy, the British stoked the very communist insurgency they had earlier attempted to avoid. Before the outcry against the Malayan Union, Malay political engagement had generally

---

[5] UMNO's charter was formally approved, with Onn as the party's first president, on 11–12 May 1946. (Stockwell 1977: 492).

lagged behind the mobilization of the peninsula's Chinese minority. Japanese antagonism during the occupation period had pushed Malaya's Chinese into organizations of resistance, foremost among them the Malayan Communist Party (MCP), "the best organized and most powerful political force immediately following the war" (Means 1976: 70). The MCP "overshadowed all other political groups" in its control over labor strikes and its infiltration of other movements, raising British concerns that the MCP's target constituencies not be disadvantaged by the provisions for Malayan statehood (Stockwell 1977: 486). When the British capitulated to Onn and the Malay sultans, they triggered a violent backlash from the predominantly Chinese MCP (Hwang 2003: 40). Soon after the Federation of Malaya was inaugurated, the MCP shifted from conventional organizing to guerilla warfare, beginning with the assassination of high-ranking British officials (Goodwin 2001: 96). In June 1948, the British declared a state of emergency, which formally lasted until 1960 (Stubbs 1979: 78).[6] The prolonged but ultimately successful counterinsurgency campaign eliminated the MCP as a force in Malayan politics. During its most violent phase from June 1948 to June 1952, the MCP lost nearly half of its combatants, with 3,149 killed (von Vorys 1975: 87). The MCP's resort to militancy isolated the movement from negotiations over independence, ceding the political arena to UMNO and, soon after, its Chinese and Indian partner organizations.

In the process of scuttling the Malayan Union, UMNO had become Britain's principal negotiator for the peninsula's route to independence (Ongkili 1985: 52). The Emergency solidified this role, with Onn and his organization presenting the ideal partner: a nonviolent, moderate political movement with national support. Indeed, satisfied with the Federation of Malaya, Malay leaders sought a gradual transition to sovereignty, during which their political dominance would become further ensconced as British forces suppressed the MCP's uprising (Stockwell 1977: 510). The Emergency expanded a bureaucratic apparatus staffed by British-educated Malay civil servants, thereby benefiting the class that formed UMNO's core (von Vorys 1975: 91). Hence, the same communal fears that had pitted the members of UMNO against the British in 1946 now made them close allies of the British during the Emergency, particularly given

---

[6] On 23 July 1948, the British banned the MCP, although political exclusion was not unprecedented (Means 1976: 78). The outspoken Malay Nationalist Party was forbidden from operating until the peak of the Emergency had past, further cementing UMNO's role as the presumptive representative of Malays' interests (Jomo 1984: 243).

Britain's newfound willingness to defer to Malay interests in the affairs of an interim government. Along with UMNO, the Malaya Chinese Association (MCA), formed on 27 February 1949. Comprised of Chinese capitalists who disdained the MCP, the MCA joined the dialogue about Britain's eventual departure (Hwang 2003: 40). Relations between UMNO and the MCA soon became a bellwether for the prospects of peaceful coexistence between Malays and non-Malays after independence, a continual concern of British administrators keen to prevent ethnic strife and preserve Malaya's economic vitality.

At the outset of the federation period, population growth among the earlier immigrant populations placed peninsular Malays at demographic parity with non-bumiputras. A 1947 census showed Malays making up 50 percent of the population of Malaya, with Chinese comprising 38 percent and Indians 11 percent (Jomo 1984: 325). Malay concerns about the country's demography were compounded by Malays' marginal role in domestic labor and business. Chinese workers manned a burgeoning tin-mining industry, whereas the vast majority of Malays remained peasants, working in subsistence agriculture under the traditional royalty of their respective states. Those Malay aristocrats who might have formed an indigenous bourgeoisie were drawn instead into the civil service, creating a class of "statist capitalists" who drew their wealth from positions in the new political apparatus (Jomo 1984: 209–210). With Malays in either state administration or traditional agriculture, Chinese businessmen and laborers acquired a centrality to the economy far beyond their already substantial portion of the population. Indians, too, in plantation agriculture more than in private enterprise, were an important economic constituency. These communities viewed participation in the Malayan Federation and collaboration with UMNO as a way of staking a claim to political influence that would last after the British had departed (Khoo 1997: 51). For his part, Onn saw cooperation with non-Malays as an opportunity for supplanting the sultans' power with an expansive, more inclusive UMNO (Ishak bin Tadin 1960: 70).

A year into the Federation of Malaya, the British, hoping to establish interethnic cooperation while sapping support for the MCP, gathered top Malay, Chinese, and Indian leaders for talks in a forum called the Communities Liaison Council. The council met for a total of twenty-three days in early 1950 (von Vorys 1975: 96). The central interlocutors were UMNO president Onn and MCA president Tan Cheng Lock. Both agreed on the need for non-Malays to actively address the problems of poverty and lack of education that afflicted the Malay masses in the countryside (von Vorys 1975: 98). During these meetings, Onn also began to favor according a larger political role to the country's minorities (Khong 1987: 30; Ishak bin Tadin 1960: 80–81). The UMNO founder did not abandon the notion of the state's Malay identity, but he shifted from the ethnicized politics of earlier mobilization toward a position of "avoiding communalism" while advancing the country to statehood (Means 1976: 124).[7] When the council recommended a combination of progressive economic (pro-Malay) and political (pro-non-Malay) policies in April 1950, Onn began to push forcefully for their approval by UMNO (Means 1976: 124–125, Ishak bin Tadin 1960: 84–85).

In the councils of UMNO, Onn initially swayed some of his peers toward the idea of full citizenship for non-Malays. But when he began appealing to the rank-and-file members, he soon faced accusations of betraying the Malay community (Means 1976: 124–125). When Onn threatened to leave the party, UMNO's General Assembly grudgingly accepted his citizenship proposal (Khoong 1987: 31). But the more he pushed, the more the rift between him and his erstwhile supporters widened. In June 1951, he observed, "Even if the principles . . . are accepted by the majority of UMNO, there would still be a powerful minority which would continue to sabotage or retard progress" (Means 1976: 126). He was especially frustrated that members would not change the party's name to the United *Malayan* National Organization (Stubbs 1979: 80). Unwilling to "force a showdown," Onn broke away from the party (Ishak bin Tadin 1960: 92).

Ever since the struggles over the Malayan Union, Onn had openly advocated constitutional monarchy, feeling the power of the people had surpassed the authority of the sultans (Cheah 1988: 25). In 1949, he had directly challenged the sultans by advocating the creation of a single, unified Malayan state. Aiming to win the monarchs' deference to UMNO as the ultimate representative of Malay public opinion, Onn instead found himself locked in an internecine struggle within the organization he had founded (Smith 1994: 100–101). Onn's bid to outflank the sultans with an even broader base of support foundered against the ironclad loyalty that bound common Malays' insecurities to their society's royalty.

On 16 September 1951, Onn established the Independence of Malaya Party (IMP), exhorting his fellow Malays to join him in a broad-based organization promoting the shared interests of all the country's communities (Hwang 2003: 57). He most likely expected that his departure would

---

[7] "Communalism" here denotes the use of ethnic identities as the basis for a pro-Malay societal hierarchy.

prompt a mass exodus of UMNO members and thereby retain for him the position of colonial interlocutor and national leader (Stubbs 1979: 80). But Malay elites would not distance themselves from the sultans. Von Vorys has described their dilemma: "The English educated Malays, however influential and powerful they might have been, could not afford to be separated from the rural, traditional hierarchy. In spite of their resources and talents, in spite of all their eloquence (in English), politically the former was, in fact, the captive of the latter" (1976: 92). The defeat of the noncommunalism advocated by Onn reinforced a political hierarchy that might otherwise have been restructured before the country reached independence. Onn became increasingly marginal as Malaya moved into its final years under British rule and UMNO, led by Tunku Abdul Rahman, reaffirmed its commitment to Malay rights.

Onn's exit from UMNO enabled the party to return to its roots as a monoethnic movement to promote Malay interests. In one decisive adaptation, however, the IMP's political breadth prompted UMNO to accept new modes of political cooperation across ethnic lines. Britain had specified that successful local elections in 1952–1953 and national legislative elections in 1955 were the prerequisites to British recognition of Malaya's sovereignty (Crouch 1996: 18; Gomez and Jomo 1999: 12). The threat of IMP victory drove Abdul Rahman to accept a Malay-dominated multicommunal coalition (Means 1976: 133). The MCP first refused to take part in elections and then, its rebellion visibly failing, sought to participate but was rebuffed by the British (Ongkili 1985: 80–81). Consequently, the primary contestants were the IMP, UMNO, the MCA, the Malayan Indian Congress (MIC, formed in 1946), and a small number of less prominent party organizations. Onn's IMP lagged in the quest for public support behind the partnership of UMNO and the MCA, which was known as the Alliance. The Alliance divided up districts in the bellwether elections of Kuala Lumpur. This strategy trumped the IMP's noncommunal appeal not only in Kuala Lumpur but across the country. In fifteen municipal elections during 1952–1953, the Alliance took ninety-four seats, independents and other smaller parties won twenty-three races, and the IMP succeeded in only three (von Vorys 1975: 109). In Johor Baru, Onn's home district, the UMNO-MCA kept the IMP from winning a single victory (Means 1976: 137). After adding the MIC to their coalition, the Alliance won a similarly impressive landslide in the national elections of 1955. The three-party Alliance attracted 80 percent of votes cast and all but one of the contested fifty-two seats (Ongkili 1985: 96). With UMNO at the helm, the Alliance government then led the country into independent statehood on 31 August 1957. The conflict between

Malay-dominant multicommunalism as advanced by the sultans, Abdul Rahman, and UMNO and Onn's noncommunal politics had been resolved decisively, with the enduring consequence that Malaysian politics would be Malay-ruled in the decades that followed.

Pluralism Persistent: Factionalized Parties in Iran and the Philippines

Unlike in Egypt and Malaysia, contentious parity between rival Iranian and Philippine elites did not give way to a decisive victory of one faction over the other. During the founding years of these countries' regimes, elites compromised with their most formidable rivals instead of decisively defeating them. They formed coalitions that perpetuated basic debates over the allocation of power. In Iran, clerical leaders disagreed about the codification of popular sovereignty and the extent to which the clergy should play a political, much less nonelected, role. Once they had bested the lay politicians who challenged them, Shi'i clergy fought among themselves over the republican nature of the nascent Islamic state. Iran's hard-liners operated beside fellow clergy who advocated republicanism with religious consultation. In the Philippines, professional politicians quarreled over government spoils as they sought to prevent one figure from monopolizing patronage over the long term. Sergio Osmeña and Manuel Roxas cooperated to balance against the popular appeal of Manuel Quezon until his death, at which point they competed against each other and split the Nacionalista Party in two.

Hierocratic Aims, Democratic Hopes: Iran, 1979–1981
In the early days of the 1978–1979 Iranian Revolution, clerical rule, or hierocracy, seemed unlikely. A broad array of social forces, including students, traditional parties, and religious leaders, had assembled to protest Mohammed Reza Shah's increasingly brutal regime. The shah, son of Iran's prior monarch, Reza Shah Pahlavi (r. 1923–1941), had become intensely unpopular among his countrymen, even as he retained the support of Iran's chief ally and patron, the United States. In the summer of 1978, domestic opposition to the shah reached new intensity as thousands of Iranians demonstrated in the capital, Tehran. Courageous protesters exposed the regime's fragility, while leaders of the main opposition parties, the National Front and the Iran Freedom Movement, partnered with clerical colleagues of the exiled Shi'i religious leader Ayatollah Ruhollah Khomeini to devise a coalition government that would temporarily govern the country if the shah abdicated.

These initial discussions suggested a dualist arrangement in which elected secularist politicians would rule and clerics, organized in terms of their own hierarchy of scholarly qualifications, would advise the government. From his exile in Paris, Khomeini endorsed this distribution of authority, likening it to common Western traditions: "Republic means the same as it exists everywhere. The difference here is that our republic relies on a constitution, which is the Islamic law. That we call it an Islamic Republic relates to the fact that all conditions for the elections as well as the ordinances, which rule Iran, stem from Islam. The choice is by the people, however, and the form of the republic is as it exists everywhere" (Rajaee 1999: 225). He also commented: "The ulama [clerical scholars] themselves will not hold power in the government. They will exercise supervision over those who govern and give them guidance" (Schirazi 1997: 24).

But rapid developments on the ground soon swept away this pluralist rhetoric. The shah left Iran on 16 January 1979, and Khomeini returned from exile on the first of February. The immediate postmonarchical government embodied earlier deliberations about politicians and clerics sharing power. A provisional executive body, the Islamic Revolutionary Council (IRC), divided seats equally between Khomeini's clerical allies and nonreligious figures like the Iran Freedom Movement's leader, Mehdi Bazargan (Arjomand 1988: 135). Khomeini's national popularity soon tipped the balance, however, in favor of the council's religious half (Arjomand 1988: 135). Soon, traditionalist clerics were leading a national campaign against their erstwhile coalition partners in the old political parties. Domestic politics immediately after the revolution thus revolved around clerical efforts to monopolize power and the waning capacity of lay politicians to stop them. As in Egypt, antipathy toward the monarchy in Iran had spurred a broad opposition movement, yet few participants reaped their anticipated rewards. In Iran, the clergy, bent on religious oligarchy, steered the country not toward the democracy many hoped for but toward a new form of authoritarianism. Traditionalist clerics steadily assumed an unrivaled dominance over the Iranian state by exploiting their affiliation with Khomeini and systematically suppressing popular calls for accountable, elected government.[8]

---

[8] Seminary-trained Shi'a clerics have constituted the bulk of the Islamic Republic's ruling elite since its inception, controlling the Leadership, half the Council of Guardians, and, until 2005, the presidency. Furthermore, these same theologians comprised most of the membership of two main political factions competing between 1984 and 1992 (discussed

Proponents of clerical rule waged two principal political battles for control over the nascent regime: They campaigned against their former opposition partners in the revolution, and they attempted to defeat republican-oriented clergy in their own ranks. These struggles, like the campaigns launched by Nasser and the Revolutionary Command Council, shaped the immediate distribution of political power and the long-term prospects for a ruling party and sustainable coalition.

The IRC cultivated national support as it slowly strengthened its control of the state in 1979. Iran's large landowning class had already been disrupted by the shah's land reforms, and thus the IRC, unlike the RCC in Egypt, did not have to contend with an entrenched aristocracy in the countryside (Katouzian 1998: 188). A vast network of local agents performed both law enforcement and service distribution (Arjomand 1988: 135). Deploying local revolutionary committees (*komitehs*), the IRC replaced suspected loyalists of the ancien regime with IRC agents. By allowing the *komitehs* to act as neighborhood militias dispatching revolutionary justice, the IRC built ties with Iran's youth and rural population while neutralizing real and imagined threats; morality police (*hezbollahis*, "partisans of God" deployed as plain-clothes thugs) and enforcers known as *baseej* provided auxiliary personnel to regulate society (Bakhash 1990: 59). An additional vehicle for managing popular mobilization against alleged enemies of the revolution was the Corps of the Islamic Revolutionary Guards, or *pasdaran* (guardians), which operated as a parallel repressive apparatus apart from the traditional military (Moslem 2002: 22). The *komitehs* and *pasdaran* signaled the inception of a radical shakeup in government personnel. While nurturing their local ties, IRC leaders attacked the state, aggressively removing residual loyalists. During the summer of 1980, the IRC replaced tens of thousands of civil servants, teachers, and soldiers with partisans of the revolution (Arjomand 1988: 144). Purges of the media and intelligence services soon followed (Rouleau 1981: 7).

The IRC's clerical cadre waged a parallel assault on their political rivals who sought to replace monarchy with parliamentary democracy. The opening salvo was fired when the IRC formally split on 4 February 1979, separating Bazargan's faction into a titular provisional government

in the next chapter) (Buchta 2000: 13–18). Yet lay politicians have been increasingly influential in the regime's middle tier, particularly the Islamic Assembly (parliament). In the Assembly's first session (1980–1984), 48.1 percent of MPs were clerics (in a 263-seat parliament). Eight years later, the same group held less than half as many seats (24.1 percent of 270 seats) (Baktiari 1996: 241).

with Bazargan at its head (Arjomand 1988: 135). The ruse of ceding autonomy to the liberal-minded Bazargan cloaked a fundamental setback for the democratic wing of the IRC: The split divorced Bazargan and his associates from actual decision making. Clerical figures filled the vacated spots in the IRC, and the council continued to rule (Bakhash 1990: 64). Having broken away from their rivals on the council, IRC clerics backed a new mass organization, the Islamic Republican Party (IRP), which attacked advocates of popular sovereignty and isolated Bazargan from the public he sought to serve.

Founded on 17 February 1979, the IRP organized clergy and their followers to overpower their opponents, such as the Iran Freedom Movement, the communist Tudeh Party, and, most formidably of all, the radical Mojahedin-e Khalq (People's Fighters) (Fairbanks 1998: 20). The party's initial cohort was led by Ayatollah Mohammad Beheshti (d. June 1981) and included Ali Khamenei and Akbar Hashemi Rafsanjani, both of whom held leading government posts through and beyond Khomeini's era (r. 1979–1989). Khamenei belonged to the country's "traditional right" faction, which privileged the Islamic Republic's religious nature over its democratic elements (Moslem 2002: 99–100). Rafsanjani was also part of the regime's right wing. The IRP called for the codification of Islamic precepts as the governing framework for society (Baktiari 1996: 55). The party's platform explicitly privileged clerical decision making over popular demands: "In cases where the wishes of the people run counter to Islamic values, officials must not heed these desires," one IRP publication stated (IRP n.d., quoted in Moslem 2002: 61). IRP elites envisioned a system known as Rule of the Jurisprudent (*velayat-e-fagih*), which concentrated power in a single figure. In addition to its clerical leaders, the party included laypeople who engaged in political activism to promote their vision of "a government guided by Islamic principles" and by trained Shi'i religious scholars (Hooglund 1984: 32).

Opposition parties struggled to halt the IRP's campaign for Islamic government but could not galvanize mass support. The IRP benefited from the Iranian public's general disdain for political movements that dated to the monarchy period. Even before the revolution, formal public participation had been waning. In the 1977 parliamentary elections, less than 19,000 of 2 million eligible voters in Tehran cast ballots (Parsa 2000: 35). Barzagan's government seemed to many to represent a continuation of the parliamentary wing of the shah's regime, as the prime minister himself observed in the summer of 1979: "The problem lies in the fact that state institutions are the creation of the old regime and 2500 years of despotism. . . . Because [all the] atrocities were committed by state institutions, the people have developed an inborn hatred, fear, and disinclination towards both the state and the government" (Moslem 2002: 21). Even though an array of centrist and leftist organizations had helped topple the shah, communist and liberal organizations could not rival the IRP's popularity as an extension of Khomeini and the IRC. As Bazargan later described, the opposition's reticence to seize power emboldened IRP leaders "in taking over the country" (Arjomand 1988: 137).

The illusion of power sharing faded in stages. The secession of Bazargan's government from the IRC badly isolated him, even as the IRP's control grew. Bazargan's meeting in Algiers with U.S. national security advisor Zbigniew Brzezinksi and U.S. president Jimmy Carter's admittance of the shah into America for medical treatment further eroded the prime minister's public stature (Bakhash 1990: 70). Meanwhile, IRP affiliates filled fifty-five of seventy-three seats for the country's constitutional drafting assembly (Baktiari 1996: 56). This overwhelmingly pro-Khomeini body (henceforth known as the Assembly of Experts) wrote a constitution that positioned Khomeini for the position of *faqih* (chief jurist) and built up antidemocratic checks on the elected national Islamic Assembly (Buchta 2000: 213). Beheshti's IRP had nearly accomplished one of its primary goals: The establishment of an Islamic state with power concentrated in the hands of Khomeini and his closest clerical associates. On 6 November 1979, two days after a group of students took over the U.S. Embassy, Bazargan resigned (Arjomand 1988: 139). Khomeini, acting as the country's de facto executive, then charged the Islamic Revolutionary Council with running the government in the fallen premier's stead (Buchta 2000: 213). IRP clerics had won a further victory.

As Bazargan was pushed aside, the democratic cause drew powerful support from a peer of Khomeni's in the Shi'i clerical hierarchy. Ayatollah Kazem Shariat-Madari advocated an Islamic Republic that conformed to Khomeini's original words from Paris – a state in which clerics would advise, while elected leaders ruled (Schirazi 1997: 25). Declaring that "power and sovereignty are rooted in the people," Shariat-Madari rallied supporters against the constitution, which vested authority in Khomeini and clerically dominated institutions rather than in the Iranian public (Schirazi 1997: 48, 51). After the constitution was formally ratified on 2 December 1979, residents of the city of Tabriz revolted, advocating Shariat-Madari's much more liberal and democratic program. Demonstrators captured several government buildings and a state radio station (Bakhash 1990: 68). But in the face of counter-rhetoric that framed Khomeini as the country's national leader, the demonstrators withdrew their demands. Despite his own convictions, Shariat-Madari also seemed to back down from open confrontation (Metz and Library of Congress 1989). IRP forces then ensured the remnant of his following was "bloodily suppressed" (Arjomand 1988: 140–141). Shariat-Madari's fledgling political organization, the Islamic People's Republican Party, dissolved and was formally banned in 1981 (Metz and Library of Congress 1989).

Under its new constitution, Iran formally became an Islamic republic. In this regime, IRP leaders hoped to hold a monopoly of positions, including the elected post of president. The entry of Khomeini's long-time colleague Abolhasan Bani-Sadr threatened these designs. During the revolution, Bani-Sadr had collaborated closely with Khomeini in Paris. In 1979, he joined the Islamic Revolutionary Council when Bazargan became prime minister of the provisional government (Metz and Library of Congress 1989). In January 1980, Iran held its first presidential election, and Bani-Sadr ran. The IRP hoped to field Beheshti as its own candidate, but Khomeini dissuaded the party from this choice. Bani-Sadr therefore faced a lackluster IRP affiliate and was swept into office with 10.7 million votes, or 76.5 percent of ballots cast (Kauz, Sharoudi, and Rieck 2001: 75). His new post made Bani-Sadr an influential rival to the IRP, but the party also took 61 percent (131 of 216 seats) of the Islamic Assembly in elections that summer (Baktiari 1996: 68).[9] After Iraq invaded Iran in September 1980, the president's stature grew. As commander-in-chief during wartime, Bani-Sadr won an enthusiastic following in the armed forces. The president also gained support from the influential traditional merchant class (*bazaaris*). Portions of these constituencies soon clashed with IRP partisans as the rivalry between democrats and hierocrats escalated.

In the winter of 1980–1981, Bani-Sadr remained widely popular and seemed capable of stopping the IRP. In November 1980, demonstrators and prodemocratic clerics expressed support for Bani-Sadr and condemned the IRP's banning of opposition newspapers (Menashri 1990: 171).[10] Yet the IRP, spearheaded by Beheshti and prime minister Ali Rajai, gradually encroached on Bani-Sadr's authority, usurping effective control over nonmilitary affairs while hampering the president's ability to conduct the war against Iraq (Menashri 1990: 173). At this point, the

---

[9] The mixed composition of the IRP's bloc in the 1980–1984 parliament, 60 percent clerics and 40 percent nonclergy, displays the party's incorporation of lay figures in its middle echelon (Baktiari 1996: 69).

[10] Grand Ayatollah Abdollah Shirazi and Ayatollah Hassan Lahuti backed Bani-Sadr in November 1980. They subsequently denounced the IRP and declared that even Khomeini's powers as *faqih* were limited (Menashri 1980: 171, 176).

Mojahedin-e-Khalq buttressed Bani-Sadr's position, providing him with invaluable street support and serving as a public counterweight to the IRP (Baktiari 1996: 75). But even with popular reinforcements, Bani-Sadr vacillated about how aggressively to push back against the IRP (Arjomand 1988: 145). The window of opportunity soon closed. A major military defeat in January 1981 damaged Bani-Sadr's prestige. In the following months, *hizbollahis* attacked Bani-Sadr's supporters. Even more damaging to the embattled president, Khomeini turned on Bani-Sadr that spring, denounced him as an ally of the West, and stripped him of his authority as commander-in-chief (Arjomand 1988: 146, Baktiari 1996: 75). Much like Bazargan the year before and Egypt's Naguib in 1954, Bani-Sadr was isolated from his supporters and neutralized. Eagerly taking its cue from Khomeini, the IRP-controlled parliament impeached Bani-Sadr in June 1981; government officials then moved to arrest the fallen leader (Baktiari 1996: 76–77).

Even as Bani-Sadr went into hiding and fled the country in July 1981, his defeat catalyzed a deadly, albeit unsuccessful, wave of resistance against the ascendant IRP (Bakhash 1990: 160). Among the beleaguered opposition currents of Iran's postrevolutionary political landscape, the Mojahedin-e-Khalq, which blended Marxist and Islamist ideologies, stood alone as the only formidable alternative to the Islamic Republican Party. In 1981, the group's membership numbered around 150,000, and these cadres were mobilized in force when parliament seemed likely to remove Bani-Sadr from office. The group's leaders called for "revolutionary resistance in all its forms" and are alleged to have initiated a series of attacks against IRP targets (Metz and Library of Congress 1989). The most notorious of these actions was the 28 June 1981 bombing of the Islamic Republican Party's headquarters, which killed more than seventy party leaders, including Beheshti (Burns 1996: 369; Buchta 2000: 214). Regardless of their culpability, the Mojahedin were subsequently targeted for brutal suppression by the state (Rouleau 1981: 8). Eric Hooglund describes the violence and its result: "An estimated 7,000 persons, mostly young people, are believed to have been killed in 1981– 1982. The severity of the government's reaction effectively eliminated as a serious internal opposition the Mujahidin" (1984: 34).[11] At the outset of the ill-fated rebellion, Massoud Rajavi, leader of the Mojahedin, fled with Bani-Sadr into exile (Buchta 2000: 214). Afterward, the group wielded

---

[11] Bahman Baktiari cites Amnesty International's figure that "2,946 executions took place in the year after the removal of Bani-Sadr; 90 percent of these from among the Mojahedin" (1996: 80).

little influence over Iranian domestic politics, morphing from a local guerilla movement into an expatriate force based abroad (Beeman 1986: 80).

By defeating Bazargan, Bani-Sadr, and the Mojahedin-e-Khalq, the Islamic republic's clerical elites had consolidated power, much as Nasser had when he rebuffed and sequestered Mohammed Naguib. The period of regime formation of 1979–1981 was a moment of political reorganization and uncertainty in which the IRP triumphed over its nonclerical rivals. Unlike in Egypt, however, this resolution of conflict between religious and lay leaders left behind substantial divisions among the clerics, cleavages foreshadowed by Shariat-Madari's abortive rebellion in late 1979. Although secularist politicians could not contest the new state's basic architecture, clerical leaders *within* the Shi'i hierarchy soon challenged the IRP's course. Many on the left wing continued to advocate a larger and more effectual role for public participation. Although they were not originally the intellectual kindred of Shariat-Madari, clerics like Mehdi Karrubi, along with nontheologians such as Mir-Hossein Musavi, soon parted ways with the IRP's founding faction. These partisans of the Islamic left resuscitated in practice many of Shariat-Madari's principles, flexing the regime's elected bodies against the restraints of its hierocratic bodies. Their efforts were embedded within and regularly contested the merger of clerical and representative institutions that the Islamic Republic embodied.

The constitution announced in November 1979 established the dominance of three religious institutions: The position of *faqih*, also known as leader (*rahbar*), filled by Khomeini; a twelve-member Council of Guardians (half of which was appointed by the leader, half by the parliament after nomination by the head of the judiciary); and an eighty-three-member Assembly of Experts charged with selecting a new leader in the event of a vacancy (Moslem 2002: 30, Buchta 2000: 59). These bodies oversaw and generally superseded the country's more publicly accountable institutions: A nominal president, a 263-member parliament (the Islamic Assembly), and an indirectly chosen prime minister who selected a cabinet and led the Islamic Assembly (Buchta 2000: 22). In this allocation of governmental authority, the Council of Guardians became a de facto upper house of parliament, frequently vetoing legislation passed by the Islamic Assembly. Thus, the new constitution inverted an earlier vision of elected government and clerical consultation: Theologians and like-minded lay persons close to Ayatollah Khomeini would rule, while popularly elected representatives would occupy subordinate posts (Moslem 2002: 11).

Although the constitution did not mention the word "democracy," its entanglement of religious and republican elements signified an ongoing struggle to reconcile Islamism and republicanism (Brumberg 2001b: 109). This debate among the clerical elite kept the question of democracy alive despite Bani-Sadr's failure. In some respects, Bani-Sadr's defeat actually fueled the growth of religious left factions that came to share Shariat-Madari's outlook but saw the programs of Bazargan and Bani-Sadr as overly Westernized (Brumberg 2001b: 100). Left-wing nationalists who were loyal to Khomeini balked at the right wing's economic agenda and rejected some of the rightist clerics' more accomodationist foreign policy stances. These ideas slowly pushed clerics into a reformist posture that solidified only after Khomeini's death in 1989 and the inauguration of open elite conflict. Long before then, however, the IRP's incipient rival factions vied for control over the same parliament that had overwhelmingly ejected Bani-Sadr.

Dueling Patrons and Abortive Autocracy: The Philippines, 1899–1946

During four decades of American colonialism and indirect administration, leaders from the Philippines' historic aristocracy captured hold of the budding state and established themselves as a national oligarchy. As in Egypt, Malaysia, and Iran, elites' pursuit of power necessitated supporters who would help their patrons exclude capable rivals. Much like Malaya's experience, elections linked provincial populations to locally popular aspirants for national office. Yet Philippine elites – constantly competing among themselves for state resources – remained deeply factionalized throughout the process of regime formation. Unlike Malays, they did not rally around a collective political cause reached by their leaders. In this respect, Philippine politicians resembled the feuding clergy of Iran's postrevolutionary regime more than the ideationally unified leaders of UMNO. Despite the drive by the country's first president, Manuel Quezon, to turn the country into a dictatorship and thus consolidate power, much as Nasser would do twenty years hence, elites from different regions continued to quarrel for control, thereby splitting the highest levels of government. The decade-long transition period before independence – interrupted by Japan's occupation in 1942 – intensified this competition and displayed the fissures of patrimonial politics that would alternately elevate and cripple Philippine presidents in the second half of the twentieth century.

The Philippines' protracted experience under American rule began in 1898, when Admiral George Dewey of the U.S. Navy easily dispatched

Spanish forces in Manila Bay (Karnow 1989: 78–79). Up until Dewey's triumph, Filipinos had lived under Spanish rule for more than three hundred years (1565–1898).[12] Although territorial conquest had not been an original goal of the American navy's incursion, victory in the Spanish-American War enabled the United States to annex the Philippines the following year, disappointing Philippine leaders who had hoped and expected to be granted national sovereignty (Smith 1994: 39–41). When American designs of long-term occupation became clear, much of the population arose to resist. Would-be revolutionary Emilio Aguinaldo declared an independent Philippine Republic in 1899 and then mounted a broad insurgency to eject the Americans (Anderson 1988: 9). Nearly 200,000 Philippine soldiers and civilians, as well as 4,300 American soldiers, lost their lives in the conflict before Aguinaldo surrendered in 1901 and his compatriots began resigning en masse (Cullinane and Paredes 1988: 73; Wurfel 1988: 6).

The failed campaign for national liberation produced leaders who engaged the United States not through violent struggle but via political channels installed by American administrators.[13] Similar to Malay administocrats who evinced ambivalence and ambition as they negotiated eventual statehood, Philippine leaders challenged and then colluded with the colonizer to heighten their domestic influence (Paredes 1988a: 9). The extraordinary duration of America's presence in the Philippines depended largely on these new elites' not simply accommodating but actually abetting U.S. designs in the archipelago, principally by facilitating its access to the country's sugar plantations and its maintenance of a strategic military outpost in the Pacific Ocean. The United States slowly transplanted American-style political institutions to the Philippines, gradually opening local government to cooperative indigenous leaders. Yet even as U.S. administrators consciously emulated the structure of their own traditions, these institutional transplants had an antidemocratic effect, buttressing local elites and preserving their constituents in the role of dependent clients (Hutchcroft 2000: 284).

Despite the tremendous destruction wrought by internal war, patterns of social authority and wealth distribution from the Spanish period endured. U.S. forces failed to reorganize local class relations. Instead, the

---

[12] The islands that compose the Philippines were the "last major imperial acquisition" of Spanish Emperor Felipe II, from whom the country takes its name (Anderson 1988: 5).

[13] From 1901 through 1935, a series of governors appointed by the U.S. president and serving under the Secretary of War held executive authority over government in the Philippines. See, among others, Paredes (1988b), Hutchcroft (2000).

American administration expropriated 400,000 acres of "friar estates" previously held by the Catholic Church and put them up for sale. This measure, which was intended to generate a class of independent small farmers, instead funneled property to those who could afford it: an educated upper class across the country, the Philippines' nascent aristocracy (Anderson 1988: 10–11). Stark inequalities between plantation owners and peasants grew; these disparities then became the elitist foundations of electoral politics and clientelist parties that connected provincial leaders to the capital. The patrons were landowning elites or wealthy urbanites, their clients peasants who depended on the landed class for their livelihood. Elections compounded economic inequality, as landlords bought the votes of rural populations with material rewards and promises of future patronage (Thompson 1995: 16).

Through elections of escalating importance, political aspirants across the country won government posts by rallying an incipient electorate they pledged to serve. Municipal elections in 1902, 1904, and 1906 generated municipal councils whose members chose governors of their respective provinces the following February (Cullinane 1988: 74).[14] The front-runners for these posts seldom quarreled over national independence, opting instead to pursue a cordial and mutually beneficial relationship with Americans as they established themselves in the provisional government. Thus, the most viable candidates were seldom differentiable by their ideological positions. Instead, competition was driven by the material logic of acquiring government spoils and delivering them to the victor's local clients.

As the United States "Filipinized" the colonial administrative staff and leadership, inaugurating a national legislature in 1907 that became bicameral in 1916, it birthed a rivalrous political class housed in the prevailing Nacionalista Party (*Partido Nacionalista*, NP) (Lande 1965: 28; Wurfel 1988: 8).[15] NP leaders in the countryside had been preserving their horizontal ties among their constituents as they ascended "vertically" from

---

[14] Severe restrictions on the franchise were the backdrop of an additional dimension by which the presumptive national elite preceded the Filipino masses as participants in electoral politics. Mimicking America's own experience of phasing in voting rights, the initial electorate comprised only literate property holders (Lande 1965: 18–20). As a result, "only 1.4% of the country's 7.6 million population [was] registered to vote" in 1907 (Paredes 1988b: 44). Restrictions on male suffrage were gradually lifted. Philippine women were not enfranchised until 1938 (Lande 1965: 28–29).

[15] In comparison to British practices in nearby Malaya, the United States indigenized the Philippine civil service with remarkably alacrity. Of 14,000 posts in 1921, 90 percent were held by Filipinos. By the time the Commonwealth was declared in 1935, the share

village- to municipality- to province-level posts (Lande 1965: 28–29). As national elections approached, the well-networked patrons on the periphery closed in on the country's center, steadily encroaching on appointed elites in the capital (Cullinane 1988: 74). Compared to their peers across the country, Federal Party leaders operated primarily in Manila and lacked a regional clientele that could make them competitive.[16] Their detachment from Philippine society was largely a product of their origins: Whereas provincial elites had built their influence by nurturing local ties, Federalistas were beneficiaries of close relations with the American rulers and thereby enjoyed a double-edged autonomy that undercut them in national elections (Lande 1965: 30; Banlaoi and Carlos 1996: 53; Cullinane 1988: 99). Moreover, because Manila sent only two representatives to the eighty-member Assembly, any faction in the capital that aspired to national power had to ally with candidates elsewhere. It was these electoral exigencies that originally spurred a collection of anti-Federalista groups operating in Manila to form the Nacionalista Party and link it to already successful local politicians in the countryside (Cullinane 1988: 98–99). By the 1907 legislative polls, the NP had built an unprecedented cross-regional electoral alliance and displaced the Federal Party (Cullinane 1988: 98–99).

In the 1907 elections, NP candidates took 72 percent of contested seats, ending the Federal Party's status as primary interlocutor with the U.S. administration (Lande 1965: 31). Although the Federal Party would continue to contest elections under the moniker of the Progressive Party (*Partido Progresista*), it never regained the mantle of party preeminence. Through the pre-Commonwealth period, the NP held a commanding majority of votes, while the Progressive Party (and its successor, the Democrat Party [*Partido Democrata*]), remained in opposition (Lande 1965: 27). The NP assumed the status of the dominant political organization, seamlessly continuing the FP's tradition of elite collaboration with the Philippines' American rulers (Cullinane 1988: 99, 101–102). Spearheading the Federal Party's electoral rout and presiding over the elite who would eventually negotiate Philippine independence were governors Sergio Osmeña of Cebu province and Manuel Quezon from the province of Tayabas. After the NP's overwhelming victory, Osmeña assumed the

had reached 99 percent, with education-related offices the largest remaining bailiwick of American civil servants (Anderson 1988: 11–12).

[16] U.S. administrators had further weakened the Federalistas' electoral competitiveness by delaying Manila's local elections until 1908, thereby depriving Federalista Party leaders of valuable experience in courting their constituents (Paredes 1988b: 52).

Assembly's speakership, while Quezon became majority leader (Cullinane 1988: 101). National elections thus not only ushered in a period of one-party rule but also began an era of intraparty struggles in which Osmeña and Quezon were each the other's most influential allies and fiercest competitors. As the colonial relationship continued during the 1910s and 1920s, Osmeña and Quezon shared a conservative outlook on national affairs: Far from demanding independence, both leaders relied on U.S. administrators to promote their positions as national-level patrons (Paredes 1988b: 42). The NP's electoral and legislative dominance preserved their access to resources in the capital while preventing left-wing forces from turning the national agenda against the landed class that essentially controlled the Assembly.

Within the confines of this hegemonic elite, however, factional rivalries were incessant. Unlike UMNO's debate over communal politics, alignments within the NP pivoted on the axis of personal ambition and the competition between Osmeña's and Quezon's factions (Lande 1965: 40–41). In 1916, the Philippine Assembly split into a bicameral legislature, and Quezon won the presidency of the new Senate (Library of Congress 1991). Holding the two highest offices yet granted the Philippines, House Speaker Osmeña and Senate President Quezon postponed ultimate confrontation as they cooperated to preserve NP rule and favorable relations with the Americans. When personal tensions prompted Quezon to break from the NP in 1922, the party's two wings soon reunited against the common challenge of the Democratic Party (Banlaoi and Carlos 1996: 68).[17]

American rule in the Philippines had proven lucrative for the sugar-plantation aristocrats who managed domestic affairs and could cheaply export their products to the U.S. market. Accordingly, Osmeña and Quezon were at most half-hearted advocates of national sovereignty, hoping to preserve their economic advantages for as long as possible without appearing to compromise their countrymen's interests. In the United States, however, the stock market crash of 1929 and the subsequent crisis of the Great Depression caused certain politicians to view the Philippines as a liability for the United States in economic, political, and security terms (Friend 1965: 81; Anderson 1988: 12). The expansion of Japanese

[17] At the time, Quezon accused Osmeña of concentrating power and ruling undemocratically, a charge Osmeña would return in 1933 (Friend 1965: 127). In the process, Osmeña committed what he would later call his "greatest error in politics," leaving the House to challenge Quezon's control of the Senate (Friend 1965: 47). Unsuccessful, he served a short time as Senate president pro tem, while Quezon ally Manuel Roxas assumed the House speakership.

power in the Pacific made the U.S.-held Philippines a target rather than an effective outpost. Furthermore, the influx of cheap Philippine agricultural produce, mainly sugar, seemed to hurt American farmers. As progressive anti-imperialists and parochial isolationists decried the U.S.-Philippine relationship, farming lobbies joined the sundry voices advocating Philippine independence. Osmeña and Quezon belatedly sought to outpace the wave of American discontent by delivering independence to their own people while securing the Philippines' long-term trade privileges. They pursued this complicated goal, rallying the Philippine masses while ensuring the economic interests of the elite, through personal missions to Washington, D.C., and direct appeals to the U.S. Congress and president Herbert Hoover (r. 1929–1933).

In the climactic race for the mantle of national liberator, Quezon took an early advantage over Osmeña and Manuel Roxas, an old ally of Quezon's who swung over to Osmeña's side during the reluctant campaign for independence. In a flurry of cables and trans-Pacific voyages, Quezon outmaneuvered his competitors and took credit for the Commonwealth agreement reached with the United States in 1933 and 1934 (Friend 1965: 146). He then easily won the NP's nomination for presidential elections the following year (Banlaoi and Carlos 1996: 75–76). The long-time rivalry between Osmeña and Quezon might have ended there had their partnership not been critical for continued NP success. While Osmeña initially distanced himself from elections for seats in the new commonwealth government, the Nacionalista Party eventually proposed a joint Quezon-Osmeña slate for president and vice president (Friend 1965: 153). Together again, the two won in a landslide (Hartmann, Hassall, and Santos 2001: 225, 229).

Ineluctably paired with Osmeña and formally beholden to an American high commissioner, Quezon nonetheless strove to establish a one-man dictatorship. His efforts to enlarge executive power – despite being curtailed when World War II intruded on Philippine politics – anticipated Ferdinand Marcos's power grab thirty years later (McCoy 1988: 117). The agreement that made the Philippines a commonwealth of the United States set the island nation on a ten-year course to full independence. During this period, the Philippine president would wield powers on par with those of a state governor in the United States: He had final executive authority over internal affairs but no independent voice in the management of foreign policy. Additionally, Quezon officially answered to the American high commissioner, who served at the discretion of U.S. president Franklin Roosevelt (McCoy 1988: 120). Quezon bristled at these

restraints, defying any forces, local or foreign, that obstructed his conquest of the emerging Philippine state (McCoy 1988: 121). Meanwhile,
the Nacionalista Party's electoral supremacy preserved patron-based elite
rule against genuinely mass-based alternatives.

As president, Quezon used his control over government resources to
establish a national network of clients (Friend 1965: 154–155). By the elections of 1940–1941, his investment in local-level supporters had paid off
handsomely, delivering forty-one of forty-three governorships and ninety-
five of ninety-eight Assembly seats to the NP (McCoy 1988: 122–123,
125).[18] But single-party rule also concealed intraparty dissent: At the middle and lower echelons, regional leaders vied with each other for the NP's
imprimatur, and further up the hierarchy would-be rulers gathered against
Quezon (McCoy 1988: 123, 127). In 1940, Quezon initiated his most flagrantly autocratic maneuver, amending the Commonwealth Constitution
to permit a second term in office by replacing a single, nonrenewable six-
year term with two four-year terms (Friend 1965: 155). A committee of top
politicians voted five-to-four against the proposal, which initially entailed
changing the president's six-year nonrenewable term to a single term of
eight years (McCoy 1988: 138). U.S. high commissioner and perennial
Quezon detractor Francis Sayre assailed the move as setting "a precedent . . . for any strong president who desires to become a dictator to prolong his tenure indefinitely" (McCoy 1988: 138). Despite these protests,
Quezon's measure passed in a national plebiscite that summer (McCoy
1988: 147). No longer a lame-duck president, Quezon threatened to keep
the presidency out of Osmeña's reach indefinitely (Friend 1965: 155). Signaling the public reemergence of the Quezon-Osmeña rivalry just months
before the Japanese invasion, Osmeña and Roxas attended a dinner for
the high commissioner that Quezon had explicitly staged as a protest
event from which he and the rest of his cabinet abstained (McCoy 1988:
150). Given that both the president and the vice president were forced by
the Japanese to flee the country for the United States shortly afterward, it
is impossible to know how their competition might have played out had
the Philippines escaped the tribulations of war. It is reasonable to expect,
though, that Osmeña would have challenged Quezon.

Beyond the Nacionalistas' ranks, Quezon's strongest critics came from
the radical Popular Front (*Frente Popular*), a collection of peasants' rights

---

[18] Pro- and anti-Quezon wings of the Nacionalista Party had joined together in 1937. The
following year, national legislative elections produced a parliament uniformly affiliated
with the NP.

organizations that became increasingly coordinated in the 1920s and
1930s (Kerkvliet 1977: 46). The movement originated in the region of
Central Luzon, encompassing four provinces and approximately 10 percent of the country's population (Kerkvliet 1977: 1). Its grassroots networks posed an increasing challenge to Quezon's autocratic rule. Despite
President Quezon's deploying government troops to skew the 1940 local
elections, the Popular Front took about a third of the contested seats in
Pampanga province and Manila (McCoy 1988: 123). Resorting to more
aggressive measures, Quezon placed Central Luzon under constabulary
control the following year. The crackdown prompted Popular Front leader
Jose Abad Santos to decry Quezon's corrupt administration and withdraw
his own candidacy from presidential elections that fall (McCoy 1988: 139–
140). Santos's withdrawal presaged a long-term trend of marginalization.
Although leftist movements associated with the Popular Front continued
to grow through the period of Japanese occupation and beyond, they were
essentially pushed to the periphery of electoral politics (Kerkvliet 1977:
67, 238, 240).

Quezon passed away in 1944, and Osmeña formally succeeded him
to lead the government-in-exile (Banlaoi and Carlos 1996: 93, 100;
Hartmann, Hassall, and Santos 2001: 226, 230). The United States mili-
tarily defeated Japan in 1945, restored the exiled Osmeña to office in the
Philippines, and finally granted the commonwealth independent state-
hood on 4 July of the following year. Elections for the presidency immediately reignited the internecine struggles of the country's political elites.
Senate president Manuel Roxas led erstwhile Nacionalistas in the new
Liberal Party. Essentially replicating Quezon's jump from the Senate to
the presidency, Roxas defeated Nacionalista standard-bearer Osmeña
(Lande 1965: 34, 40). But Roxas's victory did not usher in a period of
LP hegemony. Instead, it formalized the bifactionalism of earlier decades
in the shape of a two-party duopoly: Identical in their programs and
the social backgrounds of their leaders, the NP and LP competed for
the House, Senate, and presidency, with neither gaining lasting advantage
over the other. Both parties remained mechanisms by which elites collected
votes, captured political power, and fed resources back to their clients. The
resources of the parties were those of the candidates, their campaigns the
speeches given by individual office seekers, and their platforms the latest
views and goals of the party's politicians (Friend 1965: 124). Rotation of
offices among these professional politicians, most of whom belonged to
the country's landed aristocracy, created a two-party democracy revolv-
ing around personal competition rather than programmatic distinctions.

Consequently, the Nacionalista and Liberal parties came to emblemize the fecklessness of many postcolonial parties, in which politicians bore no allegiance to parties beyond the elections in which they could win office (Huntington 1968: 412).

Yet the Philippines seemed to provide political pluralism despite itself. For two decades, the constant struggle for the presidency prevented leaders from either party from consolidating the kind of broad power Quezon had sought. While many scholars have portrayed this period as a phase of rowdy and fragile democracy, one also glimpses in the experience of Quezon and his successors the inverse of this image: An unconsolidated autocracy fraught with factionalism and perpetually susceptible to the vagaries of unbridled elite ambition. The irresolution of early elite conflict and unceasing bifactionalism continued to plague both elected presidents and antidemocratic usurpers (roles often filled successively by the same person). Unmollified by a cohesive ruling party that would serve their ambitions, influential self-promoters regularly rallied against power-hungry presidents.

Conclusion

In the wake of momentous changes – a military coup, a popular revolution, and protracted negotiations for national independence – rival actors in Egypt, Iran, Malaysia, and the Philippines collided as they crafted new political systems. Driven more by self-interest than ideology, they reached conflicting answers to the question of who would rule and who would be ruled. Thus, across all four countries, what can be broadly termed an antidemocratic or exclusionary faction vied to constrict political power to a small group of close confederates. In Egypt, midranking military officers who distrusted the public and the traditional parties feared a return to the barracks. Clerics similarly skeptical about mass involvement in Iran's national decision making reached for new roles as executives, not just advisors, of government. Malay sultans and civil servants eschewed ceding political power to non-Malays. And landed aristocrats in the Philippines countered movements seeking economic emancipation for the country's struggling peasantry. At the time, these projects were self-serving but not unusually sinister; differently positioned leaders sought to enhance and enshrine their influence. Their relative success at achieving these aims established enduring political trajectories, which became apparent in the short term and ultimately affected the lives of millions in future generations.

On one course, leaders succeeded in blocking rivals and consolidating power in a small set of elites; on an alternate path, similarly motivated political actors found themselves hemmed in by peers who favored greater mass involvement. Between the two divergent paths, each country's course depended primarily on the countervailing efforts of elites following similar strategies to push for political inclusion. Typically, those leaders promoting a broader and more egalitarian vision of politics – figures like General Naguib and Dato Onn – adopted such positions defensively, as a way of thwarting their rivals and preserving their own influence. Still, their efforts carried deep implications for government and society. Naguib's sequestration and Onn's marginalization sounded the death knell for republicanism in Egypt and nonethnic politics in Malaysia. Victorious leaders thereby embedded their new regimes in a foundation of elite conformity and insularity.

The formative conflicts of the political regimes of Egypt, Iran, Malaysia, and the Philippines were enmeshed in the social turmoil that accompanied national political change, but their outcomes were not simply determined by that wider context. Even as they rallied mass constituencies to their cause, leaders were periodically daunted by similarly influential rivals. Intense social turmoil thus accompanied elite conflicts but did not independently determine their results. In these rare periods of flux and uncertainty, the resolution or perpetuation of competing elite ambitions remained atypically contingent. Piercing the "thicket of social conflict" and elite rivalry that accompanies the birth of a new political order (Chaudhry 1997: 16), this chapter has shown how certain leaders triumphed decisively over their competitors, whereas others were forced to accept a less hegemonic stalemate. The outcomes of their conflicts in turn shaped the institutional configurations that would regulate elite coalitions and state-society relations. Resolution of elite conflict in Egypt and Malaysia accompanied the development of ruling parties with an antipluralist agenda and an enduring coalition to support it. In contrast, persistent elite factionalism in Iran and the Philippines kept open the debate about popular sovereignty. As discussed in the next chapter, this parity and pluralism had the institutional consequence of undermining the long-term viability of a single ruling party.

3

Institutional Legacies and Coalitional Tensions

When the dust of early elite conflict had settled, elites in Egypt, Malaysia, Iran, and the Philippines were all using parties of some form, yet only regimes in Egypt and Malaysia would maintain those parties through the end of the twentieth century. Institutional variation was both the product of earlier events and the prelude to later contrasts between durable authoritarianism in Egypt and Malaysia and opportunities for democratization in Iran and the Philippines. This chapter bridges the previous chapter's analysis of regime formation and the subsequent chapters' accounts of recent political development in Egypt, Iran, Malaysia, and the Philippines. Continuing the format of the prior chapter, the following narratives extend from the aftermath of early elite conflict through the maintenance or dismantlement of parties. The case studies also cover the inauguration of limited multiparty elections in all four regimes, elections in which incumbent elites dominated and opposition movements were severely disadvantaged. Prima facie similarities notwithstanding, the regimes reached electoral supremacy by means of widely divergent paths: On one track, ruling parties accommodated otherwise disparate elite factions; on the other, leaders deactivated parties to neutralize dissenters and tighten their hold on power.

These variations in behavior and their long-term consequences at the national level emerged from similar interests and dissimilar contexts. As demonstrated in the comparison of regime origins, elites seek to maintain their influence as national-level agenda setters. Additionally, they work to exercise and, when possible, expand that influence. Yet institutions constrain actions in the present, even as they provide long-term collective benefits by regulating behavior. Not surprisingly, then, regime leaders are often hostile to institutions, attempting to dispense with them or undermine then when they become inconvenient. As Atul Kohli has written about Indira Gandhi subverting the Congress Party, "Those who are already in power, and especially if their power rests on personal popularity, tend to find rules, procedures, and a robust second tier of leaders, unnecessarily constraining; they often view institutions more as obstacles and less as facilitators of effective rule" (1994: 95). The subjects of this study illustrate this pattern: Actors in all four cases sought to maintain power and, like politicians almost everywhere, disdained institutions that seemed to limit their autonomy and reach.

Given the double-edged character of institutions – their ability to both bolster and bother leaders – it is intriguing that rulers in Egypt and Malaysia ultimately kept their parties around, while their counterparts in Iran and the Philippines completely eliminated them. The reason must be sought in the conditions in which rulers operated: The legacies bequeathed by the regime's inception. Leaders operating in the contexts passed on by their predecessors faced different threats from within their parties and responded accordingly. The following case studies map these political trajectories. For Egypt and Malaysia, they illustrate how rulers benefited from institutions they would not have built themselves and, indeed, against which they periodically chafed. For Iran and the Philippines, they show how leaders in both parties ultimately opted to dispense with party organizations and rule directly, without an organization mediating between different factions. These decisions had the immediate benefit of concentrating power around the ruler and his clique, but they also carried the seeds of instability and dissension. When supportive elites felt their positions threatened, they opted to exit from the coalition and seek new partners. Thus, the comparative histories show why Khamenei in Iran and Marcos in the Philippines undermined the very organizations on which their power depended. While seemingly imprudent in retrospect, such decisions are entirely explicable given the chronic infighting that entangled party leaders at the time.

Robust Ruling Parties and Elite Dominance in Egypt and Malaysia

During the mid-1950s, leaders in Egypt and Malaysia quelled intraelite factionalism. The resolution of elite conflict provided their political parties, the Liberation Rally and UMNO, with a cohesive corps of figures who would seek to preserve their own power while suppressing alternative currents. This ballast for authority enabled leaders to preserve the early, exclusionary contours of national politics. Thus, through their initial victories, Nasser and Abdul Rahman not only curtailed the democratic trends advocated by Naguib and Onn, they also established the infrastructure for durable authoritarianism. These regimes were not perpetually unified or harmonious; indeed, leaders in Egypt and Malaysia grappled with serious rivals over the long term. Yet their organizations provided a structure for reconciling differences and renewing their coalitions during difficult times. By the end of the 1970s, both Egypt and Malaysia had come to experience constrained multiparty competition, with their respective ruling parties enjoying steady dominion over their disadvantaged opponents. The electoral hegemony that crystallized during that period foreshadowed enduring party control under Hosni Mubarak and Mahathir Mohamad in the decades that followed. While the third wave was claiming its first victims, Egypt and Malaysia already exhibited the resilience that would carry them securely through the rest of the century.

From Single-Party Rule to Guided Multipartyism: Egypt, 1954–1981
Having crushed Naguib's supporters and driven the Muslim Brotherhood underground, Nasser's regime was nearly unchallenged: Landed aristocrats had been subdued, traditional parties disbanded, and the most prominent proponents of reform co-opted or marginalized. Soon, Nasser vaulted onto the world stage as a leader in the "Non-Aligned Movement" and regional affairs, all the while pairing international notoriety with domestic popularity. Nasser's earlier victory over Naguib demonstrated that political control often hinged on mass support. He therefore used the Liberation Rally and successor institutions to garner public acclaim.[1] In June 1956, Egyptians approved a new constitution that formally ended the transitional period begun three years earlier. The constitution maintained the existing ban on opposition parties while dissolving the Revolutionary Command Council into a circle of political elites centered on Nasser. A new mass organization, the National Union, replaced the Liberation Rally (Beattie 1994: 122–124). In the autumn of 1956, Nasser nationalized the Suez Canal and defied British-led attempts to maintain Western control,

---

[1] Nasser and his cohort eschewed the term "party" because of its association with the discredited parliamentary opposition of the ancien regime. Although Egypt's ruling party was not officially dubbed a party until 1978, with the NDP's inauguration, the LR, NU, and ASU were parties in function, though not in name (Binder 1966: 218).

thus magnifying his stature in Egypt and around the world.[2] Bolstered by his newfound prestige and insulated by an exclusionary political system, Egypt's president enjoyed a decade without serious domestic crisis (Beattie 1994: 146).[3]

In this period, the ruling party became an important tool for defusing conflicts and preempting challenges by his erstwhile partners of the RCC (Waterbury 1983: 308–314; Beattie 2000: 8). As maestro of the Free Officers' 1952 coup, Nasser was keenly aware of his colleagues' capacity to conduct a second power grab (Beattie 1994: 160). Even as the president introduced more civilian technocratic officials, officers-turned-cabinet ministers remained in charge of the country's vital armed forces and domestic security agencies (Dekmejian 1971: 175–178). Balancing against any potential threat from these quarters, Nasser used the party organization to broaden the regime's popular base and shift power away from military leaders (Dekmejian 1971: 165; Beattie 1994: 162). His most significant effort in this area was the creation of the Arab Socialist Union (ASU) to replace the National Union in 1962. The ASU's ostensible purpose was to advance the goals of Egypt's new National Charter (Dekmejian 1971: 144). Approved by plebiscite on 30 June 1962, the National Charter called for a socialist development path to be steered by the ASU (Beattie 1994: 164–165). In pursuit of broad support from the lower socioeconomic classes, the National Charter established a quota of one-half of elected parliament seats for peasants and workers. It also heralded a new transitional period of no more than ten years, at which point the program would be reexamined.finally, the National Charter declared that the ASU would be formed by elections from base to peak, a hopeful vision of organizational democracy that would be regularly invoked in subsequent years but barely implemented (Beattie 1994: 164).

Given that researchers often portray the ASU as abnormally weak (e.g., Huntington 1968: 418), it is notable that the union drew much broader participation than Nasser had intended. When the ASU began accepting applications in January 1963, it received nearly five million registrants

---

[2] This political victory subsumed an immediate military defeat and depended on the United States and the Soviet Union pressuring British, French, and Israeli forces to withdraw (Beattie 1994: 116).

[3] The period 1956–1967 included two major foreign policy setbacks for Nasser: Syria's secession from the short-lived United Arab Republic (1958–1961) and Egypt's costly military involvement in Yemen (1962–1967) (Beattie 1994: 118, 158, 196). In themselves, though, neither of these imbroglios brought domestic instability on the level of March 1954 and 1968.

over its first twenty days (Beattie 1994: 166). The flood of applicants threatened to corrupt the organization's ideological commitments and prompted the president to create two additional, more selective bodies: The Vanguard Organization and the Youth Organization. These organs functioned as parties within the party, monitoring the membership and covertly managing the ASU's cadres (Beattie 1994: 167).[4]

On its surface, the ASU included an impressive one out of six Egyptians, thus exceeding by threefold the per capita membership of the Soviet Union's Communist Party (Dekmejian 1971: 146). Within the organization, though, a strict hierarchy enforced by Nasser belied the ASU's pretensions of popular inclusion and participation. In pyramid fashion, the ASU comprised a set of local committees connected vertically through middle-tier regional boards to a General Secretariat and Supreme Executive Committee (Binder 1966: 219; Dekmejian 1971: 145). (See Figure 3.1.) Although Nasser promised internal elections from the party's base to its peak, his own appointees filled the ASU's upper echelons (Hamrush 1993: 181–182). Indeed, the critical Central Committee, designed to link the National Congress to the Supreme Executive Committee, was never formed, thus breaking the theoretical link between cadres and leaders (Dekmejian 1971: 153). When elections were held, party officials rigged them to promote sympathetic middle managers and cadres (Waterbury 1983: 330–331).[5]

Nasser's blend of personal intervention and organizational rules was less exceptional, however, than some accounts of the ASU have implied.[6]

---

[4] Devoid of any former RCC members except its leader, the Vanguard Organization was Nasser's personal political apparatus. Its leaders later posed a serious threat to Nasser's successor, Anwar Sadat, in 1971, by which time the organization had grown to be an estimated 150,000 strong (Beattie 1994: 167).

[5] Years later, presidents Sadat and Mubarak would "introduce" internal party elections in the ASU and NDP, respectively. These measures were similarly plagued by favoritism and fraud, allowing a patina of pluralism beneath which "elected" positions were effectively appointive.

[6] Both Iliya Harik and Clement Henry contrast the ASU with ostensibly more rigorous, rule-based political organizations. Henry, for instance, pithily remarks: "Hardly a vanguard for recruiting top political leadership, the party was more like a rearguard for retiring it" (Moore 1974: 197). (Interestingly, the source of this conclusion, R. Hrair Dekmejian's analysis of party leaders' career paths, emphasized that guaranteed retirement meant long-term security for individuals and, consequently, helped to stabilize the leadership. See Dekmejian 1971: 206.) My treatment of ruling parties builds on these earlier accounts in two respects: first, by showing that parties outside Egypt were often similarly arbitrary, and, second, by contrasting the flawed but resilient political organizations of Nasser and his successors with the counterfactual example of complete party elimination in Iran and the Philippines.

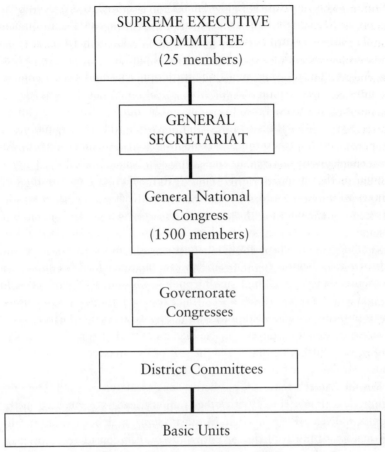

FIGURE 3.1. Organization of the Arab Socialist Union (circa 1963).
Note: Diagram constructed from Dekmejian (1971: 145–146); Harik (1973: 90–91); and Beattie (1994: 166–167).

As shown later, even the operations of a prototypical "strong" party, UMNO, have been steered by dominant individual leaders. More significantly, although Nasser demurred from putting the ASU above his own political stature, this "subordinate" party provided a mechanism for integrating competing factions and preventing public rifts (Harik 1973: 83). The ASU secretariat incorporated representatives of nearly all the major government agencies (Dekmejian 1971: 152).

Never was the ASU's role as an integrative mechanism more critical than in the wake of Egypt's devastating military defeat in June 1967, when

Israel's successful invasion of the Sinai Peninsula replaced the nationalist euphoria Egyptians had earlier enjoyed with profound disillusionment
and skepticism toward Nasser's government (Dekmejian 1971: 253). As
domestic uncertainty followed international humiliation, Nasser utilized
the ASU to buttress his own domestic popularity and then eliminate
his most capable political rival, Abd al-Hakim 'Amer, commander of
Egypt's armed forces. Preempting the public outcry over the country's
losses, Nasser offered his own resignation, while ASU leaders mobilized
demonstrators to protest this move and insist the president retain his position. This semiorchestrated acclaim reaffirmed Nasser and allowed him to
channel public outrage toward his most prominent rivals, the top-ranking
officers who had worked with him in the RCC. Of these, 'Amer was by
far the most popular and therefore the most threatening to Nasser. To a
large extent, Nasser had invested in the political apparatus of the ASU
to contain 'Amer, whose national stature made him both irksome and
indispensable (Beattie 1994: 162). The 1967 war provided Nasser with a
useful pretext for detaching himself from his long-time RCC colleague. In
the wake of the pro-Nasser rallies, 'Amer resigned his post under duress.
Three months later, he died, allegedly taking his own life (Beattie 1994:
212). Egypt's military defeat thus yielded a political victory for President
Nasser, who further demilitarized the regime by introducing new civilian
leaders (Dekmejian 1971: 178).

Despite 'Amer's removal, public protests escalated in 1968 when the
regime dealt less severely with other military leaders implicated in the
country's defeat. Egypt's High Military Court had been dramatically
lenient toward much of the air corps, the branch considered most neg-
ligent during the war. When the court issued demotions and fines carrying only light jail sentences or none at all, workers and students took
to the streets. On 20 February 1968, students at Cairo University began
demanding major political reforms. Their protests represented the most
potent public challenge to the regime since 1954 (Hamrush 1993: 202).
The clamor for reform prompted the president to reshuffle his cabinet
and include a number of university professors, a political nod to the students leading the demonstrations (Hamrush 1993: 203). Further tilting his
coalition away from the military, Nasser brought in eight new civilians
with doctorates (Dekmejian 1971: 165). By this point, nearly a third of
cabinet members held high-ranking posts within the ASU, signaling the
growing overlap between the organization and the executive's authority
(Dekmejian 1971: 208).

When diversifying his cabinet and party appeared insufficient to quell popular discontent, Nasser launched a fresh campaign of reform, much in the spirit of the March 1954 transition. On 30 March 1968, after consultation with his new ministers, Nasser announced new structural changes in the system, including the transformation of the Arab Socialist Union from base to peak and a clean-up of the government's most corrupt elements (Vatikiotis 1991: 410). The March 1968 declaration signaled a second major shift under Nasser from repression to liberalization, although its most basic promises, like those of March 1954, went unfulfilled. On 2 July 1968, Egyptians participated in a public referendum that ratified the 30 March declaration. Subsequent ASU elections were once again permeated by the president's influence (Hamrush 1993: 203–204). Meanwhile, the regime continued to repress its opponents: When students again demonstrated in late November, state security forcefully repressed them. As more than twenty lost their lives, the regime effectively retracted whatever concessions it had proffered, perpetuating violent dominance over the society it purported to lead (Dekmejian 1971: 264). In this manner, Nasser neutralized the most damaging consequences of 1967, preserving the regime he had founded even as his personal health declined.

In September 1970, Nasser died of heart complications and bequeathed a regime beset by internecine struggle. His efforts to provide a political counterweight to the RCC's former members divided the leadership between the departed president's original colleagues in the coup and his subsequent appointees. Naguib's early removal, 'Amer's later elimination, and the deaths and retirements of many other RCC members left only two original conspirators in the government: Vice President Anwar Sadat and Hussein Al-Shafei (Beattie 2000: 39).[7] Pitting themselves against the rightful successor, Sadat, Nasser's most valued political organizers deemed

---

7 The RCC had originally included eighteen officers, several of whom were soon ejected, leaving a core that roughly matched the seminal fourteen lead coup plotters of Nasser's Free Officers. Over the next decade, Nasser steadily winnowed this set down, as Dekmejian recounts: "The top officers remaining in power after the fall of Nagib were substantially the same persons that belonged to Abd al-Nasir's inner circle before the July 1952 coup d'etat.... By March 1964 only seven [including Nasser] of the original core of the Free Officers were still active at the highest levels of leadership" (1971: 217–218). By the end of 1968, only four remained: Nasser, minister of labor Kamal al-Din Rif'at, Anwar Sadat, and Hussein Al-Shafei. Significantly, Nasser, Sadat, and Al-Shafei were on the ASU's Supreme Executive. As Nasser ushered former RCC members out of power, he brought in second-tier participants in the Free Officers' Corps, thereby cultivating a set of top managers reliant on him (Dekmejian 1971: 219).

themselves the true heirs of the departed president's legacy. Initially, former ASU secretary-general Ali Sabri and his partners heading domestic
security services presumed that Sadat would simply be one among several
leaders (Beattie 2000: 40–43). Yet in a short time the new president began
to assert his autonomy, steering Egypt in a less Nasserist direction than
the Sabri group had envisioned. Beneath the ideological clashes over the
country's realignment from Soviet support to U.S. engagement lay a fundamental power struggle over who would rule after Nasser (Beattie 2000:
62–63). Sadat prevailed in this confrontation, purging the ASU of many
of its top leaders and steering the country toward a limited multiparty
system in which the president's organization predominated.

By the spring of 1971, Sadat had begun steadily undermining the positions of his ostensible coalition partners by currying favor with the second
echelon in the police and security services (Beattie 2000: 46–49). When
the president reversed land reforms and floated a peace proposal with
Israel, Sabri's faction erupted in open criticism (Ansari 1986: 161–162).
Sadat was then positioned to end the pretense of collective leadership and
preempt any coup plots that Sabri and his men might have attempted to
hatch. On 1 May 1971, Sadat announced that he would be removing those
leaders who no longer "had legitimate claims to impose their will on the
people" (Ansari 1986: 162). Ali Sabri was the first to go, stripped of his
government position and forced to resign from the ASU. His colleagues
heading the Ministry of Interior and armed forces soon suffered similar fates; notably unlike Naguib's removal, however, these resignations
did not stir a public outcry (Beattie 2000: 63–64, 68–69). By the end of
May, Sadat's "corrective movement" had swept down through the ASU
and the country's leading professional syndicates, removing or imprison-
ing his most viable challengers (Ansari 1986: 167; Hamrush 1993: 246).
Dekmejian describes the efficacy of the action: "In one stroke, Sadat had
eliminated almost everyone in the collective leadership that could conceivably pose a threat to him" (1971: 309). Cloaking his purge in the
liberal rhetoric of Nasser's 1968 declaration, Sadat established himself as
president in deed and not just in title.

This early domestic success paved the way for even more momentous
foreign policy victories. From his installation, President Sadat had gam-
bled that Egypt would reap greater dividends by removing Soviet military
advisors and turning to the Americans for assistance than by preserving
the foreign policy alignments of Nasser's final years. In October 1973,
Egypt retook the East Bank of the Suez Canal and began a protracted
process of peace negotiations with Israel. Six months later, the president

proposed a series of changes that opened Egypt's economy to international trade, expanded domestic opportunities for political participation, and strengthened the country's ties to the United States. In the October Paper, issued in April 1974, Sadat laid out a course for gradually restructuring the Nasserist state and opening the country to economic and political pluralism (Hinnebusch 1985: 112; Hamrush 1993: 246–247).

His political reform proposals not only buttressed Egypt's nascent relationship with the United States, they also provided the means for separating out the disparate ideological currents from the ASU into separate organizations. Egypt's current multiparty system took root in the aftermath of May 1971, as Sadat corralled the disparate ideological camps of the ASU and screened the union's membership (Beattie 2000: 77–79). Having already excised the ASU's most powerful Nasser-era appointees, Sadat pared down the organization and then carved off two wings into the rudiments of separate parties. The president eliminated the previously compulsory nature of membership in the ASU, by which even the practice of some professions (journalism, for example) depended on party membership (Waterbury 1983: 314). Heavily controlling party elections, the president rid himself of perceived enemies while retaining the overall organization (Beattie 2000: 80–81). Another set of rigged party elections in summer 1975 primed the regime for an end to single-party rule (Beattie 2000: 189). In 1976, Sadat introduced three competing platforms, or forums (*manabir*), a compromise between moving straight into multi-partyism, as those on the right desired, and maintaining the ASU system favored by leftists protective of the "socialist gains" under Nasser (Waterbury 1983: 358; Zaki 1995: 218; Beattie 2000: 190). These platforms, "right" (socialist liberals), "left" (progressive nationalists), and "center" (socialist democrats), then fielded candidates in parliamentary elections that October (Waterbury 1983: 366).

The 1976 elections changed the face of Egyptian politics but preserved the executive branch's supremacy over alternate political currents. The center platform was recognized as the party of the president, with Sadat's brother-in law, Mahmud Abu Wafia, as its formal head. Known as the Egypt Party, the organization included most of the president's inner circle. In addition, "[t]he media were at its disposal, and the civil service and public sector work force were assumed to be a captive electorate" (Waterbury 1983: 366). Running a surfeit of 527 candidates for 352 posts, the party won 280 seats (79.5 percent) in parliament (Beattie 2000: 199–200). The left and right platforms took 2 and 12 seats, respectively (Waterbury 1983: 366). Forty-eight independents also won election, signaling the persistence of opposition trends outside the three-party spectrum (Beattie 2000: 200). A portion of the independent bloc soon resurrected the Wafd Party, while others worked on behalf of the banned Muslim Brotherhood (Waterbury 1983: 369; Beattie 2000: 200). These resilient movements, long dormant in the arena of formal politics, became prominent participants in multiparty elections over the next thirty years. Yet rarely did the opposition's performance exceed what it garnered in the 1976 polls, the first formal competition among multiple parties in nearly a quarter of a century.

Mimicking Nasser's maneuvers in 1954 and 1968, Sadat curtailed political liberalization when it stopped serving his goals. The inauguration of limited multipartyism brought a reprieve to a regime exhausted by war and fearful of economic crisis, placating rightist critics at home and foreign backers abroad. And the new system seemed to lurch closer to democracy on 2 January 1977, when the president authorized the creation of full alternative political parties (Waterbury 1983: 367). Yet less than three weeks later, economic structural adjustments overshadowed political liberalization as tens of thousands of Egyptians rioted over proposed subsidy reductions for basic goods, including bread. Not since 1952 had the country experienced such violent mass aggravation. In restoring public order, the security forces killed at least seventy-nine people and wounded another eight hundred (Beattie 2000: 208). Thousands more accused of instigating the riots were arrested and detained in the following months (Beattie 2000: 210). At the same time as he reintroduced economic subsidies, Sadat slowed party development to a glacial pace, avowing that democracy had "fangs and claws" (Waterbury 1983: 368; Stacher 2001: 85–86). In consequence, proposals for additional parties outside the original three would have to face the daunting challenge of seeking approval from a committee run by former ASU members.[8]

After January 1977, Sadat seemed to cling to power more tightly than ever, preserving the dominance of his own party behind the fresh facade of multipartyism. In summer 1978, Sadat introduced the National Democratic Party. By virtue of the NDP's having a new chairman (despite retaining the same president), Sadat hoped to erase his regime's association with the bread riots (Beattie 2000: 236–237). The NDP was formally approved in October 1978 and quickly attracted the bulk of the Egypt Party members of parliament (Beattie 2000: 237, 239). The Egypt Party

---

[8] Law 40 of 1977 effectively places party formation under the executive branch. Restrictions on party formation have since become a central target in the opposition's calls for reform.

thus fell by the wayside, departing the scene completely with early parliamentary elections in 1979. Those polls, timed to reinforce the president's position after the March 1979 Camp David Accords with Israel, increased the ruling party's parliamentary majority to 84 percent of elected seats. Sadat also appointed forty more MPs, thirty women and ten Egyptian Christians (Copts) (Waterbury 1983: 371–372). Although the Wafd had officially re-formed the prior year, it failed to revive the electoral strength it had enjoyed before the 1952 coup (Waterbury 1983: 370).

During Sadat's final years in power, the president's earlier promises of pluralism gave way to the stark reality of government repression. Increasingly alienated from the public, particularly by his rapprochement with Israel, Sadat lashed out against real and suspected domestic foes, eventually jailing thousands of activists from across the political spectrum in September 1981. Though he avoided the fate of Iran's shah, Sadat's crackdown brought tragic consequences (Beattie 2000: 273). Before the president could engineer another ruling party victory at the polls, a group of Islamist militants assassinated the president on 6 October 1981. Vice President Hosni Mubarak, a former air force chief of staff and deputy war minister, became the country's new chief executive (Hopwood 1985: 184). Like his predecessor, Mubarak would promise gradual political opening and the continuation of government support for the lower classes, all the while retaining control over party operations, elections, and civil society.

UMNO's Alliance and National Front: Malaysia, 1957–1981

After leading the campaign for independence in Malaya (known after 1963 as Malaysia), UMNO survived electoral challenges and contained the interethnic tensions that lingered long after the Emergency formally ended in 1960. From independence through the beginning of Mahathir Mohamad's premiership in 1981, the ruling party managed internal dissent, prevented broad public rifts, and strengthened its electoral advantages over rival parties. As they guided the new state from under British control, UMNO leaders worked to quell Malay economic discontent while preserving a multiethnic coalition. Elections under the British had initiated UMNO's leaders in the "racial arithmetic" that subsequently allowed the party to sustain electoral majorities (through the Alliance) and retain the support of lower-income Malays in the countryside (Milne and Mauzy 1980: 4). Joining UMNO with its junior coalition partners, the Malaya Chinese Association and Malayan Indian Congress, the Alliance defeated Onn's IMP and PAS (the Islamic Party of Malaysia), a moderate Islamist opposition group. At the same time, control over government preserved UMNO's national position as the official promoter of Malay interests. Initially, as UMNO restricted opposition activity and circumscribed political competition, party dominance fed electoral victory and was fed by it in turn. Yet with economic disparities between rural Malays and affluent Chinese continuing, the electorate soon dealt the Alliance a major setback at the polls, spurring ethnic riots and prompting a national freeze on parliamentary politics.

Initial elections foreshadowed many of the techniques UMNO would continue to deploy throughout Malaysia's modern statehood. Their results similarly presaged the shape of ruling party hegemony. Highly advantageous districting enabled UMNO's coalition to translate popular vote victories of 51.8 percent in 1959 and 58.5 percent in 1964 into overwhelming majorities of 71 and 86 percent in the country's House of Representatives (*Dewan Rekyat*) (Tan 2001: 144, 155, 174). Thus, after independence, as before, the Alliance proved capable of besting the most viable monoethnic competitor organizations, principally PAS and the Chinese-led Democratic Action Party (DAP). UMNO took full advantage of its control of the state, deploying government patronage to needy areas and exploiting state-run television to tout its programs and candidates (Funston 1980: 186–187). Opposition candidates not only faced an uphill battle in those terms, they were also harassed, detained, or otherwise muzzled by government officials who judged them too vocal in their criticisms (Funston 1980: 187; Khoo 1997a: 52).

In this context of restrained oppositional activity and glaring economic inequality, social tensions persisted. Ever since the Federation of Malaya agreement under the British, Malay and Chinese leaders (often joined by representatives of the arguably less pivotal Indian minority) had cooperated in efforts to improve rural Malays' economic status without threatening domestic (primarily Chinese) or foreign capitalists. By 1969, it had become apparent that this pact – which, with the exception of a small number of government welfare agencies, remained largely informal – was failing to produce a Malay middle class (Jomo 1984: 253–254; Gomez and Jomo 1999: 15). Despite steady growth in the postindependence economy, poor Malays had benefited little; as social immobility set in and the income gap within ethnic groups widened, popular discontent with the Alliance rose (Gomez and Jomo 1999: 19). In elections on 10 May 1969, PAS, the DAP, and the Chinese-backed Gerakan held the Alliance to an unprecedentedly weak performance: The UMNO-led coalition won only 66 of 104 seats (63.5 percent) (Means 1976: 396). The three-party Alliance had garnered only 48.4 percent of votes in peninsular Malaysia, a result that stunned politicians and the masses alike. The prospect of an Alliance rout emboldened opposition supporters among non-Malays, who publicly celebrated UMNO's loss of the two-thirds majority that enabled the party to amend the constitution unilaterally (Means 1976: 396–397).

Chastened, the ruling party's supporters took to the streets as well. On 13 May 1969, UMNO organizers in Kuala Lumpur responded to their exuberant critics with counterdemonstrations that quickly became violent. Overwhelmingly anti-Chinese rioting gripped the capital, eventually claiming the lives of an estimated 196 people, with an additional 439 wounded (Funston 1980: 208–209). That evening, Prime Minister Abdul Rahman declared a state of emergency for Selangor state. The following day, the state of emergency was extended nationwide, conventional politics were suspended, and the country was placed under the administration of a National Operations Council (NOC) headed by the deputy prime minister, Tun Abdul Razak Hussein (Means 1976: 398; Funston 1980: 211–212). Elections in Sabah and Sarawak on the island of Borneo were frozen as UMNO scrambled to retain even a simple majority (Ongkili 1985: 202).[9] For the next twenty-one months, the NOC's ten members were the government of Malaysia. Midway through this crisis period, Prime Minister Abdul Rahman, citing personal reasons but also under sharp criticism for not advancing Malays' economic status, stepped down from his post and was succeeded by Tun Abdul Razak (Means 1976: 399). The NOC focused on restoring order by "reestablishing tolerance among the communities of West Malaysia" (Ongkili 1985: 215). Yet its means were increasingly autocratic, including an extended ban on political activities and new restrictions on speech. Constitutional changes then codified many of these new strictures, recasting Malaysian politics even after parliament reconvened in early 1971 (Funston 1980: 214– 215).[10]

---

[9] Parliamentary elections in Sabah and Sarawak were held the following year, after UMNO had coaxed influential local parties to join its coalition (Crouch 1996: 53). The results then gave the Alliance a slim majority of 53.5 percent (77 of 144 seats) (Tan 2001: 174).

[10] The relatively limited role of military figures in Malaysian politics, even during this period, bears noting. In comparison to Egypt, the Malaysian military has maintained a low profile in national political life. In the decade before Malaya's independence, the British had filled the country's military and police forces with trained Malays, just as it had staffed the civil services (Crouch 1996: 17). But Malay leaders' nonviolent and gradualist pursuit of independence encouraged the institutionalization of a repressive apparatus that would remain modest in size and stay under civilian control. Further, familial ties between UMNO elites and the armed services reinforced a shared vision of Malay leadership in a peacefully managed multiethnic society (Milne and Mauzy 1999: 2–3).

As important as the NOC's political response to the 13 May riots were its economic prescriptions for treating Malay discontent. Freshly defeated MP Dr. Mahathir Mohamad faulted Prime Minister Abdul Rahman for not remedying Malays' economic deprivations (Milne and Mauzy 1980: 86–87). Although his critique prompted UMNO to expel Mahathir temporarily from the party, his concern resonated far beyond the circle of Malay nationalist "ultras" whom he epitomized (Means 1986: 399). Other party leaders interpreted their electoral losses and the sub-sequent riots as a sign that Malay interests remained insecure: Government would have to intervene more aggressively to deliver socioeconomic equality with the non-Malay minority to Malays (Ongkili 1985: 217). In response to these concerns, the NOC issued the New Economic Policy (NEP), which aimed at general economic improvement "by raising income levels and increasing opportunities for all Malaysians, irrespective of race." But the NEP also spoke of "accelerating the process of restructuring Malaysian society to correct economic imbalance, so as to reduce and eventually eliminate the identification of race with economic function" (Ongkili 1985: 224). Although this language did not explicitly mention targeted supports, Malays, as the group lagging behind in education, income, and employment, were the NEP's understood beneficiaries. Cultural policies making Malay the national language and privileging Malays' citizenship status further demonstrated UMNO's commitment to defending Malay identity. Abdul Rahman's resignation and the rise of Razak to UMNO's presidency and Malaysia's premiership reinforced this shift.

In its relations with other parties, UMNO recalibrated its coalition to avoid a repeat of the 1969 elections. The Alliance expanded to include additional non-Malay parties and even the Malay party PAS. Dubbed the National Front (NF, *Barisan Nasional*), this capacious assemblage extended UMNO's reach into the very communities that had turned against the Alliance (Crouch 1996: 33). By broadening the coalition to include more parties, UMNO strengthened its position as ultimate arbiter and manager. UMNO leaders could now concede less to their subordinate partners, demand more from them, and, when necessary, push dissenting parties out of the NF without losing power. The three-party Alliance had not been nearly as malleable. Creation of the National Front substantially reduced the influence of the previously central MCA and MIC. Harold Crouch explains, "While the Alliance could have been characterized as a partnership (although an unequal one), the NF was in effect a façade for UMNO rule" (1996: 34).

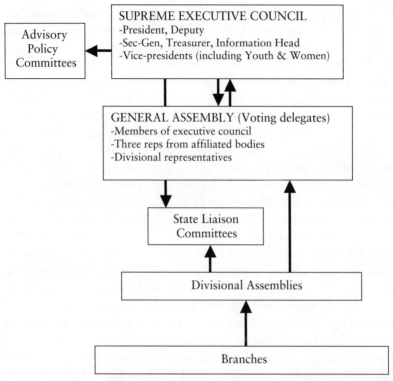

FIGURE 3.2. Organization of the United Malays National Organization (circa 1966).
Note: Diagram constructed from Funston (1980: 169–171).

Within UMNO, the party's structure resembled the ASU in Egypt, but it was more regulated in terms of the elections that fed the organization from local units to its national peak (Figure 3.2).[11] The base unit was the branch, which elected representatives to the Divisional Annual Assembly. Divisional representatives sent delegates to the national General Assembly, although the division's relations with the General Assembly were mediated by another body, the State Liaison Committee. The General Assembly met annually, as well as more frequently when circumstances required, and according to Funston it had "extensive" powers "in the crucial areas of policy-making, constitution-framing and discipline" (1980: 169). Although the General Assembly was formally "the highest authority in UMNO," it was often superceded by UMNO's Supreme

---

[11] The following discussion is based on Funston (1980: 168–171).

Executive Council (Funston 1980: 169–171). The Supreme Executive Council included the president, his deputy, the party's secretary-general, the information head, the treasurer, five vice presidents, and up to twenty-seven "ordinary elected members" (Funston 1980: 170). Because the president could fill as many as eleven of the Executive Council's thirty-seven posts through appointment, his office was extraordinarily strong (Funston 1980: 171). Through UMNO's hierarchy, the president ran the party; through the National Front, UMNO overwhelmed the opposition.

In the 1974 parliamentary elections, the first national polls since the post–13 May state of emergency, NF candidates took 88 percent of the seats (135 of 154), a historic high for the period following the establishment of statehood (Tan 2001: 174). Outside the NF, the DAP and a regional organization, the Sarawak National Party, each won only nine seats. Even though the National Front practically ensured hegemony for UMNO through its very breadth, UMNO assiduously manipulated the bounds of multiparty competition (Crouch 1996: 30).[12] The party dominated the national media, distributed government funds for local projects, monitored voting behavior (down to the level of the polling station), and mobilized government workers to vote for NF candidates. It continued to deploy these tactics even as it shuffled coalition partners in later years. Elite cohesion despite conflicts sustained UMNO's control of the National Front and the multiparty elections it contested.

Just as UMNO leaders had rallied around Abdul Rahman and, above all, the cause of Malay rule in the years before independence, the party's top officials remained loyal to the organization in the face of internal feuds

[12] Social scientists have tended to treat 1969 as a turning point in Malaysia's postindependence history, during which the regime crossed the threshold from democratic to authoritarian practices (see, among others, Crouch 1996; Slater 2003). To an extent, the contrast between earlier and subsequent elections supports such claims. Indeed, a leader of the NOC declared soon after the Council began its work: "Democracy is dead in this country. It died at the hands of the opposition parties who triggered off the events leading to this violence" (Funston 1980: 212). Yet such an account also raises the counterfactual question, Was the UMNO regime more willing to accept an opposition victory in 1959 or 1964? Or were the 1969 polls simply the first time its readiness to share power was really tested? Following this line of reasoning, I treat the events of 1969 and their aftermath as revelatory more than transformative. Having previously intimidated its opponents and manipulated electoral processes to its own advantage, the regime showed in 1969 that when pressed it would go even further to hold onto power. Crouch's claim about *post*-1969 politics thus applies to the entirety of Malaysia's independent statehood: "Apparently democratic practices were permitted only so long as they did not actually undermine the power of the ruling elite while they were quickly modified or abolished when elite interests were threatened" (Crouch 1992: 21, quoted in Khoo 1997a: 49).

in the mid-1970s. Prime Minister Razak's health began declining soon into his tenure. By 1975, he was already grooming Dato Hussein Onn, his deputy and the son of UMNO founder Dato Onn Jaafar, to succeed him. Yet even Hussein's imminent promotion was viewed as a stopgap measure, given that he suffered from a preexisting heart condition. Consequently, competition at the next echelon was especially fierce. In June 1975, UMNO's internal elections advanced three party leaders into the coveted vice presidencies that lay just beneath the deputy premiership. Among the victorious candidates was Mahathir Mohamad, who had reclaimed a seat in parliament and garnered a cabinet post in parliamentary elections the prior year. Placing third, Mahathir edged out Selangor chief minister Datuk Harun Idris (*Far Eastern Economic Review* 4 July 1975).

Despite his loss within the party, Harun commanded a strong following for his work as head of UMNO Youth and remained a likely contender to succeed Razak (Crouch 1996: 100). Razak and Hussein, apparently threatened by Harun's influence, soon distanced him from that opportunity. In November 1975, soon after Harun declined an ambassadorial appointment – effectively political exile – Razak charged Harun with corruption, prompting the Selangor leader to turn from his state-level duties to preparing his legal defense (Leifer 1976: 158; Tilman and Tilman 1977: 144–145). Razak passed away during a medical treatment trip to England in January 1976. Yet after assuming UMNO's presidency, Hussein continued and even accelerated the campaign against Harun: On 18 March, Harun was stripped of his party membership; a week later, he lost his post as chief minister; and on 18 May he was convicted and sentenced to two years in prison (Tilman and Tilman 1977: 145). Although he subsequently received amnesty and was welcomed back to UMNO, Harun had been effectively marginalized during a critical phase of succession maneuvers (Mauzy and Milne 1983–1984: 619). Hussein had chosen the notoriously pro-Malay Mahathir as his deputy, thereby settling the debate over who would be next in line for command of the party and government. In an act of historic irony that was in no way accidental, then, Hussein perpetuated and relied on the notion of Malay preeminence that his father had challenged (Leifer 1976: 156). And just as Onn had found himself isolated outside of UMNO, as the organization exerted a centripetal force on Malay elites, so too did the otherwise powerful Harun prove ineffectual when defying the party.[13]

---

[13] The resolution of conflict should not be read retrospectively to minimize the intensity of that episode. At the time, one analyst described Hussein and Harun's showdown as a

By suppressing Harun's challenge, Hussein primed UMNO for another strong electoral performance. In 1977, UMNO expelled PAS from the National Front because of the Islamist group's defiance in its traditional strongholds of Kelantan and Terengannu. Yet the ruling party went on to retain essentially the same share of parliament (84.4 percent) in elections the following year as in the previous election, losing only four seats (Crouch 1996: 65, 75; Tan 2001: 174). Unity within UMNO had renewed its strength against the opposition; elite cohesion then translated into electoral control through manipulation of the national media and local politics. UMNO dominated the airwaves and gerrymandered the ground game, disadvantaging its competitors both before and during elections. Already excluded from the broadcast media, opposition parties like PAS and the DAP suffered further from a prohibition of open-air public rallies. Finally, state patronage helped to buy votes strategically and thereby further shut out what little support oppositionists may have curried at the local level (Crouch 1996: 30). Blocking the opposition's limited avenues for engaging the public proved a reliable guarantor of UMNO dominance, a way of recalibrating in the wake of the 1969 crisis. In July 1981, Hussein resigned due to health problems, and his deputy succeeded to the premiership (Tan 2001: 181). Sustaining the trend of the 1970s, Mahathir went on to rule for more than twenty years, carrying the UMNO/NF coalition through five more electoral triumphs.

Elite Dissent and Party Deactivation in Iran and the Philippines

Unresolved conflict in Iran and the Philippines sent political developments on a trajectory of institutional decline that departed from patterns in Egypt and Malaysia. Whereas the initial struggle for power left Nasser and Abdul Rahman with relatively unified coalitions, the vicissitudes of regime formation placed Iranian clerics and Philippine politicians in a less advantageous position. Early, incessant rivalries within each regime undermined the building of long-term organizations that could harness otherwise disparate interests. The Islamic Republic's would-be hierocrats operated beside fellow clergy who sought to incorporate the public in a genuinely plebiscitary regime. Their standoff escalated within

major threat to UMNO itself: "The removal of Harun Idris openly polarized the UMNO party, particularly between the increasingly voracious and powerful UMNO youth wing and the older guard.... Thus, in the long term, *it is clear that the ability of UMNO as the ruling party in the country to work as a united party is now very much open to question*" (MacAndrews 1977: 306, emphasis added).

the country's parliament and the Islamic Republican Party, then continued after the IRP's deactivation. Intraelite factionalism among Philippine elites also trumped institutional longevity. The Philippines advanced to independent statehood with personal rivalries between Osmeña and Roxas cleaving the Nacionalista Party and preventing any one faction from entrenching itself in power. In 1972, Ferdinand Marcos seemed to break this trend when he essentially reprised Quezon's earlier power grab. But the president-turned-dictator then dispensed with the Nacionalista Party and froze all party politics, thereby denying rival politicians the organization under whose banner he had twice been elected.

Leader Ali Khamenei and President Marcos ultimately came to view their parties as liabilities rather than assets. Hoping to eliminate the nuisance of elite dissenters, they dispensed with party institutions and operated instead through loose networks of personal allegiance and tactical cooperation. This bid to concentrate power brought immediate benefits by unfettering the rulers; it sequestered political gadflies and made the ruling circle more homogenous and more tightly wedded to the top leader. Yet newfound autonomy delivered the illusion of power more than its substance. The decision to disband the ruling party, far from pulling influence toward the ruler's clique, instead fragmented the authority Khamenei and Marcos had sought to magnify. When they abandoned their parties, each man planted the seeds of elite defections and electoral defeats.

The Right Wing's Climb and the IRP's Decline: Iran, 1981–1992
At the end of the tumultuous year of 1981, Ayatollah Khomeini was still chief jurist and leader; the right-wing cleric Ali Khamenei was president. Members of the Islamic Republican Party controlled a solid majority of the Islamic Assembly, and figures loyal to the fallen Beheshti dominated the Council of Guardians, which supervised the legislature. IRP affiliates also retained fifty-five of the seventy-three seats in the Assembly of Experts, the body that had approved the constitution and would choose Khomeini's successor in the event of his death (Baktiari 1996: 56). In September 1981, parliament formally banned non-IRP organizations and placed the creation of new parties under a clerically dominated oversight board (Fairbanks 1998: 20). Nearly completely excluding alternative movements, the IRP's cleric-politicians and their lay allies had achieved the preeminence Bazargan and Bani-Sadr had sought to obstruct.

Despite the ruling clerics' victory over Bani-Sadr and the Mojahedin-e-Khalq in 1981, consensus in government proved elusive. Clerical control over the regime's religious and republican factions had been achieved, but discord among the clergy intensified. While Iranian leaders established the Islamic Republic and occupied its top posts, they clustered into distinct factions based on their vision for the new regime. Some elites changed or intensified their stances based on the positions they occupied, particularly after Khomeini's departure in 1989, when the dissonant factions lacked a recognized mediator. Some of the forerunners of the reformists were opportunistic democrats who promoted the "republican" elements of the regime (that is, the elected parliament) because their sole power base in post-Khomeini Iran lay there.[14]

Such strategic shifts notwithstanding, three main factions could be discerned in the country's postrevolutionary elite.[15] The most consistently antidemocratic of these groups was the so-called traditionalist right, which centered on Khamenei (president 1981–1989) and the founding corps of the IRP. Traditionalist right clerics favored pure hierocracy and accepted but did not embrace the notion of elected offices accountable to the broader public. In economic policy, they favored limited state involvement, low taxes on the business class, and minimal subsidies for the poor. The urban-based merchant class (*bazaaris*) arguably constituted their most influential social constituency.

Closely linked to the traditionalist right was the "modernist right" led by Hashemi Rafsanjani (speaker of the parliament, 1980–1989). In the early years of the Islamic Republic, Khamenei's traditionalist right and Rafsanjani's modernist right were scarcely differentiable. During the 1980s, the right-wing factions were joined by their distrust of plebiscitary politics. Fueling their elitism was the right wing's dependence on the Council of Guardians, which was largely insulated from public opinion and often blocked the proposals of populist parliamentarians from the Islamic left (Baktiari 1996: 91–92). The modernist right's views later diverged from those of the traditionalists, however, as the nation struggled to rebuild its infrastructure and attract foreign capital in the early 1990s. At that point, the modernist right began to call for "rationalizing"

---

[14] For example, some members of the "Islamic left," the predecessor to the reform movement of the late 1990s, initially favored exclusionary candidacy requirements designed to marginalize so-called liberal parties, such as the Iran Freedom Movement, in the 1984 parliamentary elections. When essentially the same standard – evaluating candidates based on their loyalty to the Supreme Leader – was deployed to block Khamenei's critics in 1992, the same leftist politicians decried the tactic (Baktiari 1996: 109–110).

[15] The following categories are drawn from a broad reading of elite politics in the Islamic Republic. Among many other valuable works, the principal sources here are Baktiari (1996), Buchta (2000), and Moslem (2002).

the state and economy, attempting to conform to a neoliberal model of structural adjustment and bureaucratic retrenchment.

Over time, the Islamic left reinvigorated the republican aspirations submerged in the revolution's wake. Much of this cohort believed deeply in the idea of *velayat-e-faqih* and had adhered to Khomeini's leadership during his rule. At the same time, their vision for a religious state revolved around popular participation and government support for the masses (Baktiari 1996: 81). The Islamic left sought to include the Iranian public in national decision making and pursued redistributive economic policies that aided the lower classes. During the 1980s, its political stronghold was the elected parliament. Their most prominent leaders included Mir-Hossein Musavi, a civil engineer by training whom Khomeini had appointed to the Islamic Revolutionary Council in mid-1979. From 1981 through 1989, Musavi served as prime minister and spearheaded the Islamic left's policy agenda. He was aided by progressive cleric Mehdi Karrubi (deputy speaker of the parliament, 1981–1989). In the wake of Khomeini's death in 1989, Karrubi and his affiliates reignited the political torch lit by Shariat-Madari in his abortive call for popular sovereignty. They believed that the clergy had a role to play in government, but as Khamenei and Rafsanjani's power grew, the Islamic left became concerned about the rise of an unelected oligarchy that seemed to disdain the masses.

As the Iran-Iraq war was being waged, Khomeini constantly mediated between the factions and cautioned against any disunity that might weaken the nation. During this period, it is conceivable that the divisions between factions could have been bridged or eliminated through either a formalized compromise or the right wing's suppression of leftist clerics (Banuazizi 1994: 4). But instead of imposing consensus or backing a definite winner, Khomeini "spent much energy and political capital to ensure that the opposing factions were kept in rough balance" (Banuazizi 1994: 4; Moslem 2002: 4). Unlike in Egypt, where the regime cohered around Nasser's coalition and the broad organizations that sustained it, Iran charted a less steady course. Khomeini's mediation held Iran's factions in parity. The Islamic Republic's leader regularly made broad noncommittal pronouncements that competing politicians then parsed to their side's advantage. In turn, the regime's primary political organization, the Islamic Republican Party, emblemized this dissonance and housed a functional but fractious multifactional alliance.

After the 1980 Islamic Assembly elections and the parliament's regulation of alternative parties, the IRP enjoyed unrivaled dominance. Despite

valiant attempts to challenge it, even old parties like Bazargan's Iran Freedom Movement struggled for purchase in the new system. But within the
IRP, clerical cooperation against the proverbial enemies of the revolution
gave way to infighting even before the first parliamentary session of 1980–
1984 had concluded (Moslem 2002: 62). Prime Minister Musavi and his
allies on the Islamic left advocated "the strengthening of the public sector... at the expense of private enterprise," challenging the right wing's
vision of the state's role (Baktiari 1996: 89). As early as 1983, President Khamenei admitted that "there were differences of opinion among
the members of the [party's] central committee" while hastening to add
that "both camps agree on most issues" (Moslem 2002: 68). The following year, Rafsanjani publicly identified "two main groups within the
IRP" that disagreed on the proper extent of government involvement in
the country.[16] The party's more conservative leaders had begun to feel
threatened by so-called radicals (Islamic leftists) within the organization,
who seemed poised to extend their already substantial influence over the
Islamic Assembly into the IRP itself.

By 1984, the first parliament was nearly evenly split, with around
eighty MPs in the right wing's camp, seventy favoring the Islamic left,
and close to eighty more who were less attached but generally divided
between the two (Baktiari 1996: 107). Baktiari describes the situation:
"Since the Rafsanjani camp controlled the speakership and the governing
board, and the radicals controlled the government, executive-legislative
relations were virtually at a standstill. The parity of influence was also
greatly affected by the leadership style of Khomeini, who did not allow
any faction to gain the upper hand" (1996: 108). Elections in 1984 tipped
the composition of parliament in the left wing's favor. Drawing a strong
national turnout (over 24 million people reportedly participated), the
elections increased the size of the Islamic left's bloc. At the same time,
rightist politicians such as Speaker Rafsanjani retained their leadership
posts, largely through Khomeini's rhetorical intercessions on their behalf
(Baktiari 1996: 113–115). By buttressing Rafsanjani, Khomeini helped to
deflate the victorious Musavi and dash hopes that the left wing's popular
mandate would swiftly translate into policy accomplishments (Baktiari
1996: 118–119). The IRP continued to reflect the intractable divisions
of parliament, a situation deemed unacceptable by Rafsanjani and President Khamenei, who was reelected to a second four-year term in 1985

---

[16] "Rafsanjani Predicts Struggle With 'Arrogant Powers'" *IRNA*, 28 December 1984, FBIS-
SAS-84-252, 31 December 1984.

(Baktiari 1996: 124). The next year, the speaker and president proposed to Khomeini that the IRP be dissolved, but at that point the leader rejected the idea. Nonetheless, the two IRP headmen began formally scaling back the party's operations.[17] Rafsanjani and Khamenei's fears were fed by the Islamic left's victory in passing several progressive economic measures that targeted merchants in the cities and benefited peasants in the countryside. Left-wing leaders had also gained control over the IRP's official newspaper, *Jomhuri-ye Islami* (Islamic Republic) (Baktiari 1996: 139). The premier leaders of the right wing interpreted these achievements as harbingers of the Islamic left faction's growing influence: "[W]ith party resources in their hands," they feared, "the faction could now impose its perspective on practically every legislation possible" (Baktiari 1996: 139). In 1987, Rafsanjani and Khamenei wrote to Khomeini, again asking him to dissolve the party (Baktiari 1996: 140). They contended that the party had played a vital role in consolidating the revolution but was no longer needed; indeed, the party's continued operations could actually harm the country. They concluded: "Therefore, it is felt that the existence of the party no longer has the benefits of its early days and on the contrary party polarization under the present conditions may provide an excuse for discord and factionalism, damaging the unity of the nation."[18] This time, Khomeini agreed, and the organization formally ceased its activities on 2 June 1987 over the lone objection of Prime Minister Musavi (Baktiari 1996: 140).

The IRP's dissolution immediately released right-wing elites from an increasingly cumbersome and antiquated coexistence with the Islamic left, but the IRP's demise inaugurated a new phase of public competition among Iran's clerically led movements, one that did not initially favor Rafsanjani and Khamenei. With the IRP gone, Iran experimented with formal multiparty politics. The government entertained party applications from December 1988 through March 1989, but the major political forces generally avoided the official approval process administered by the Ministry of Interior. Instead, they worked as factional groupings with affiliated newspapers that served as their public face (Fairbanks 1998: 21–22; Buchta 2000: 14). The right wing's faction called itself the Society of Combatant Clergy (SCC). The SCC's conservative clerics had a history of informal collaboration dating back to prerevolutionary meetings about

---

[17] "Hashemi-Rasanjani Holds News Conference," *Tehran Domestic Service*, 4 June 1987, FBIS-NES-87-111, 10 June 1987.
[18] "Khomeyni Agrees to Disbanding of Political Parties," *IRNA*, 2 June 1987, FBIS-NES-87-105, 2 June 1987.

Khomeini's writings (Baktiari 1996: 111). In 1984, the SCC had fielded a list of candidates that largely overlapped with the IRP's main standard-bearers (Baktiari 1996: 112). Opposed to the SCC was the leftist Association of Combatant Clerics (ACC). In the parliamentary elections of 1988, the first since the IRP's dissolution, the ACC expanded the Islamic left's representation in parliament while encroaching on the bloc loyal to Rafsanjani (Baktiari 1996: 147–150). Buoyed by an uncharacteristically lucid defense of the poor by Khomeini as well as by war fears that suppressed turnout in Tehran, the Islamic left commanded a majority of parliament, while Rafsanjani's faction won barely one-third (Baktiari 1996: 150, 162, 164).

Events the following year reversed the leftist faction's fortunes and brought the right-wing SCC a momentous victory. In the summer of 1989, Ayatollah Khomeini died, and Ali Khamenei assumed the post of supreme leader. Khamenei's succession to the country's highest position followed the political defeat of left-wing supporter Grand Ayatollah Hossein-Ali Montazeri. Montazeri was Khomeini's official heir apparent until Rafsanjani managed to drive a wedge between the two clerics in the mid-1980s (Baktiari 1996: 171). In late 1986, Rafsanjani was implicated in the Iran-Contra negotiations with the United States. At that point, Khomeini deflected criticism away from Rafsanjani, who then spearheaded a backlash against one of his chief critics, Montazeri's son-in-law Mehdi Hashemi. Hashemi's arrest and subsequent execution isolated Montazeri and prompted him to decry the regime's excesses more stridently and to advocate political reform, including the relegalization of the Iran Freedom Movement (Baktiari 1996: 136–138, 171).[19] Bristling at his protégé's criticisms, Khomeini drove Montazeri from his position as designated successor on 28 March 1989 (Baktiari 1996: 171). Just over two months later, Khomeini passed away. The Assembly of Experts met the following day to begin selecting a successor. With Montazeri essentially disqualified, Karrubi pushed in vain to broaden the selection beyond senior clerics. But the religious left wing did not command the influence over the Assembly of Experts that it held in the elected Islamic

---

[19] Baktiari records one especially dramatic example of the chastened Montazeri's advocacy for human rights in the Islamic Republic, a letter from 1 October 1988 in which the cleric declares: "We will get no results with frequent arrests, harshness, punishments, detentions, and killings. Besides, we will cause discontent among the people who are the country's and the revolution's capital assets. We will cause irreparable injustice to many people because of the narrow-minded and uncaring officials in charge of the ministry of security and information" (1996: 172).

Assembly. In a short time, the Assembly of Experts selected right-wing stalwart Khamenei to succeed the departed Khomeini as leader (*rahbar*) (Baktiari 1996: 175–176).[20]

Although Khamenei's rise spelled a setback for the ACC, constitutional changes that boosted Rafsanjani's power proved even more damaging to the Islamic left. A 30 July 1989 referendum inaugurated Iran's "second republic" through a set of forty-five amendments designed to reinforce the right wing's position. The revised constitution's most influential provisions granted the leader powers that Khomeini had possessed informally by virtue of his position as the Islamic Republic's first jurist, including appointment of the head of the judiciary, the chiefs of the security services and revolutionary guards, and the Council of Guardians' six clerical figures (Ehteshami 1995: 49). The amendments also abolished the post of prime minister (Musavi's stronghold since 1981), transferred the premier's responsibilities to a newly created president, and greatly curbed the Islamic Assembly's ability to interpellate the executive and his cabinet (Ehteshami 1995: 38; Baktiari 1996: 185). To fill the presidency, a fresh election was held. The Council of Guardians had screened out all but two of eighty applicants: Rafsanjani and a token contestant. Swept to victory with 94 percent of the vote amid 55 percent turnout, Rafsanjani then joined with Leader Khamenei to accomplish their long-time goal of defeating the Islamic left (Buchta 2000: 36–37).

The next three years pitted Khamenei and Rafsanjani against the ACC-controlled parliament as the right and left wings debated postwar reconstruction and economic recovery. The Islamic Republic's long war with Iraq had formally ended in summer 1988, after an estimated six hundred thousand had perished (Baktiari 1988: 153). Iran's infrastructure was devastated, and its economy seemed headed toward crisis. Unemployment estimates ranged from an official rate of 14 percent to private claims of 26 percent. Meanwhile, overemployment had bloated the state bureaucracy: The public sector accounted for nearly one-third of all jobs. Manufacturing was down, and nonoil exports comprised a paltry 10 percent of foreign exchange receipts (Baktiari 1996: 193).

Seeing this bleak macroeconomic picture, Rafsanjani pushed to rationalize and modernize the Iranian state, trimming subsidies, enforcing fiscal

[20] Immediately after his appointment to the post of leader, Khamenei was dubbed an *ayatollah* in the country's media, a precipitous and controversial promotion given his lack of the proper scholarly credentials for that higher post. Until that point, he had shared the ranking of *hojjatoleslam* (one rank below *ayatollah*) with both Rafsanjani and Karrubi (Baktiari 1996: 176; Buchta 2000: 12, 17).

discipline, expanding the private sector, and attracting foreign capital. Now in the post of speaker of parliament, Karrubi and his fellow MPs from the Islamic left balked at Rafsanjani's proposals to scale back state support for the urban and rural poor and rejected any realignment of Iran's foreign policy in pursuit of stronger ties with the West (Baktiari 1996: 194–195; Buchta 2000: 17). While Karrubi's bloc thwarted many of the president's plans, the leftist parliamentarians were not much more successful at implementing their own programs. The Council of Guardians, operating as a de facto upper house for the right wing, vetoed 40 percent of the legislation passed by the Islamic Assembly (Buchta 2000: 21). By the time the next parliamentary elections approached in 1992, Rafsanjani was demonstrably irritated by the left wing's subversion of his domestic and foreign policy agenda; during Friday prayer sermons, the president denounced his parliamentary foes as power hungry and backward (Baktiari 1996: 215).

Khamenei aided his beleaguered ally, employing the Council of Guardians to shatter not only the policy deadlock but also the political presence of the Islamic left. Through three sessions of the Islamic Assembly, the Islamic left had constituted a formidable and sometimes dominant presence. Accordingly, the leader and president saw the upcoming 1992 elections as a chance to rid the ACC of its primary institutional base and thereby remove the only major obstacle to implementing their own agenda.[21] Before the elections, Rafsanjani and Khamenei turned the Council of Guardians' "approbatory" power – its authority to veto potential candidates – into a screen against some to the Islamic left's most viable candidates. Asghar Schirazi describes the opening they exploited: "Article 99 of the constitution includes amongst the powers of the Guardian Council supervision of elections to parliament, to the Assembly of Leadership Experts, for the president and of national referendums. *But it is not clear what exactly is meant by supervision*" (Schirazi 1997: 88–89, emphasis added). During Khomeini's years as leader, the council had prohibited secularists and moderates opposed to the Islamic Republic from running. Marxists were blocked in the 1980 elections, for example, and members of the Iran Freedom Movement were disqualified in 1984 (Schirazi 1997: 87). But in summer 1991, Rafsanjani's faction succeeded in amending the constitution to make a candidate's loyalty to the leader a precondition for his standing for office. Khamenei then obligingly took advantage of the change to impair his and Rafsanjani's opponents (Baktiari 1996: 216).

---

[21] "Khamene'i Sides with Council of Guardians," *Keyhan International*, 20 February 1992, FBIS-NES-92-055, 20 March 1992.

Cognizant of what the change portended, ACC leaders in the Islamic Assembly attempted to circumscribe the council's new powers, but the council overruled the parliament and reaffirmed that only appropriately qualified applicants would be allowed to run (Siavoshi 1992: 46–47; Schirazi 1997: 89). By that point, "[t]he vehement protests of the majority in parliament and of their allies...were of no avail" (Schirazi 1997: 89). Khamenei reinforced the expansion of the council's powers and called its members the defenders of parliament's integrity: "The health of our government depends on preserving its Islamic direction and observing the Constitution in it, and this is achieved through the presence of the Council of Guardians.... Therefore, you who are now charged with observing these regulations in the elections are performing a very important task. You must therefore observe the regulations carefully. A deputy who comes into the Majles must be a good and pious person." Although he did not specify what the standard for such piety would be, Khamenei mentioned that the council should reject all those who were "corrupt," "troublemaker[s]," or "in opposition to the government on any pretext."[22] At that point, even the left-wing minister of the interior, Abdollah Nuri, conceded, "With the announcement of the view of the leader, every kind of ambiguity in this regard has been resolved for the Ministry of the Interior."[23]

When candidate applications opened for the 1992 elections, the Council of Guardians dutifully exercised its new powers. In past elections, the number of aspirants to parliament had been increasing, from 1,100 in 1984 to 1,960 in 1988.[24] In 1992, applications numbered a record 3,150. Yet, on 1 April, the Council of Guardians announced it had approved only 2,050 (65 percent) for candidacy (Ehteshami 1995: 61). Even more significant, the disqualifications fell primarily on the left wing's strongest candidates. Almost half of the left's most influential candidates had been screened out (Moslem 2002: 181). Forty sitting MPs, including deputy speaker Asadollah Bayat, did not qualify for candidacy and a chance at reelection (Baktiari 1996: 218). Karrubi and the ACC protested the council's decisions in vain. Rebutting complaints that popular contenders were being prevented from running, Khamenei disingenuously replied, "Well, you must trust your officials. They are trustworthy. Maybe they detected

---

[22] "Role of Council of Guardians in Majles Elections," *Resalat*, 23 February 1992, *FBIS-NES-92-057-S*, 24 March 1992.
[23] "Paper on Rivalry for Control of the Majles," *Keyhan*, 20 February 1992, FBIS-NES-092-052, 17 March 1992.
[24] "Majles Speaker Urges Fairness in Elections," *IRNA*, 17 March 1992, FBIS-NES-92-054, 19 March 1992.

something, and so they have rejected the candidate."[25] Khamenei was far
from impartial during the campaigning and voting: The leader used public
addresses and prayer sermons to promote the SCC and deride the Society's
competitors (Ehteshami 1995: 61).[26] At the same time, President Rafsanjani's brother controlled the state radio and television networks, providing
the right wing easy access to the nation's airwaves, while the Islamic left
suffered from a limited presence beyond its newspapers (Siavoshi 1992:
47; Baktiari 1996: 215).

On 10 April, 18 million Iranians voted in the truncated contest that
realigned the Islamic Republic's parliament.[27] By the conclusion of the
8 May runoff, the SCC, in conjunction with allied independents, had
taken a commanding parliamentary majority of 150–160 of the 270 seats
(55–59 percent). Suffering a precipitous loss in influence, the left wing had
only 20 successful candidates (7 percent of seats).[28] One defeated leftist
MP described the elections as an "organized political purging of the revolutionary forces" (Baktiari 1996: 219). This historic reversal ended the
Islamic left's long-running control over the Islamic Assembly and ratified
the end of factional parity enforced during Khomeini's years as leader.
Khamenei and Rafsanjani seemed to have cemented a new alliance and
achieved the power that had almost eluded them. First, they had deactivated the IRP, stripping the Islamic left of an opportunity to use that organization. Next, they had assumed the country's top position of leadership
following Khomeini's death. And finally, they had dispersed the ACC's
parliamentary bloc, pushing the left wing into the political hinterland.

Yet as omnipotent as Khamenei and Rafsanjani appeared in April 1991,
their dominance would very quickly prove brittle. Before the next parliamentary elections passed, the tactical alliance among the right wing would

---

[25] "Khamane'i on Palestinians, Majles Elections," *Voice of the Islamic Republic of Iran,* 27
March 1992, FBIS-NES-92-61, 30 March 1992.

[26] In a 27 March address, the leader called voting a "religious duty; a necessary duty." Five
years hence, Rafsanjani used similar words to subvert the traditionalist right's standard-
bearer. At the time, though, the president approved of the process, commenting, "Fortu-
nately, the candidates are those whose competence has been approved. They are committed, competent, and revolutionary individuals. They will surely abide by the regulations.
The people are free to choose, they will vote for whoever they decide is competent."
"Khamane'i on Palestinians, Majles Elections," *Voice of the Islamic Republic of Iran,*
FBIS-NES-92-061, 30 March 1992; "Hashemi-Rafsanjani Interviewed on Elections,"
Voice of the Islamic Republic of Iran, 1 April 1992 FBIS-NES-92-64, 2 April 1992.

[27] "Interior Minister Views Election Turnout, Runoffs," *IRNA,* 14 April 1992, FBIS-NES-
92-73, 15 April 1992.

[28] "52 Elected Nationwide," *IRNA,* 12 April 1992, FBIS-NES-92-072, 14 April 1992;
Future Alliances Country Intelligence Unit (1996: 15).

crumble, pitting the leader and president against each another amid the same kind of intraelite factionalism that had ailed the IRP. Thus, in the regime's second decade, an antitraditionalist coalition would revisit the promise of popular sovereignty that the revolution had left unrealized.

Presidentialism Run Amok: The Philippines, 1946–1978

Long before the country won its independence in 1946, Philippine parties were characterized by the utilitarian attachments of their members. In the party duopoly that followed, politicians behaved just as capriciously, pursuing their ambitions for higher office through whichever party would nominate them. This jockeying for advantage among national-level patrons and their networks of clients did not conform to lines of ideational debate, as in Iran. Yet fundamental elite divisions that remained after the regime's creation did feed factional conflicts, rather than being harnessed by party organizations. The preindependence rivalry between Manuel Quezon and Sergio Osmeña had brought local factionalism to the national level and foreshadowed the two-party competition over state resources that characterized Philippine politics until martial law was introduced. Power in the capital was the ultimate prize for the politician-patrons who governed the country, for it allowed them to deliver material goods to constituents/clients even as they protected their own property and positions in the landed aristocracy. Largely free of American encroachment after World War II, Philippine leaders competed vigorously via the two parties that had pursued the presidency in 1946: the NP and LP. Like two well-matched teams, neither party could easily trump the other: Nacionalista presidential candidates won election three times (1953, 1957, and 1965), and so did Liberal candidates (in 1946, 1949, and 1961) (Thompson 1998: 209; Hartmann, Hassall and Santos 2001: 226–227). Party parity stemmed from their members' penchant for being "political turncoats" (*balimbing*), switching between parties in pursuit of advancement. Volatility within the parties, however, coexisted with their joint control of the political system. Together, the NP and LP captured 94 percent or more of the popular vote in congressional elections from 1946 to 1961 (Lande 1965: 35). Leftist organizations such as the Democratic Alliance and Communist Party of the Philippines were marginalized or suppressed, channeling political careerists into the NP-LP nexus (Goodno 1991: 42–47).

Within the organizations, the material logic of patron-client relations swamped any potential for the parties to adopt differentiable, programmatic positions. Asked to contrast the two parties, one Philippine student ruefully observed, "I don't believe one species of mud can be very different from another" (Wurfel 1988: 97). Indeed, the Nacionalistas and Liberals were kindred spirits, sharing an unabashed voracity for government resources and the dirty means by which they could sate it. From local councils to the presidency, political posts were filled through elections marked by violence and bribery. As many have observed, the triumvirate of Philippine politics was "guns, goons, and gold." But the two-party hegemony thinly concealed intense rivalries between oligarchic families. Landlords assembled localized armies that performed the double function of suppressing mass demands when they arose and manipulating elections through force and fraud (Anderson 1988: 15). On average, thirty-nine people were killed during each of the four presidential elections between 1955 and 1967 (Thompson 1998: 211). Corruption was just as rampant as violence, with vast portions of the population involved in the parties' patronage networks. An estimated quarter of Filipinos sold their votes during elections (Thompson 1995: 23). From the countryside to the capital, Philippine electoral politics was distinguished not by party positions but by personal ambition.

Neither the Nacionalista Party nor the Liberal Party spent much time outside of campaign periods cultivating a mass membership (Wurfel 1988: 95). In presidential election years, however, their conventions were of paramount importance (Wurfel 1988: 96). Party nominations were the penultimate step in the race for the Philippine presidency. As such, they epitomized politicians' tendency to put expediency before party loyalty. Ambitious figures had the chance to win their own party's nomination, but, failing that, they might try to be nominated by the ostensible rival party. In 1965, Ferdinand Marcos took the second course, leaving the Liberal Party, for which he had served as both a congressman and senator, to receive the Nacionalistas' nomination. In doing so, he challenged his former party chief, Philippine president Diosdado Macapagal, who was seeking reelection. Marcos not only succeeded in winning the NP's nomination and the presidential race, he also managed to be reelected in 1969, a feat previously accomplished only by Quezon (Goodno 1991: 54). Yet the 1969 elections were unusually tainted by charges of vote buying, violence, and distorted election results. These problems evinced the strains Marcos had already placed on Philippine electoral democracy before his second term in the presidency.

By 1970, President Marcos had become the consummate product of the Philippines' mercurial party duopoly. Having reached the pinnacle of national politics, he schemed to remain there beyond the two-term limit defined by the constitution. Again treading the path of Quezon, Marcos tried to transform an ostensible lame-duck presidency into an indefinite tenure. His main method was, perversely enough, to call a Constitutional Convention (known idiomatically as the "ConCon") that most of its participants hoped to use to reform Philippine politics, strengthen government accountability to the public, and address long-neglected social justice concerns (Wurfel 1988: 108–109).

Voters sent 320 delegates to the ConCon through unusually pluralist elections that the president did not succeed in dominating (Wurfel 1988: 109). In June 1971, the convention opened. For much of the next year, the delegates tried to remedy the problem of excessive executive power. Many ConCon participants favored a shift to a parliamentary system (with an indirectly elected prime minister) coupled with a specific prohibition – targeted at Marcos and his wife, Imelda – against a sitting or former president, or any of his close relatives, holding the government's top executive office (Wurfel 1988: 110). Courting the delegates with cash payments and other incentives, the president and first lady succeeded in derailing this initiative, but delegates did agree to the parliamentary system on 7 July 1972 (Wurfel 1988: 111). Still, much work remained before a final constitution would be published. Marcos's second term was winding down, and he feared that he might be out of office, with a new president in place, by the time the constitution was formally ratified (Wurfel 1988: 111).

On 23 September 1972, Marcos declared martial law and indefinitely suspended the country's two-party system. Purporting to preserve national security, Marcos's actions toward the Constitutional Convention – which had proved pliant but too plodding for the president – revealed baser motives. Citing a communist threat to the nation's stability, Marcos jailed hundreds of his critics, including more than a dozen ConCon delegates. A cowed and controlled convention then hastily approved new documents ceding to Marcos the combined powers of the new premiership and the old presidency (Wurfel 1988: 115). Signed by Marcos on 30 November, the constitution of the Philippines' emerging autocracy reversed in two months the reform trajectory of the prior two years (Wurfel 1988: 115). Flawed but competitive elections had been the currency of Philippine politics since independence. Marcos ended the two-party system, allowing only an occasional plebiscite to legitimize his legalistic dictatorship (Thompson 1995: 49). Rule by martial law continued as the president muzzled the country's media, kept his political enemies detained, and established a new network of military and political affiliates bound to him through patronage.

When he replaced the parties' duopoly with one-man rule, Marcos effectively deactivated the Nacionalista Party, under whose banner he had twice won the presidency (Wurfel 1988: 95). Given the NP's role for Marcos as a bridge to power rather than a political instrument, the organization seemed at least as dispensable during the martial law period as the Liberal Party he had abandoned in 1965. Ensconced in the presidency, with no need for a future electoral nomination, Marcos traded party politics for personal networks originating with his closest family members and friends (Thompson 1995: 50). The president and first lady formed the hub of these networks, which extended from both sides of the family into the government's top ministries: Customs and Internal Revenue (run by a brother of Imelda Marcos's), the Central Bank and Ministry of Agriculture (under Imelda's sister), and the Medicare Commission (headed by the president's brother) (Thompson 1995: 53). Ferdinand Marcos's cousin, Major Fabian Ver, was given control over the armed forces, a move that undermined military professionalization even as it gave Marcos a reliable agent for suppressing the opposition and preempting dissent (Thompson 1995: 54). In addition to employing family members in many top government posts, Marcos attracted a broad set of former party politicians who relied on the president as their new chief patron. The outer ring of material allegiance included Liberal and Nacionalista politicians as well as key business leaders (Thompson 1995: 61). For decades, Philippine politics had revolved around the pursuit of material rewards through clientelism between differently situated local and national politicians. Marcos's regime epitomized this pattern.

His remapping of patronage networks bought him new loyalists, but it also cost him support among earlier affiliates. Putting his family and friends before parties solidified Marcos's personal authority over the political class and repressive apparatus at the same time that it irked aspiring politicians who expected to advance through one of the two parties. Even while serving his earlier elected terms, Marcos had alienated high-ranking NP politicians like the brothers Salvador and Jose Laurel. "[Marcos] did not pass state patronage around as incumbent presidents usually did but concentrated it in the hands of his family and friends," Mark Thompson points out, thereby "turning the NP (Nacionalista Party) into the [de facto] MP (Marcos Party)" (1995: 43–44).

In the period after 1972, while wielding authoritarian powers, Marcos completely dispensed with the Nacionalista Party. His reasoning was similar to Khamenei's and Rafsanjani's when they dissolved the IRP, as Marcos's defense minister at the time, Juan Ponce Enrile, explained: So long as the organization continued to operate, senior leaders like the Laurels could challenge Marcos from within the party.[29] Despite assurances to some top Nacionalista figures that he was just setting aside the NP so it could reawaken at some later date, the party never regained its position in Philippine politics (Rocamora 1998: 11).[30] Nor was the NP's formal rival, the Liberal Party, any more successful at surviving the martial law period. While some Liberal leaders, such as Benigno Aquino Jr., remained staunch opponents of Marcos, others abandoned political life altogether or joined the president's tentacular network of clients (Thompson 1995: 61).

The Philippines' traditionally feisty political class languished for six years as Marcos refused to hold national elections and kept some of his harshest critics behind bars (Rosenberg 1979: 153–154; Thompson 1995: 58). Only in 1978 did the president reintroduce multiparty elections under what he dubbed a "new constitutional order." The primary impetus for this republican façade was Marcos's need to maintain international monetary support. From 1972 to 1976, U.S. assistance, which went primarily to the country's armed forces, rose from $18.5 million to $43.0 million (Thompson 1995: 65). (Two years later, the country was receiving $250 million in foreign aid from around the world, a figure that grew during Marcos's remaining years [World Bank 2002].) In October 1976, the Philippines hosted the annual meetings of the heads of the International Monetary Fund and the World Bank. Chagrined "by the absence of any legislative institutions" and calls by former president Diosdado Macapagal for a restoration of parliamentary rule, Marcos held a referendum on the continuation of martial law and announced plans for legislative elections in March 1977 (Wurfel 1988: 128; Franco 2000a: 210). The referendum, which conspicuously occurred just before the conference, provided a thin veneer of progress, suggesting that the Philippines' prospects for political competition were relatively strong compared to those of other Southeast Asian nations at the time (Wurfel 1988: 122). Even so, Marcos subsequently postponed the elections and then promised anew, before an international human rights conference held in Manila in August, that they would take place in 1978 (Wurfel 1988: 129).

In April 1978, after an unprecedented hiatus from voting, Filipinos returned to the polls, and Marcos's minions flooded the scene. Since Marcos had swept away his original party, the impending elections

---

[29] Interview with Juan Ponce Enrile, 28 May 2003, Manila.
[30] Interview with Salvador Laurel, 30 May 2003, Manila.

prompted the president-cum-dictator to cobble together a loose umbrella organization under which his associates could run. Two months before the elections, the president announced the New Society Movement (*Kilusan Bagong Lipunan*, KBL). A public mantle for Marcos's existing web of clients, the KBL did not formally meet for another two years, well after its affiliated politicians had assumed their positions in the National Assembly. Its function as an election list more than a political organization was a symptom of Marcos's continued aversion to party building. The KBL's policies and resources were those of Ferdinand Marcos (Delury 1987: 890). Marcos entertained his clients' requests personally, foregoing any attempt to create a pyramidal organization to enhance dyadic ties between the periphery and Malacañang, the presidential palace.[31] Enrile described the KBL circa 1978 as "a movement used as a vehicle by those people who ran in that election to identify themselves when they went to the electorate," explaining that "[i]t was only later on, after the election, that the [KBL] was organized formally as a party."[32]

In spring 1978, Marcos's candidates were set to fill a new unicameral National Assembly (*Batasang Pambansa*), which replaced the defunct Senate and Congress. Unlike earlier Philippine elections, which were modeled on the American system of single-member districts, candidates competed in multimember districts by open lists (Bonner 1987: 235). The assembly's 165 elected representatives and 35 presidential appointees were then to oversee the long-promised transition from martial law. At that time, KBL candidates included former Nacionalistas Salvador and Jose Laurel as well as thirteen of twenty-four governors who were former members of the Liberal Party (Thompson 1995: 62). Challengers to the KBL were few and originated mainly among those whom Marcos had deemed too adversarial to recruit as patrimonial adjuncts. The strongest figure in the field of challengers was former Liberal Party senator Benigno "Ninoy" Aquino. Unlike previous referendums and local elections under martial law, in which alternative candidates were prohibited, the 1978 National Assembly elections permitted Aquino's new LABAN party (*Lakas ng Bayan*, or People Power, whose acronym means "fight") and other opposition movements to participate.

LABAN faced an uphill struggle from the start. Marcos had announced the date of elections only two months before they were to take place, offering a small window for opposition campaigning. Consequently, LABAN

---

[31] Interview with Imee Marcos, 21 May 2003, Manila.
[32] Interview with Enrile, 28 May 2003, Manila.

activists carefully confined their election work to the country's most accessible area, the capital and its environs. Although their expectations for electoral victory were modest, opposition leaders figured that highly populated metropolitan Manila would be less susceptible than the countryside to government tampering (Wurfel 1988: 131; Goodno 1991: 73). Their primary candidates were Liberal Party figures, but members of the Philippine Communist Party were also represented (Thompson 1998: 74–75). Social democrats backed the LABAN campaign but did not field candidates (Goodno 1991: 74). Aquino, under a death sentence at the time, campaigned from jail, with his wife, Corazon, and his daughter speaking on his behalf at rallies. Modest at first, LABAN's popular appeal steadily grew, and the party's preelection drive culminated in a gathering of ten thousand supporters on 30 March (Thompson 1998: 76).[33] The night before the election, Manila residents joined in a noise barrage to express their support for LABAN.[34] The capital seemed poised on the brink of change, and survey data suggested that Aquino as well as some of his fellow LABAN candidates would win (Wurfel 1988: 132).

Whereas LABAN's reform campaign resonated with many Filipinos, the KBL made more prosaic appeals, wooing voters with political payoffs and material rewards. The president guaranteed housing and salary increases for the city's 280,000 public school teachers, who served as monitors of the voting process.[35] An incentive of 50 percent pay raises for other public workers expanded the base of clients who turned out for Marcos.[36] Flooding the campaign with state resources, President Marcos knowingly predicted his party would "shut out" the opposition across the twenty-one-seat district.[37]

In the 7 April 1978 election, fraud was "brazen and massive,"[38] KBL partisans ejected election monitors and fabricated vote tallies, sometimes awarding their party's candidates votes in excess of the number of registered voters (Wurfel 1988: 132). Inflated numbers came from a

[33] "Opposition Candidates Stage 'Huge' Rally in Manila," *AFP*, 30 March 1978, FBIS-APA-78-63, 31 March 1978.
[34] "Laban Produces '100 Fake Election Returns'," *AFP, FBIS-APA-78-74*, 17 April 1978.
[35] "Marcos Looks to Presidency for 6 More Years," *AFP*, 29 March 1978, FBIS-APA-78-62, 30 March 1978.
[36] "Free, Clean, Honest Election Promised," *Manila Domestic Service*, 4 April 1978, FBIS-APA-78-66, 5 April 1978.
[37] "Opposition Candidates Stage 'Huge' Rally in Manilla," *AFP*, 30 March 1978, FBIS-APA-78-63, 31 March, 1978.
[38] "Aquino: 'Brazen and Massive Cheatings', *AFP*, 10 April 1978, FBIS-APA-78-69, 10 April 1978.

combination of methods, including the stuffing of ballot boxes with fabricated votes and the eager participation of a reported two hundred thousand "flying voters" bussed in from outside Manila and paid to vote
for KBL candidates (Bonner 1987: 238). There were also ample opportunities for Marcos's clients to intervene without filling boxes. One of
Imelda Marcos's confidants related to U.S. Embassy staff that the president's wife claimed "it would be 'in the counting and not in the casting of
votes that the election [would] be decided'" (Bonner 1987: 237). Not surprisingly, the first lady, who headed the KBL slate of candidates, emerged
as the top vote winner for metropolitan Manila. The city's domestic news
service reported the day after voting ended that "Mrs. Marcos moved
to the top spot from the fourth rank...displacing Foreign Secretary
Carlos P. Romulo...in the initial canvass of votes. The first lady garnered some 106,300 votes while Secretary Romulo polled 106,026."[39]
Marcos would not be denied the shutout he had forecast. According to
LABAN observers, three polling stations recorded zero votes for Aquino
out of some four hundred votes cast – a transparently manufactured result
in a city that had clamored for the imprisoned politician days earlier.[40]

As the KBL swept metropolitan Manila, a modicum of competition
touched other parts of the country. Marcos and his affiliates were bent
on defeating LABAN but recognized that a certain level of pluralism was
needed to maintain the façade of gradual political development. Hence,
the president tolerated smaller opposition groups' taking seats in less
prominent areas of the country. Thompson notes a strong correlation
between lack of KBL supporters penetrating a region and opposition success at the polls, writing, "In areas where Marcos or his cronies were the
dominant political forces, no major opposition was formed.... But where
the opposition did organize, it performed surprisingly well" (1998: 79–
80). One interpretation of this finding is that the opposition should have
contested more areas. An alternate view, supported by the metropolitan Manila experience, is that the presence of KBL networks reduced the
opportunity for opposition victory. Evidence outside the capital also backs
this second notion. KBL candidate Salvador Laurel, who had campaigned
in the rural constituency of Batangas, reflected, "This wasn't really a race,
since we had no competition" (Joaquin 1985: 262).

[39] "KBL Maintains 21-0 Lead Over Laban in Manila," *Manila Domestic Service,* 10 April
1978, FBIS-APA-78-70, 11 April 1978.
[40] "Laban Produces '100 Fake Election Returns,'" *AFP,* 14 April 1978, FBIS-APA-78-74,
17 April 1978.

With Marcos's strongest opponents excluded, the 1978 elections turned the president's clients into subservient legislators. The New Society Movement controlled 83 percent of seats in parliament (Hartmann, Hassall, and Santos 2001: 221). Thus, the KBL became the president's new rubber stamp for pushing "revolution from the center," a vague political program said to defy the old oligarchic elites and the country's active communists. Within its ranks, the movement continued the politics of patronage and personalism concentrated around the president and his preferences. One former KBL congressman described the benefits of membership as follows: "It's nice. Like any political grouping you want to be able to bring something home. You don't want to go home empty-handed. And at that time all funds were controlled by Malacañang. Despite Congress appropriating the money, yet the releases are controlled by Malacañang, since they decide what money gets released. Now, if you're in the opposition you don't get anything."[41] A former leader in the organization recalled, "Every time political leaders would go to Malacañang there was an expectation that they would receive something, even cash. Often cash."[42] While times were good for those who enjoyed the president's favor, other politicians began to chafe under Marcos's autocracy and to seek fresh opportunities for advancement.

Conclusion

Early elite politics in Egypt, Iran, Malaysia, and the Philippines indelibly marked party institutions in all four countries. Whereas Egypt and Malaysia moved forward with ruling parties that contained conflict, Iran and the Philippines witnessed leadership rivalries that superceded the available organizations. Nasser and Sadat manipulated but maintained the Arab Socialist Union and the National Democratic Party. UMNO offered a mechanism for Malay dominance and steady leadership succession from Abdul Rahman to Abdul Razak to Hussein. In 1981, when Mubarak and Mahathir took office in their respective states, the ruling parties were in place for managing new issues while consistently excluding the opposition. At the level of national politics, Iran and the Philippines projected a similar image of autocratic domination. By discarding the IRP and the NP, Khamenei and Marcos sought to consolidate their positions and concentrate power. In the short run, they were successful and enjoyed electoral success on par with their peers in Egypt and Malaysia.

[41] Interview with Rudolph Albano, 26 May 2003, Manila.
[42] Interview with Gabriel Claudio, 26 May 2003, Manila.

In all four countries, the first multiparty elections of the third wave period – Egypt's in 1976 and 1979, Iran's in 1992, Malaysia's in 1974 and 1979, and the Philippines' in 1978 – severely favored incumbents and disadvantaged the opposition. Cooperative elites, through parties in Egypt and Malaysia and factions in Iran and the Philippines, were the guarantors of electoral control and the guardians of regime stability. Yet maintaining that support depended on cross-factional collaboration best preserved through long-term political bonds, not through tactical, expedient partnerships. Consequently, the members of Khamenei's and Marcos's leadership circles soon found themselves at odds with one another. Their disagreements escalated, driving former partisans – daggers drawn – to ally with the opposition. Their counterparts in Egypt and Malaysia succeeded in mending similar rifts and sustaining a cohesive elite. The next chapters address why these authoritarian regimes fared differently during the 1980s and 1990s. In this discussion, it is important to remember that that divergence was rooted in an earlier period, a time when institutions grew or withered based on a political context imparted from the regime's founding and the choices of subsequent leaders as they coped with that legacy.

Finally, it bears noting that in exploring the relationship of party institutions to individuals, we should not overstate the impact of even the most prominent leaders in these cases. When tracing the role of political parties in stabilizing elite coalitions in Egypt and Malaysia, individual leaders necessarily loom large. Yet the apparent preeminence of Nasser and Sadat in Egypt or Tunku Abdul Rahman in Malaysia accords with the underlying resilience of party institutions. Through parties, these leaders exercised a form of power that eluded their peers in Iran and the Philippines. Moreover, subtle differences in the fates of specific leaders illuminate the effective influence of institutions over individuals. It is conceivable, for example, that had Sadat responded differently in 1970–1971, he might have been replaced by Ali Sabri or another member of the pro-Nasserist faction.[43] In essence, he could have met the same fate Abdul Rahman encountered in Malaysia, when the NOC ushered him out of the premiership and installed Razak. Similarly, Sadat's hypothetical ouster

---

[43] Such a turn of events could have hinged on a more calculated response by Ali Sabri and his confederates, although even more prudent strategizing would have been needed to surmount the Sabri faction's ill repute among most Egyptians (Beattie 2000: 72–73, 75). Whatever the conditions needed for one to envision it in Egypt, the counterfactual case of a leader's removal (Tunku Abdul Rahman in Malaysia) further illuminates why parties function not just as tools in the hands of elites but also as the molds of elite relations.

would not automatically have transformed the overarching structure of regime politics. The maintenance of ruling parties and their preservation of elite dominance does not depend on particular individuals but on the broader institutional contexts in which those individuals are embedded and interact.

4

Ruling Parties and Regime Persistence

Egypt and Malaysia during the Third Wave

During the 1980s and 1990s, as dictatorships in Latin America, Eastern Europe, Africa, and Asia collapsed, Egypt and Malaysia's autocracies stood firm. Although opposition movements across the developing world vaulted into power through dramatic election victories, President Mubarak and Prime Minister Mahathir thwarted kindred campaigns against their rule. Both rulers seemed to exercise almost unparalleled domination and to have an extraordinary ability to preserve their own incumbency while preparing the way for their chosen successors. And although each man held power longer than any of his predecessors, their extended tenures were less the product of individual guile or charisma than the continuation of a historical legacy each inherited: a functioning ruling party organization that neither would have elected to develop but from which each benefited enormously.

This chapter concludes the causal narratives of Egyptian and Malaysian political development that began with early elite conflict and continued through the party maintenance and leadership successions covered in Chapter 3. In contrast to many studies of domestic regime change and democratization during the third wave era, the following accounts show a pattern of autocratic endurance and opposition defeat. Despite the opportunity of multiple elections in which they could compete, antiregime activists repeatedly failed to marshal elite support or to translate their popular constituencies into political power. The linchpin of Mubarak and Mahathir's shared success at preserving themselves and rebuffing their critics was a ruling party through which disparate elites cohered within the regime and controlled the electoral arena available to the opposition. By mediating among elites, the NDP and UMNO each maintained a broad coalition of leaders who in turn drew on distinct and potentially competing social bases of power. The organizations of the NDP and UMNO have largely alleviated elites' fears of permanent exclusion from the ruling clique. Embedded within the party, conflicting elites can settle issues of significance without having to separate themselves publicly from the party or seek outside allies. These settlements are rarely egalitarian, and the head of the party can be a fickle arbiter. But occasional departures notwithstanding, the overall pattern is that losses are sufficiently diffuse and opportunities for future gains sufficiently attractive to make continued loyalty preferable to campaigning for reform from the outside.

I demonstrate this trend by assessing the Mahathir and Mubarak regimes from the early 1980s through the start of the twenty-first century. I show why ruling parties brought elite cohesion and electoral control across six limited multiparty elections in each country. The narratives focus on moments of tension inside the NDP and UMNO that reveal the internal dynamics of elite conflict and the way in which both parties bound elites together and prevented broader public rifts. First, I consider the opposition's performance in typical elections during which the ruling coalition was not especially strained and the ruling party's influence was correspondingly latent. These elections demonstrated the limited reach of opposition groups, even when they challenged an unpopular government. The next section moves from the conventional to the extraordinary, analyzing the resolution of intraelite conflict in Egypt (1999) and Malaysia (1987) and the elections that followed: Egypt's in 2000 and Malaysia's in 1990 and 1995. These experiences shook the Mubarak and Mahathir regimes but did not dislodge either ruler from power. Political concessions offered through the party enticed leaders to remain rather than break away. As the coalition regrouped, the regime reasserted its electoral controls and restored the power asymmetry that had typified prior electoral contests. The final section moves to the most recent stage of ruling party politics, which culminated in the renewal of the Egyptian and Malaysian regimes through preparations for leadership succession.

Elite Cohesion in Typical Egyptian and Malaysian Elections

When the opposition occupies only the margins of national politics, as in Egypt and Malaysia, it is easy to treat this debility as the cause of regime endurance. The following comparison shows why such logic should be reversed – why opposition weakness should be seen as a product of enduring autocracy. When opposition movements are suppressed for decades, as they have been in Egypt and Malaysia, we must examine the ways in which power holders have undermined the organization of dissent and denied opportunities for democratization.

Deliberalization under Mubarak: Egypt, 1981–1998

The man who would eventually rule Egypt longer than either of his predecessors, Muhammad Hosni Mubarak (r. 1981–present), began his presidency with a fresh political opening, a grace period toward the opposition that had been severely repressed by Sadat. Mubarak relaxed the "red lines" governing activism, released political prisoners, and permitted the press to criticize government ministers. (Mubarak himself remained off-limits.) Nongovernmental associations proliferated, and professional syndicates provided additional forums for demanding civil liberties and political rights. The multiparty system bequeathed by Sadat also bloomed – albeit briefly. These gestures of liberalization took place under the continuing shadow of a state of martial law, the safety net of a chief executive unwilling to loosen his grip permanently. Under emergency rule, the president had the power to detain political opponents indefinitely without charge and to try civilians in military courts. Sadat had lifted the country's state of emergency just months before his death, but his successor reinstated it as soon as he assumed office. Mubarak initially used few of his emergency powers and spoke of giving "democracy in doses," (Mustafa 1997a: 27) but before his first decade in office was over, the president had reversed direction and reverted to the autocratic mode of his predecessors.

Early barometers of Mubarak's tolerance for opposition activity were the growth of new parties and the outcome of elections for the People's Assembly – developments that earned the country the mantle of being a "trailblazing" case of liberalization in the Arab world (Hudson 1991: 408). Although the first development has attracted attention, the second of these indicators is more informative. Today, few of the country's some two dozen parties exist beyond the papers on which they are registered to operate. Within the vast field of nominal parties, a small cluster of weak but active parties formed a nascent opposition to Mubarak distinct from what Sadat had faced in 1976 and 1979. Feeble in comparison to their counterparts elsewhere, these organizations in the Egyptian political arena are the closest analogues to opposition parties in other developing countries like the DAP and PAS in Malaysia. During the 1980s, five parties and one quasiparty competed with the NDP: the center-right Wafd Party, which had reemerged in 1978; the Arab nationalist Nasserist Party; the left-wing Labor Party; the National Progressive Unionist Party (NPUP, the left branch of Sadat's original platforms); and the Liberal Party (the right branch of the same program). In addition, the Muslim Brotherhood operated and continues to function as a de facto political party.[1]

During Mubarak's first term in office, Egypt's opposition parties registered the strongest electoral successes yet achieved against the National Democratic Party. Elections in 1984 were held under a new system of proportional representation based on party lists – a shift that prompted the Muslim Brotherhood to partner with the Wafd. The electoral law change benefited the opposition by aggregating votes that were otherwise dispersed across NDP-favored districts (Pripstein-Posusney 1998). Overall opposition representation rose to 13 percent. Afterward, Egypt's Supreme Constitutional Court, an institution then largely independent of the president's influence, invalidated the list system because it did not permit individual candidacies. In response, parliament passed another electoral law that mixed proportional races (for 400 seats) with individual contests (for 48 seats) (Pripstein-Posusney 1998). Regime leaders miscalculated the opposition's popularity and assumed that non-NDP parties would not meet the required 8 percent threshold to enter parliament in the proportional races (Kienle 2001: 26). Instead, the opposition performed even more strongly under the combined system. One hundred non-NDP candidates were elected, a record 20 percent of parliament's elected seats. The Wafd won thirty-six seats; the Labor Party and Brotherhood, running on a combined list, took fifty-six; and opposition independents won eight seats (Zaki 1995: 80).

The elections seemed to cast sparks of competition into Egyptian politics, but Mubarak stamped these out in his second term (1987–1993). Using executive decrees, military courts, and the broad deployment of security forces, the president retracted his tolerance toward alternate movements and denied his critics the limited security they had briefly enjoyed. In 1990, the Supreme Constitutional Court changed Egypt's electoral system yet again, this time to the benefit of the NDP. The SCC ruled

---

[1] The regime claims the Muslim Brotherhood cannot be formally recognized because the Political Parties Law of 1977 explicitly forbids parties based on a religious platform. Nonetheless, during Mubarak's time in office, the Brotherhood has regularly participated in elections and other political forums. Despite, or perhaps because of, its quasiparty status, the MB has been the only opposition group to demonstrate a strong popular following that exceeds the popularity of individual candidates. Still, genuine support among portions of Egyptian society has been insufficient to bring the Muslim Brotherhood into control of parliament, even when it allied with other opposition groups.

the mixed voting system of 1987 unconstitutional on the ground that it "limit[ed] the right of candidates to run as independents" (Zaki 1995: 92–93). By itself, the decision seemed to help the opposition's chances of competing, since they were no longer confined to lists or constrained by thresholds for getting representatives into the People's Assembly. As implemented by the NDP government, however, the change promised to reduce competition to the level of the 1970s, principally through the regime's control over districting. Moheb Zaki writes: "Although the opposition welcomed the return to the original electoral law, they were enraged by modifications introduced by the government on the electoral districts. The changes smacked of a clear attempt at gerrymandering which threatened to further reduce the already small representation of the opposition parties in parliament" (1995: 93). In response, the opposition called for judicial supervision of the election process, a procedure stipulated in the 1971 constitution yet never implemented. The regime took no such measures.

Expecting a flagrantly unbalanced contest, the Wafd, Liberal, and Labor parties, along with the Muslim Brotherhood, boycotted the elections, arguing that participation would only legitimate a biased system. Breaking the boycott, the National Progressive Unionist Party participated and won six seats (Zaki 1995: 93). In addition to the small NPUP faction, the 1990–1995 People's Assembly included 56 independents and 385 NDP MPs (Zaki 1995: 94). Among the independents were fourteen Wafd members, eight representatives from the Labor Party, and four from the Liberal Party (Kienle 2001: 54). The opposition's delegitimation strategy had largely failed. The boycott did not prompt the regime to make the process fairer, and, axiomatically, it decreased the opposition's presence in the Assembly.

In 1993, Mubarak won reelection by single-candidate plebiscite to a third six-year term and demonstrated his continuing commitment to concentrating power. When the People's Assembly neared the conclusion of its session in 1995, the opposition chose to rejoin elections. It hoped to break the NDP's two-thirds majority in parliament and thereby deny the president a rubber stamp for his decisions and a ready tool for amending the constitution (Mustafa 1997a: 31). Even this plan seemed ambitious, however, given Mubarak's record of tight control over the election process. As one Labor Party member commented: "We boycotted the last elections to pressurise the government into allowing free and fair elections. The government, however, ignored us. This time, we are participating with no illusions. . . . we are aware that this time round government malpractice will be even more intense" (Kassem 1999: 108). This expectation was borne out: Government interference in the 1995 elections exceeded the levels of fraud and coercion exhibited in the previous five parliamentary polls.

Shortly before the 29 November voting, the regime jailed fifty-four Muslim Brotherhood members, including much of the organization's leadership. Sixteen of those convicted were candidates, and fourteen had served in the 1987 People's Assembly (Makram-Ebeid 1996: 128). Thousands more MB campaign supporters were detained without charge. The formal opposition parties were frustrated by other restrictions, such as a ban on campaign meetings in public areas (Kienle 2001: 58–59). During the campaign period, the government-controlled media overwhelmingly favored the NDP (Egyptian National Committee 1995: 63). Each opposition party was allocated two forty-minute slots to present its political platform, but the NDP controlled the remainder of airtime. Hence, the speeches by non-NDP candidates comprised a meager portion of the media coverage (Kienle 2001: 58). Opposition parties nonetheless fielded hundreds of candidates across the country. Even with dozens of its members in prison, the Muslim Brotherhood ran approximately 100 candidates, while the Wafd put forward 182. The Labor Party had 120 seeking office, the Liberal Party 61, Nasserists 65, and NPUP 35. In all, 3,989 candidates participated, 80 percent of them independents (Makram-Ebeid 1996: 129).

Despite the broad field of contenders, the most influential participants in the 1995 elections were Egypt's state security agents, who intervened early and often to ensure a landslide for the NDP. The campaign period had shown the system's tremendous bias for the ruling party, and regime interference escalated once voting began. Government agents threatened voters and candidates, blocked opposition delegates from monitoring the voting process, and excluded independent figures from observing the tallying (Egyptian National Committee 1995: 45, 55–57). State security forces delivered boxes filled with completed ballots (Kienle 2001: 60). At other times, they worked with what they had on site, as in one polling station where "the police ejected the opposition, shut the police stations and filled the ballot boxes to the brim" (Makram-Ebeid 1996: 131). So brazen was the manipulation of the vote that the regime rarely bothered to conceal its fraud. One independent candidate reported that state police had approached him on the eve of the election and contritely explained that they would be rigging the vote against him the next day.[2] Regime agents also tried to influence the ballots being cast. A grassroots election

---

[2] Interview with Hossam Badrawi, 19 July 1999, Cairo.

monitoring team reported that in one area, "ready-to-use" ballots with NDP candidates checked off were exchanged for unmarked ballots along with a bribe of twenty Egyptian pounds (US $6.00 at the time). The electoral client could vote for the ruling party and walk away with a handful of extra cash (Egyptian National Committee 1995: 45).

Layers of fraud (outside the polling station, in the queue, at the ballot box), the presence of security forces, and the vicious rivalries of local leaders produced what was reportedly Egypt's most violent election since the country's first experience with national voting in 1866. The Ministry of Interior reported that 36 people were killed during the elections and 411 injured, four times the number wounded in 1990. The Wafd counted sixty-four killed (Egyptian National Committee 1995: 62–63). This carnival of force, fraud, and intimidation brought the NDP its biggest majority ever and decimated the opposition. Final results gave the NDP 417 seats, a flagrantly artificial 94 percent majority. The official opposition parties won thirteen seats, while the Muslim Brotherhood succeeded in only one race (Ries 1999: 344). The regime's sixth multiparty election showed that oppositionists were no closer to controlling government than they had been in 1976. The third wave of democratization had circled the world but barely grazed the Mubarak regime.

Mahathir's Initial Victories: Malaysia, 1981–1986

In comparison to contemporaneous events in Egypt, Malaysia's leadership succession in 1981 was notably peaceful. In its wake, the political trends of the 1970s continued, and the National Front consistently blocked its most viable rivals. Whereas Mubarak allowed the opposition a nominal honeymoon period, the political arena remained essentially fixed during Mahathir's first years. Unlike Mubarak, who focused on domestic political stability, Mahathir was initially more troubled by the threat of an economic crisis. When he took control of UMNO in 1981, his countrymen were concerned about a possible economic downturn. Many developing countries were beginning to suffer from a debt crisis with potential international aftershocks. In order to ward off such a blow and buttress his own political authority, the new premier called early elections the following year. UMNO's coalition again dominated the field, winning an 85 percent share of parliament. PAS, the DAP, and independents together took twenty-two seats (14 percent) (Ramanathan and Adnan 1988: 18). Rather than imperil the government during rough times, elections had provided Mahathir a vessel for traversing economic torpor and strengthening his hand. Under Mahathir's direction, the UMNO-dominated regime persevered despite further economic setbacks.

When Malaysia's economy continued to flounder in the mid-1980s, elections once again rejuvenated Mahathir's government, deflecting criticism and preserving the ruling party's power. Malaysia's GDP growth dipped to −1.1 percent in 1985, rising modestly to 1.2 percent the following year (Searle 1999). Hoping to stay ahead of any further deterioration in the economy, Mahathir dissolved the House of Representatives on 19 July 1986 and announced that elections would be held 2 and 3 August. (Voting in the rural portions of Sabah and Sarawak began a day before general polling across Malaysia and in Sabah and Sarawak's urban areas.)[3] Mahathir's timing caught the opposition off guard, and it also provoked litigation. Claiming that the nomination period fell short of the legally required period of four business days, DAP leader Lim Kit Siangh went to court to stop the elections. Kuala Lumpur's High Court, a perennial ally of the ruling Malay elite, refused to freeze the process and the elections proceeded with a ten-day campaign period, the shortest in Malaysia's history to that point (Ramanathan and Adnan 1988: 47).[4]

By abridging and accelerating the process of electoral preparation, Mahathir exercised one of the many semilegal techniques at his disposal for disadvantaging the opposition. Like Egyptian opposition parties, non-NF parties were banned from holding "open-air public rallies" and confined to smaller gatherings held indoors (Crouch 1996: 60). The government also implied that opposition victories would spark communal conflict and, more overtly, threatened to withdraw development funds from areas that supported the opposition.[5] As William Case points out, "Election day propriety" was observed by UNMO, but it made little difference, given that "district malapportionment, a short campaign period, bans on opposition rallies, and the government's highly partisan use of media outlets, state equipment, and development grants, all unchecked by the electoral commission" had effectively put the opposition at a disadvantage before any votes were cast (1996: 448).

During the campaign, the DAP and other opposition parties joined forces for the first time against the National Front. Their common goal was to break the two-thirds majority UMNO held in parliament through

---

[3] "Election Set for 3 August," *Kuala Lumpur Domestic Service*, 18 July 1986, FBIS-APA-86-139, 21 July 1986; "Mahathir Announces Dissolution of Dewan Rakyat," *Kuala Lumpur Domestic Service*, 18 July 1986, FBIS-APA-86-139, 21 July 1986.

[4] "High Court Dismisses Application to Delay Poll," *Kuala Lumpur International Service*, 22 July 1986, FBIS-APA-86-140, 22 July 1986.

[5] "Parties' Election Prospects, Issues Viewed," *AFP*, 31 July 1986, FBIS-APA-86-148, 1 August 1986.

the NF.[6] Because of PAS's explicitly pro-Malay platform (it pledged to establish an Islamic state if victorious), DAP leaders refused to formalize an electoral pact with the Malaysian Islamic party, but the groups coordinated to cover distinct nonoverlapping constituencies: The DAP worked on urban areas, while PAS sought support among rural Malays in the northeast.[7] Generally agreeing to run in separate districts, the two parties fielded competing candidates in only thirteen races.[8] Their cooperation proved insufficient, however. By early morning on 4 August, it was clear the NF had maintained its legislative supermajority, with UMNO taking eighty-three of the eighty-four seats it had contested (Ramanathan and Adnan 1988: 50). All had gone according to Mahathir's plans, or at least the premier implied as much when he boasted:

I am proud to say that we can hold a general election in our country in a peaceful and perfect manner. This is because our country's people have matured and understand democracy. . . . There were some surprise victories in several constituencies, but in terms of the number of seats we have won so far, I thought we would win more or less by such a margin.[9]

By strategically engaging areas supportive of the opposition, Mahathir's party was able to deprive the 20 percent of voters who supported the DAP and the 15 percent who turned out for PAS of a countercoalition against the NF in parliament (Ramanathan and Adnan 1988: 54). Following the election, UMNO held 148 of 177 positions in the House.[10] In these first elections, as in those of the decade that followed, Mahathir's success depended more on the allies he retained than the adversaries assembled against him.

Elite Conflict and Its Resolution in Egypt and Malaysia

Initial elections under Mubarak and Mahathir maintained the pattern of ruling party dominance and opposition marginalization. The NDP and UMNO's electoral hegemony depended on elite cohesion, the

---

6 "Commentary Lauds Ruling Party's Policies," *Kuala Lumpur International Service*, 28 July 1986, FBIS-APA-86-146, 30 July 1986.
7 "Mahathir Predicts Election Landslide Win," *AFP*, 30 July 1986, FBIS-APA-86-148, 1 August 1986.
8 "National Front Takes 6 Seats by Default," *Kuala Lumpur International Service*, 24 July 1986, FBIS-APA-86-145, 29 July 1986.
9 "Mahathir Views Elections," *Kuala Lumpur Domestic Service*, 3 August 1986, FBIS-APA-86-149, 4 August, 1986.
10 The elections were the first held after an increase in electoral districts from 154 to 177. In 1974, a similar, demographically based change raised the number of House seats from 104 to 154 (Ramanathan and Adnan 1988: 43).

underpinning of a legalistic and repressive network that dampened competition. Yet these organizations were also sites for contentious debate. When the inner coalition began to fray, the system of electoral controls also showed strain. In the 1980s and 1990s, both ruling parties defused intraelite conflict through political negotiations and prevented the opposition from taking power.

By managing the interests of the ruling cadre through a system of regularized advancement, ruling party regimes are well-equipped to prevent open dissension. On the occasions when elites pursue their interests apart from the regime, they may be successful as individuals. But in most of these instances, the ruling party stems the flow of defectors and mends any intraregime rifts. Isolated rebels then find themselves unable to change the system they left, and they often return to the fold. This was the general pattern when the NDP and UMNO managed their coalitions during times of elite disagreements. What made these regimes more resilient than their counterparts in Iran and the Philippines was the ruling parties' ability to contain contestation before it spread too far into the public arena. To the extent that residual elite conflict leaked into the public arena, regimists-turned-oppositionists were successful only in individual local races.

The phenomenon of noncritical elite breakaways and incumbent losses suggests a counterfactual answer to the question, "What would have happened had the parties *not* moderated elite discord?" In the Egyptian elections of 2000 and the Malaysian elections of 1990, the ruling parties performed worse than they had in the previous twenty years of multiparty elections. Those results followed the resolution of intraelite conflict in both countries – the successful merger of Old and New Guard and the incorporation of "NDP-independents" within the NDP in Egypt and the failure of the opposition party Semangat '46 to establish itself as the new UMNO in Malaysia. These particular outcomes of regime recovery in the context of obvious public dissatisfaction (as exemplified by subsequent electoral setbacks) indicate that were it not for ruling parties in Egypt and Malaysia, politics in those countries would have looked much like the politics in Iran and the Philippines. These moments when rulers averted instability evince the links between elite cohesion, electoral control, and regime endurance.

Generational Merger in the NDP: Egypt, 1999–2000

With opposition parties and civil society organizations severely disadvantaged by the strictures of martial law, conflicts within the NDP arguably form the fulcrum of Egyptian national politics. The recent ascendance of a "New Guard" within the National Democratic Party therefore has both historical precedents and lasting ramifications. As a reincarnated business class began to assert its political voice in government, Mubarak's regime faced the challenge of economic reform and bureaucratic retrenchment. Elections to parliament were one entry point by which younger, ascendant capitalists pushed their way into the ruling coalition. Elected status as a parliamentarian promised both legal immunity from prosecution and a hand in policy making (Zaki 1995: 97). The rise of these businessmen-politicians as independent candidates and then as ruling party apparatchiks delivered the sequel to Sadat's economic opening, as wealth translated into political influence through the party.

Overlapping cleavages caused by generational and policy differences surfaced during the elections of 1990 and 1995. The shift to individual candidacies in 1990 brought larger parliamentary majorities for the NDP, but it also created advancement opportunities for junior party members and outsiders. Since seats were no longer reserved for competition between official party standard-bearers, ambitious politicians not nominated by the NDP could run as independent candidates. If successful, they had the option of reaffiliating with the party in place of its defeated representatives. Mubarak even encouraged this limited competition as a sort of open primary for NDP status (Al-Khawaga 1997: 96), and the regime's parliamentary bloc soon included a large number of "NDP-independents." In 1990, an estimated ninety-five (22 percent) elected MPs had this profile, and in 1995 the number was around one hundred (23 percent) (Zaki 1995: 96; Mustafa 1997b: 45). The entry of NDP-independents intersected with the government's vow to reform the economy by undertaking IMF-prescribed structural adjustment and privatization. Growth rates rose steadily, and the Paris Club forgave Egypt half its debt for its assistance in the 1990–1991 Gulf War. The United States released the country from an additional $7 billion of debt (Sullivan 1992: 27).

The growing economic importance of Egypt's business elite did not translate automatically into greater recognition from the ruling party's veterans. Long-time power holders were slow to cede organizational influence to the up-and-coming capitalists. The NDP's highest steering committee, made up of Kamal Al-Shazli, Safwat Sherif, and Youssef Wali, opposed any disruption to the government's bloated civil service and system of state-owned enterprises. By 1995, an estimated 400,000 state employees had to be laid off as state-owned enterprises were privatized (Aidi 2003: 2). The constituencies of Egypt's socialist past stood behind the old leadership, which threatened to obstruct rapid reform.

The stage seemed to be set for public elite conflict, as politically ambitious business leaders sought to dislodge the NDP's entrenched managers. In the summer of 1999, apparently responding to the senior leadership's intransigence, a proposal circulated about the creation of a second ruling party. The Future Party, as it was to be called, would compete with the NDP and provide a platform for the ascendant business faction (*Al-Ahali*, 16 June 1999). Some leaders of the opposition saw the proposal as an opportunity for the opening of a "small space for democracy" to lead to broader changes.[11] To the dismay of those hoping for a regime split, however, the proposal was not publicized, and the party never emerged (*Agence France-Presse*, 19 September 1999). The Future Party was part hope, part bluff – a trial balloon of what business-oriented politicians envisioned if their concerns were not allayed. One NDP member of the Consultative Assembly (upper house) recounted that the idea was never formally pursued: "It's a party created by some people whose intention is reforming the top of the party. This was a big question among everybody. I don't know what happened. I don't know if this was real [or] if it was not true. There wasn't a decision."[12] But from the perspective of one advocate of the Future Party, the project's goals were pushed as far as seemed viable and then accomplished through accommodation rather than autonomous organizing. "I wanted to create a different party with young people and a future vision," he explained to me. He continued: "After speaking with people, we arrived at the conclusion that this would be difficult considering the political situation of the country. So we decided upon a course to reform the party from within, after much debate." Following this decision, Gamal Mubarak, the president's son and a leader among the Future Party group, joined the NDP as a representative of the New Guard.[13]

A political correspondent for Egypt's leading English weekly corroborates this account, describing the Future Party as a proposal whose goal of business interest promotion was pursued through other means:

[T]his was an idea. I think it was suggested for the first time by Gamal Mubarak, but they let the leftist party newspaper publish this and see what the reaction of the people will be to it. The [old guard] group of Youssef Wali, Kamal Al-Shazli and Safwat Sharif began to react quickly and to find out what's going on, if there's any attempt to get rid of them or not.... But at the end the idea was cancelled by the president and his son, who found that it is better to join the party's ranks to

---

[11] Interview with Rifaat Al-Said, 22 July 1999, Cairo.
[12] Interview with Sherif Wali, 25 April 2002, Cairo.
[13] Interview with Hossam Badrawi, 30 April 2002, Cairo.

take a leading position in the party and to play a stronger role in reforming the party. They found [that] it is not good to establish a new party, but it is better to remain in the party and to exercise an influence over the party to move it into a more democratic way of doing things.[14]

Attention turned to the existing Future Foundation, led by Gamal Mubarak since 1998, which aimed to provide affordable housing for young Egyptians, and to the Future Generation Foundation, also headed by Gamal Mubarak, which focused on training Egypt's youth for entering the job market (*Al-Ahram Weekly On-Line*, 10–17 December 1998). When asked about the Future Party, President Mubarak reportedly said, "The Future? This is the name of a non-governmental organization led by Gamal Mubarak."[15]

Even as the Future Party became history, room was made within the NDP to promote Gamal Mubarak and his allies in the business community, such as Mohammed Abul-Einein and steel magnate Ahmed Ezz. The upwardly mobile New Guard moved to the National Democratic Party's fore. In February 2000, the NDP's General Secretariat brought aboard Gamal Mubarak, Ezz, and another prominent business leader, Ibrahim Kamel. One member of the General Secretariat said the decision reflected the party's recognition of the business community as "part of the country's social forces" (*Al-Ahram Weekly On-Line*, 10–16 February 2000). Differences persisted between the proposed leaders of the Future Party and the traditional leaders of the NDP, but by incorporating not only the president's son but also a broader set of politically ambitious business leaders, the NDP had renovated its coalition to reflect demographic and economic changes.

The 2000 parliamentary races spurred debate in the ruling party's highest ranks about developing a more meritocratic system of membership promotion. At issue was how many business elites the NDP should nominate as official candidates. The value of NDP candidacy appreciated further when the Supreme Constitutional Court belatedly ruled on the 1990 case concerning judicial supervision. Dealing a blow to conventional electoral rigging, the SCC ordered that members of the judiciary should monitor elections in all of Egypt's polling stations. Since it portended a fairer process, the decision put a premium on the ostensible prestige of NDP candidacy over running as an independent and joining the party once elected. Thousands of applications for nomination were submitted to the

[14] Interview with Gamal Essam El-Din, 17 April 2002, Cairo.
[15] Ibid.

party. When the leadership completed its selections, the slate of candidates showed 42 percent turnover from previous choices. This transformation symptomized strains in the new coalition. One local analyst reported, "The changes in names reflected strong internal disagreement on the selection of candidates, as this percentage change was the largest in the history of the NDP." It showed "undisclosed disputes inside the party" between the followers of Gamal Mubarak and "traditional leaders" who backed Secretary General Wali and Organizational Secretary Al-Shazli. The analyst described the dispute: "Gamal Mubarak preferred selecting younger candidates who gave a new image to the party. This was rejected by the party's traditional leadership that had always controlled the selection process" (Ouda, El-Borai, and Abu Se'ada 2001: 57–58). Rather than split into two organizations along the lines of traditionalists versus technocrats, the NDP accommodated the partisans of the Future Party proposal.[16] The disagreement yielded a mix of traditional and fresh candidates, with one hundred of the candidates aged thirty to forty (*Middle East Economic Digest*, 29 September 2000). Although NDP leaders did not curtail the problem of NDP-independents, they had mended what was potentially the most destabilizing rift at its source. Approximately fourteen hundred party members who were not chosen tried their luck outside the party as NDP-independent candidates.

To enable Egypt's judiciary to cover 15,502 polling stations, the 2000 elections were staggered in three stages over a month's time. National Democratic Party candidates faced two sets of challengers. On one front stood the official opposition, including nearly seventy candidates from the Muslim Brotherhood and more than two hundred from the Wafd. On the other side were the NDP-independents, an average of six per race. Hoping they could still rig the process, ruling party candidates were frustrated to find judiciary members would not let unregistered voters cast ballots, nor would they turn over ballot boxes to policemen offering to "help" transport them to the tallying stations.

Still, with a typical lag time of six days between the three stages of voting, the NDP found ways to manipulate the outcomes of later races. It intervened outside the polling stations, where the judiciary did not reach.[17] Because judges were confined to monitoring the casting of

---

[16] "New Guard" member Dr. Hossam Badrawi was among the official nominees and recalled that "most of" the group was nominated. Interview with Hossam Badrawi, 30 April 2002, Cairo.
[17] Interview with Nasser Amin, 2 June 2002, Cairo.

ballots, they were helpless to prevent state security forces from obstruct-
ing or harassing voters. As the rounds progressed, the Ministry of Interior
increasingly employed uniformed and plainclothes thugs to suppress voters. Monitoring and repression produced the spectacle of a clean process
inside the polling station accompanied by often bloody clashes in the surrounding streets. At one point, a judge went outside to investigate why
no voters had shown up by midday. He found state security forces blocking all voters who tried to approach. On questioning a nearby soldier, he
was told, "Your responsibility ends at the door of the school [the polling
station]. Once you step outside you are not a judge and I do not recognize
you."[18]

State security concentrated on stopping supporters of the Muslim
Brotherhood from voting, particularly in the last third of polling, which
was contested by several of the organization's senior leaders (Egyptian
Organization for Human Rights 2000). One NDP leader explained what
had happened candidly:

Wali: When I was saying 80% [clean] I meant it, because it was not all clean
elections. Sometimes we had to stop the Muslim Brothers from emerging.
Interviewer: Had to stop them from getting too many seats?
Wali: Yes. Especially a lot in the third stage [of voting], because in the first stage
not a lot of people [i.e. MB-inclined voters] entered [the process]. In the second
stage they entered and they found themselves successful. So in the third stage
they didn't believe it, so they began [turning out in greater numbers]. They were
moving like hell![19]

Despite the obstacles placed in its path, the Muslim Brotherhood won
seventeen of the sixty-three races in which it ran candidates, a marked
improvement over its showing in 1995 and a sign of the judicial monitors'
efforts to improve the process (Mustafa 2001b). The overall opposition
performance was much worse. Aside from the MB, the official opposition
parties took a modest twenty-one seats, including several that went to
independents who were informally affiliated with particular opposition
movements (Rabei 2001: 195).

The competition between the NDP and NDP-independents did not help
the opposition, but it did create heavy turnover in the ruling party's roster
in the People's Assembly. Eight committee chairs lost, including founding
NDP member Mohamed Abdellah (Reshad 2000: 151). Only 172 (39
percent) of the NDP's official candidates were successful. Another 181

[18] Interview with Amin, 2 June 2002, Cairo.
[19] Interview with Sharif Wali, 25 April 2002, Cairo.

NDP-independents who had not publicized their affiliation despite their unofficial status were elected and rejoined the party (Abdel Maguid 2001: 99). Thirty-five genuine independents also entered the ruling party's bloc, giving it 388 of the contested seats (87 percent), more than the two-thirds needed to pass legislation and rubber stamp the president's decisions by a comfortable margin (Abu Rida 2001: 74).

Thus, unanticipated levels of competition at the district level troubled the NDP leadership but did not produce an opposition government. The traditional and new wings of the party had reconciled their differences; scattered electoral defeats did not aggregate into national change. Afterward, the NDP continued to exert control over the elections, subverting future judicial supervision through ongoing voter suppression. Despite the judiciary's prominent effort to guarantee meaningful polls, contestation in Egypt's elections returned to levels that proved unthreatening to regime partisans.

The Defeat of Team B and Semangat '46: Malaysia, 1987–1996

A decade before the abortive Future Party proposal in Egypt, UMNO curbed a breakaway movement within its own ranks. Malaysia's elites were not rent by the same issues that clove the Egyptian leaders, and they used different strategies of electoral control. But the subject of elite debate and the techniques of electoral victory mattered less than the institutional context in which those debates occurred. When Mahathir's rivals challenged him, the party provided a structure for accommodating dissatisfied leaders. Their subsequent reaffiliation reinforced the regime's command of national politics as UMNO pulled back from the brink of defeat and retained its parliamentary predominance.

Having survived rounds of elections against the opposition, Mahathir faced discontent in UMNO. The premier was accused of backing extravagant national projects while favoring family members and close friends (Crouch 1996: 118). Accusations of mismanagement were particularly damaging as Malaysia weathered an extended recession (Shamsul Amri Baharuddin 1988: 174). According to figures released by the Asian Development Bank at the time, only the Philippines (at 0.2 percent) had lower GDP growth than Malaysia (0.5 percent) among states in the Asia-Pacific region for 1986 (*Sydney Morning Herald*, 27 April 1987). Unlike in Egypt, where long-standing policy differences over structural adjustment threatened to polarize the government's leading politicians, the growing challenge to Mahathir focused on the style of his leadership. It culminated in a contest over control of the party that harkened back to Harun Idris's failed bid in 1976.

The unrest began with a split between Mahathir and his second-in-command. In February 1986, Deputy Prime Minister Musa Hitam formally resigned his post, citing personal differences with Mahathir. Musa's resignation capped three years of speculation that tensions between him and the premier were rising (Crouch 1996: 117). Ignoring rumors that he felt Mahathir had targeted him for exclusion, Musa attributed the estrangement to the premier's unwarranted suspicions: "When I resigned I claimed that it was just genuinely on democratic principles. When the prime minister accused me of attempting many times to kill him politically I said, 'I cannot be your deputy. We've got a system. I have to be your backup. I will not be comfortable.... I will not be able to do my job well when my boss says I'm trying to kill him [politically]...' So I resigned and people said, 'Oh, he must be trying to undermine Mahathir.'"[20] Subsequent events support the interpretation that Mahathir was threatened by Musa's popularity and sought to insulate himself from potential challengers. Unlike the policy divisions between New Guard and Old Guard in Egypt's NDP, Mahathir and Musa had no great ideological differences (Crouch 1996: 117).

Upon Musa's resignation Mahathir replaced several senior members of his cabinet and filled Musa's position with a lesser known figure, Ghafar Baba. The cabinet shuffle amplified the worry of some high-ranking UMNO figures that Mahathir was concentrating his power and focusing precious business opportunities on a narrow circle of clients (Gomez and Jomo 1999: 238–239). In response, an anti-Mahathir faction coalesced within the party. Trade and Industry minister Tengku Razaleigh Hamzah, a long-time aspirant to the prime ministership, partnered with Musa to challenge Mahathir and Ghafar in the party's triennial elections in 1987. Razaleigh and Musa criticized the prime minister for keeping Malaysia in an economic crisis, indulging in extravagant government-sponsored projects like the creation of a Malaysian automobile, and permitting corrupt dealings among his personal friends (*Sydney Morning Herald*, 24 April 1987; Milne and Mauzy 1999: 44). Razaleigh contested the party presidency in the 1987 triennial elections, while Musa ran to remain in the vice presidency, a post he had retained even after leaving the cabinet. The race split UMNO's voting members into two groups: "Team A," led by Mahathir and Ghafar, and "Team B," the faction of Razaleigh and Musa

[20] Interview with Jan Sri Musa Hitam 11 June (2003), Kuala Lumpur.

(Ramanathan and Adnan 1988: 70). This challenge was serious enough to prompt Mahathir to declare, in blatant defiance of UMNO convention, that he would remain prime minister even if he lost his post as head of the party. The vow irked many UMNO members who saw Mahathir as "flouting the laws of the tribe ... [and] acting un-Malay by saying he might not accept the wishes of the party" (*Wall Street Journal*, 22 April 1987).

Despite his controversial threat, Mahathir prevailed by skillfully distributing cabinet and party positions to undecided electors (Shamsul 1988: 185). In the race for party president, he took a narrow majority of votes (761 to 718). By an even slimmer margin (739 to 699), Ghafar also beat Musa (Ramanathan and Adnan 1988: 71). Team A candidates performed similarly well in the races for UMNO's governing board, the Supreme Council, winning seventeen of the available twenty-five seats (Ramanathan and Adnan 1988: 72). Yet Team B continued to fight. Razaleigh and newly appointed minister of foreign affairs Rais Yatim resigned their posts the following week. For the top contestants, the election's aftermath was initially a "winner-takes-all" standoff (Shamsul 1988: 181). Mahathir purged the cabinet of seven remaining Team B affiliates. The resulting discord threatened to rip UMNO apart. One news story reported, "The Razaleigh-Musa faction ... now claims to represent almost half of the nearly 1,500 most important UMNO activists" (*Sydney Morning Herald*, 28 April 1987).

The burgeoning dissident movement began to contract, however. Mahathir's reelection deterred potential Razaleigh supporters and rallied the rank and file around Team A. Still in the midst of a national economic slowdown, many UMNO members opted to stick with the party and its valuable patronage networks rather than gamble on Razaleigh (Crouch 1992: 33). As the dust settled after the internal party elections, more and more elites gravitated to their official leader. Early supporters of Razaleigh crept back to Mahathir, and all of the top Team A members remained steadfast in their loyalty to the premier (Milne and Mauzy 1999: 43). The ruling party's centripetal pull not only drained Razaleigh's cadre, it also broke his provisional partnership with Musa. After Team B's formal exit, Razaleigh strove to pry UMNO from Mahathir's grasp, whereas Musa adopted a more neutral posture.

Unsuccessful at contesting the party presidency from within, Razaleigh tried to capture the organization from outside. He launched his challenge with a court case that temporarily froze UMNO's organization. Both Razaleigh and Mahathir then attempted to claim the party's name and assets. Eventually, the court ordered UMNO dissolved, but the prime minister managed to hold onto UMNO – temporarily renamed "UMNO Baru" (New UMNO) – and most of its membership. Denied the UMNO title, Razaleigh and his partisans formed a new party called Semangat '46 (Spirit of '46), a name that recalled UMNO's explicitly pro-Malay origins under British rule. As Razaleigh moved further away from UMNO, his alliance with Musa weakened. Crouch writes, "While Razaleigh remained adamantly opposed to compromise with Mahathir, some of Musa's supporters were inclined to look for a modus vivendi" (1996: 119).

In the fall of 1988, a by-election signaled that the consequences of Musa's estrangement could be dire. Protesting against Team A, Musa ally Shahrir Ahmad resigned his UMNO seat in parliament and called a new election in Johor. Johor was not only Musa's home state, it was also the site of UMNO's founding and the party's traditional stronghold (*Japan Economic Newswire*, 26 August 1988). Yet Shahrir trounced the Team A candidate by a margin of more than twelve thousand votes. For UMNO this landslide raised the troubling prospect of losing the state's seventeen other seats in a future election (*The Economist*, 13 October 1990). Johoreans had proved incredibly loyal to their native son and would doubtlessly follow Musa with even greater passion. In addition to this regional support, moreover, Musa had national backing among the country's teachers thanks to his prior work as Minster of Education. Therefore, both regional and national voting patterns hinged on the former UMNO deputy's orientation. A shift by Musa to the opposition threatened to have countrywide repercussions.

In early October 1988, Musa underlined the message sent by Shahrir, physically distancing himself from UMNO by sitting with the independents in parliament (*New Straits Times*, 3 October 1988). Mahathir soon reached out publicly to both Musa and Razaleigh, announcing: "I would like to invite Tengku Razaleigh Hamzah and Datuk Musa Hitam to be members of my Cabinet as Ministers without portfolio. This is a sincere invitation. . . . [I]t's a step towards mending the rift among the Malays and Umno members. . . . [F]or the sake of unity, we are prepared to accept these two leaders into the Cabinet" (*New Straits Times*, 31 October 1988). Musa initially declined. The following month, he and Shahrir led a group called the Johor Malay Unity Forum, which issued a six-point proposal for reconciling Mahathir's offer with the demands of Musa's supporters in Johor (*New Straits Times*, 1 November 1988; *New Straits Times*, 19 December 1988). The program provided for the reinstatement of marginalized officials from Team B to their posts as branch and divisional heads. It also included "the automatic acceptance of former UMNO members" into the party (*New Straits Times*, 19 December 1988). UMNO's supreme council accepted the proposal on the condition that the forum's participants would recognize the elected party leadership (*New Straits Times*, 14 January 1988). In December, 1,300 Johoreans rejoined UMNO, and Musa publicly returned to the party on 31 January 1989 (*New Straits Times*, 21 January 1989; *New Straits Times*, 1 February 1989). He reasoned that Mahathir had "given in to quite a lot of suggestions and demands" (Lai Kwok Kin 1989). "Slowly but surely," Musa reflected, "the [UMNO] leadership had taken a softer and softer line" (*Reuters*, 31 January 1989). Shahrir's by-election and the Johor Malay Unity Forum displayed a willingness to support UMNO but a distaste for Mahathir. Even after Musa and his followers rejoined the party, campaign flyers with Mahathir's picture were strategically taken down during the election so as to minimize the damage of Mahathir's unpopularity among Johoreans.[21]

Mahathir had wooed Musa and his partisans back before they could compete separately in the next parliamentary election. The arrangement probably served both sides, but the prime minister benefited most of all. As the bulk of Team B reaffiliated with UMNO, they reinforced Mahathir's previously vulnerable position. The UMNO president had accomplished a personnel shift that he had sought since the 1986 parliamentary elections. His main rivals were weakened, while the party's general cadre remained loyal.

The return of Musa's camp to the party proved critical to UMNO's performance in the 1990 elections, which witnessed one of the strongest opposition campaigns survived by a ruling party during the third wave of democratization. While Musa was negotiating to rejoin, Razaleigh had been assembling UMNO's foes in an opposition alliance of unprecedented diversity. The ultimate failure of this movement and its reabsorption within UMNO demonstrates the insufficiency of fervent opposition activism without a critical mass of elite defectors – the very ingredient Mahathir deprived Razaleigh of when he wooed Musa's faction back.

Razaleigh collected the disparate monoethnic parties that had twice failed at defeating Mahathir. His principal affiliates were PAS and the DAP, with which Semangat '46 built two distinct but cooperative electoral alliances against the NF. Having been trounced already, both groups saw benefits in coordinating with Razaleigh. The Islamic PAS seized the chance

---

[21] Interview with Tan Sri Musa, 11 June 2003, Kuala Lumpur.

to retailor its radical image from 1986, when the party had advocated the creation of an Islamic state. Keen to improve on its earlier performance, PAS leaders regarded an alliance with Semangat as the only way to capture the votes of Malays disenchanted with UMNO (Khong 1991b: 9). Calling their partnership the Muslim Unity Movement (*Angkatan Perpaduan Ummah*), Semangat and PAS jointly courted the Malay majority, UMNO's primary constituency.

Like the message of Shahrir's victory in Johor, by-elections during 1988 and 1989 revealed Semangat's strengths and weaknesses. Primarily, they showed that the party needed to court non-Malay voters who might otherwise flock to the NF (Crouch 1992: 34). In response, Semangat formed an alliance with the DAP and several smaller opposition parties, which they dubbed the People's Concept (*Gagasan Rakyat*). The Muslim Unity Movement had not been able to agree on a common manifesto of shared political positions, but the People's Concept members proved more coherent, a Semangat-led foil to the UMNO-dominated National Front. It was an alliance of unequals, and the non-Malay participating parties were voluntarily subordinate to Semangat, the representative of Malay interests (Khong 1991b: 11). With the People's Concept on one side and the Muslim Unity Movement on the other, Razaleigh's movement seemed poised to succeed where previous anti-UMNO efforts had failed. Khong Kim Hoong explains, "Ever since the debacle in the 1969 elections, the ruling coalition had seemed quite unshakeable. However, in 1990, the ruling Barisan Nasional coalition appeared vulnerable" (1991b: 13). The next elections promised a chance for the opposition not simply to expand its share in parliament but to take control and establish a two-coalition system (Crouch 1992: 34). Far exceeding previous levels of opposition coordination, the assembled parties had candidates for 131 of the 180 seats in parliament, all but one of the peninsular seats (Crouch 1996: 128).

On 5 October 1990, Mahathir dissolved parliament and called new elections for 20–21 October. Campaigning would last only nine days, giving the opposition even less time to prepare than in 1986 (Khong 1991a: 178). UMNO candidates benefited from the abridged campaign period, as incumbent officeholders had already been politicking in their official positions, whereas the opposition had to struggle to communicate its message nationally (Khong 1991b: 21). Opposition candidates were also limited by lack of space, as they were permitted to publicize their programs only at indoor meetings (*Reuters*, 5 October 1990). Meanwhile, UMNO's control over the country's media allowed the party to make extensive use of the "religious card," portraying Razaleigh on television and in print as weak on Malay rights (Khong 1991b: 7). The media's pro-government bias was one of the principal irregularities cited by a commonwealth election observation team (*Reuters,* 5 October 1990). Distortions were so egregious that at one point Razaleigh's comments were clipped to make him say, "The opposition is in disarray" (*Japan Economic Newswire,* 16 October 1990). UMNO leaders also employed civil servants as campaign workers and offered farm subsidies and other state supports to key constituencies (Khong 1991b: 21–22). Where indirect intervention failed, the regime relied on vote buying to win key races, a method unavailable to Semangat because of its relative lack of access to state resources (Khong 1991b: 42).

UMNO also continued to exert a gravitational pull on Razaleigh's band. "By winning back supporters of the Semangat 46," Crouch points out, "UMNO was able to weaken the key component of the opposition front" (1992: 40). Although Semangat's supporters still included "two surviving Prime Ministers, former chief ministers, and members of the royal households," the overwhelming share of Razaleigh and Musa's faction eventually reaffiliated, foremost among them Musa himself (Crouch 1996: 121). Further boosting UMNO's position was the government's recovery from its earlier economic woes. In 1990, Malaysia's GDP growth reached a dynamic 9.4 percent (Khong 1991a: 179).

Razaleigh's Muslim Unity Movement and People's Concept lost ground in the final days before voting (Crouch 1996: 127). Semangat itself fielded candidates in 61 of the 180 single-member districts, more than any other single opposition party but significantly fewer than UMNO, which ran 86 candidates. Final results gave Semangat only 8 victories, while UMNO took 71 seats (83 percent of those it contested). The outcome nearly halved Semangat's already modest parliamentary bloc of 15 post-1987 UMNO renegades (*Reuters,* 23 October 1990). Meanwhile, the National Front took 71 percent (127 of 180 seats), sustaining its supermajority, albeit with its lowest share of parliament in more than twenty years (Khong 1991a: 164).

Elections in Musa's state of Johor played a large role in UMNO's success and Semangat's defeat. Semangat and the DAP won 36 percent of the vote in Johor compared to the National Front's 62 percent, but the result was that all of Johor's 18 parliamentary seats went to the NF (Tan 2001: 172, 179). The sweep despite the closeness of the vote count suggests the importance of Musa's return to UMNO with the Johor Malay Unity Forum. Given the opposition's performance in 1990, Musa's continued separation from UMNO could have shifted as much as 10 percent of parliament into the opposition bloc from one state alone.[22] Even that localized shift – leaving aside the potential national repercussions of a realignment by Musa – would have sheared away the National Front's two-thirds majority. Yet instead of bringing defeat to UMNO, Musa's state enabled the party to reassert its dominance.

By delivering Johor, Musa and his followers brought UMNO national victory. Razaleigh did carry his home state of Kelantan, however, causing the ruling party a localized defeat. With a 93 percent Malay electorate, Kelantan had long been a stronghold of PAS (Khong 1991b: 27). The area was also tied to Razaleigh, whose uncle held the traditional position of sultan and probably enabled Semangat's win (Khong 1991b: 25–26). Together with PAS, Semangat swept the state's thirty-nine legislative seats and thirteen parliamentary seats (Khong 1991b: 18–19; Tan 2001: 179). Nonetheless, the defeat of many top Semangat figures, including its deputy president and a number of sitting MPs, reduced the breakaway faction's chances of enduring independently (Khong 1991b: 41).

Although Semangat candidates enjoyed scattered victories, the group's poor national showing induced most of its members to rejoin UMNO. Razaleigh's partisans, like the NDP-independents in Egypt, reaffiliated when they saw that their future success depended on renewed loyalty to the ruling party rather than autonomous, ineffectual action among the opposition. Since Semangat had failed to break the NF's governing super-majority, UMNO leaders portrayed Razaleigh as a purely self-promoting politician unconcerned with the fortunes of other Semangat members (*New Straits Times*, 19 April 1995). When PAS stifled Semangat representatives in the Kelantan government, many of Razaleigh's colleagues "took up UMNO's invitation to return to its fold" (*New Straits Times*, 19 April 1995; Liak Teng Kiat 1996: 218). Subsequent legislative polls at the national and state level in April 1995 gave a record majority to UMNO's National Front and sounded the death knell for Razaleigh's ambition of an alternative government. These results augured a relapse to the electoral dominance of Mahathir's early years and ended Razaleigh's quest for a two-alliance system.

For the former UMNO figures of Semangat '46, continued political activity outside the National Front seemed futile. Even though the movement had made a decent showing in 1990, it possessed neither the influence to correct its media handicap nor the popular base to garner

[22] Interview with Edmund Terence Gomez, 6 June 2003, Kuala Lumpur.

anti-UMNO votes around the country. After April 1995, humiliated by their losses and eager to regain some level of access to the ruling party's economic and political largesse, the demoralized dissidents of Semangat ended the Muslim Unity Movement with PAS. Reconciliation between Mahathir and Razaleigh followed the next May, and Razaleigh brought most of his estimated two hundred thousand followers back to UMNO before the party's semicentennial (Khoo Boo Teik 1997b: 168).

Regime Renewal: Power Handovers in Egypt and Malaysia

Economic and political turbulence troubled many autocratic governments during the 1980s and 1990s, but leaders in Egypt and Malaysia eluded this trend and found ample cover behind strong ruling parties. Although residual political friction produced scattered defeats for their candidates, the NDP and UMNO maintained national dominance and fortified their regimes against further opposition campaigns. Electoral victories had renewed regime cohesion over the medium term, maintaining the ruling party's centrality for elite advancement. The ruling clique's stability brought additional electoral victories and ensured alternative political forces could not translate their constituent support into government authority.

Just as rulers in both countries had inherited institutions from their predecessors, by the turn of the twenty-first century they were preparing to bequeath those organizations to new leaders. As the third wave settled and a new century opened, Mubarak and Mahathir had each ruled for almost two decades and presided over a regime nearly half a century old. The focus of their organizations shifted from the quotidian containment of domestic opposition to the paramount task of regime preservation.

The New Guard's Self-Promotion: Egypt, 2001–2006

In the 2000 elections, for the first time in its history, the NDP was forced to rely on NDP-independents to retain its parliamentary majority. The prevalence of races in which NDP candidates faced off against NDP-independents gave the elections the hue of a party primary. Chastened by the defeat of their official nominees, NDP leaders debated how the party should respond. Wali and Al-Shazli downplayed the setback, portraying the results as a mere correction to their earlier selection of candidates (al-Shoubki 2001: 100–101). Gamal Mubarak, by contrast, fueled his case for organizational change by speaking publicly about the "erosion of the party's popularity" and the need for internal reforms (*Al-Ahram Weekly Online*, 15–21 February 2001).

The continued recruitment and integration of a new generation of politicians mattered more than popularity for the NDP's success. In a system where state police selectively disenfranchised voters, the electorate's preferences were a secondary concern in preventing a repeat of 2000. Party unity and electoral manipulation were more critical. The renewed fealty of the rank and file to the general secretariat would help curtail the NDP-independent phenomenon. The Ministry of Interior could further undermine the judiciary's supervisory power and assist NDP candidates in repelling their foes. The regime promptly addressed both matters, reconfiguring NDP internal procedures while retooling its electoral controls.

Soon after calling for reform, Gamal Mubarak introduced an ostensibly meritocratic method for selecting candidates within the party. Beginning with the Consultative Assembly elections and later extending to a local council races, the NDP instituted electoral caucuses (*al-mogamm'aat al-intikhabiyya*) in which party members voted for the candidates they wished to see on the ballot. The caucus system expanded the network of participants in decision making but functioned mainly as a nomination mechanism advising the General Secretariat.[23] Wali, Al-Shazli, and Sherif could still manipulate the caucus process to favor their clients (*Al-Ahram Weekly On-Line*, 3–9 January 2001; *Cairo Times*, 12–18 April 2001). In most cases, the outcome of a given electoral caucus was predetermined through informal negotiations that narrowed the range of contestants to the number of positions available. Hence, the voting validated private decisions reached among a select few (*Cairo Times*, 11–17 July 2002). Caucus results were binding on NDP members, and the party expelled those who ventured out as NDP-independents (*Cairo Times*, 10–16 May 2001). The workings of the new system are evident in the experience of Ali Shamseddin, the party's deputy secretary of youth for Cairo. Shamseddin ran against his superior, party secretary of youth Nabih Al-Alaqami, for the NDP's nomination as candidate in the Consultative Assembly elections in 2001. Shamseddin claims that the party leadership pressured delegates to vote for Al-Alaqami and also influenced the voting procedure behind the scenes, charges supported by other reports.[24] He lost in the primary and then launched an unsuccessful campaign for

---

[23] Interview with Mohammed Rageb, 4 April 2002, Cairo.
[24] Interview with Ali Shamseddin, 30 April 2002, Cairo.

the upper house seat. Shamseddin was subsequently ejected from the NDP.

While marginalizing the occasional independent-minded party member, the caucuses elevated Gamal Mubarak's faction through the NDP's ranks. Early in 2002, the party's steering committee expanded to include Gamal Mubarak, outspoken MP Zakariya Azmi, and Ali Eddin Hilal, minister of youth and former dean of Cairo University's Faculty of Economics and Political Science. This change gave the ascendant faction numerical parity against the six-member board's old guard. The NDP's party conference in September 2002 further strengthened the hand of the younger Mubarak's cohort. Safwat Sherif replaced Youssef Wali as secretary-general, and Gamal Mubarak became head of the NDP's new Policies Secretariat. Significantly, the NDP's General Secretariat grew to include more businessmen MPs (Hossam Awad and Hossam Badrawi). Elections by the six thousand delegates in attendance decisively shifted the General Secretariat to favor Gamal Mubarak's platform: The five new entrants to the governing body were allies of the young leader (*Associated Press*, 17 September 2002). Hence, the faction supportive of technocratic reforms and economic liberalization established majority control of the NDP's central board (*MEED Weekly Special Report*, 4 October 2000). Although Sherif remained the party's second-in-command after President Mubarak, Gamal Mubarak's rapid ascension over just three years' time suggested that his influence matched or exceeded Sherif's.

In March 2003, Gamal Mubarak toured New York and Washington, D.C., in a public relations blitz directed at influential American policy institutes and political forums. He reportedly made a positive impression on government officials and think tank figures concerned with Egypt's poor record on democracy and human rights (*Washington Post*, 10 February 2003). Following his visit, the younger Mubarak called for creating a human rights commission and abolishing one form of Egypt's infamous state security courts. The proposals were enacted but did little to curb the regime's penchant for arbitrary arrests and detentions (*Cairo Times*, 13–19 March 2003). More significantly, the developments of spring 2003 portended the conjunction of Gamal Mubarak's rise with the NDP's retreat from meaningful reform.

Subsequent to the 2000 elections, the Egyptian regime moved to smother the light cast by judicial supervision. Even after Gamal Mubarak praised the role of the judiciary and boasted that Egypt is the only country in the world with such an institution, government leaders weakened the judges' influence at the polls. Intervention by state security agents and hired thugs escalated after 2000, making judicial observers nearly superfluous. Supervision of the Consultative Assembly elections in 2001 was feeble, opposition participation was low, and the NDP took seventy-four of eighty-eight available seats. In January 2002, the NDP-controlled People's Assembly exempted village, district, township, city, and governorate council elections from judicial supervision, prompting the Muslim Brotherhood to boycott them entirely.[25] By means of fraud reminiscent of 1995, the NDP then took 98 percent of the seats (*Al-Ahali*, 10 April 2002; *Al-Ahram Weekly*, 18-24 April 2002).

Finally, a summer race in Alexandria showed that popular candidates could be completely blocked if the regime judged them a threat. On 27 June 2002, state security forces and local thugs stopped voters in the Al-Raml district of the city from casting their votes in a long-awaited by-election. The frustrated throngs predominantly supported Gihan Al-Halafawi and Muhammad Sayid Ahmed, Muslim Brotherhood members who had been on the cusp of victory in 2000 before a court order suspended voting. Since Al-Halafawi and Ahmed's supporters were forcibly prevented from casting ballots, these legitimate victors were left with a few hundred votes compared to the three thousand they had garnered previously (*Al-Ahram Weekly Online*, 4–10 July 2002). Unbelievably, the NDP's candidates quintupled the number of votes they had taken in 2000 (*Cairo Times*, 4–10 July 2002). The Al-Raml election decided only 2 seats out of a total of 454, and the Muslim Brotherhood controlled only 17 seats (3.7 percent) at the time. Despite the election's minimal impact on parliament, the regime intervened in force to prevent the inclusion of two more opposition members in government. In the years that followed, Mubarak's government actually reduced the Brotherhood's representation in parliament by two seats when two of the group's MPs were forced to participate in a rerun of their 2000 races. The resulting NDP production essentially replayed what had occurred in Al-Raml, and the ruling party's standard-bearers emerged victorious.

Beginning in 2003, public protests over the second Palestinian intifada and the U.S.-led invasion of Iraq morphed into rallies directed at President Mubarak and his associates. In March, an estimated ten thousand protesters occupied Cairo's central square, and chanters coupled their outrage against the United States and Israel with critiques of Mubarak and his sons (Schemm 2003). Although state security rigidly corralled

[25] Interview with Gamal Essam El-Din, 17 April 2002, Cairo.

subsequent demonstrations, the reemergence of public protests signalled broad dissatisfaction during the president's fourth term (1999–2005). Print media crystallized this discontent, with the Nasserist weekly *Al-Arabi* and the new independent *Al-Masry Al-Yom* (begun in summer 2004) assiduously exposing the regime's excesses. Street demonstrations became the most visible addition to the arena of opposition politics. In December 2004, a new organization calling itself the Egyptian Movement for Change, or Kifaya (Enough), initiated downtown rallies, demanding that Mubarak not be granted additional presidential terms and condemning the growing possibility of a hereditary succession. Kifaya's demonstrations varied in size from dozens to hundreds but seemed to embolden other groups to articulate their criticisms and manifest the depth of their popular support (International Crisis Group 2005: 10).

Alongside Kifaya and the indefatigable Muslim Brotherhood stood the newcomer Al Ghad (the Tomorrow Party). Founded in October 2004 by ex-Wafdist and twice-elected MP Ayman Nour, Al Ghad enlivened the moribund party scene with its liberal program and youthful leader. Perhaps for this very reason, the party soon found itself embroiled in legal battles and an internecine organizational struggle, precisely the same ills that had historically bedeviled other Egyptian opposition parties (Stacher 2004: 224). On 29 January 2005, the government charged the forty-one-year-old Nour with forging more than half of Al Ghad's 2,000 founding signatures. Released from jail on 13 March, Nour operated for the remainder of the year under the shadow of a potential prison sentence (ICG 2005: 2–3). Simultaneously, state-employed moles within Al Ghad debilitated the party from within. Given that half of the party's senior leaders were apparently on the dole of the ruling party, Al Ghad's subsequent decline in an allegedly liberalized political field is easily understood (El-Amrani 2005).

On 26 February 2005, President Mubarak called for parliament to introduce a constitutional amendment providing for multicandidate presidential elections, thus promising to end the prior practice of single-candidate referenda for the country's highest post (*New York Times*, 27 February 2005). Yet even as Mubarak was commended for taking a "very bold step" – popularly ratified three months later – the president's announcement stood against a backdrop of continued and even escalating repression of his domestic critics, with two thousand MB members arrested in April and May and dozens of Kefaya demonstrators assaulted (*Washington Post*, 24 May 2005). Availing himself of the opportunity that Mubarak's shift to presidential elections presented, Nour contested the September polls for chief executive and came out second. Besting his former party chief at the Wafd, No'man Goma'a, Nour took 7.57 percent of the vote to Goma'a's disappointing 2.93 percent. Mubarak won with a reported 88.57 percent. (ICG 2005: 16, fn. 118). This symbolic victory clarified Nour's position as upstart front-runner among the official opposition, yet it only intensified his problems. In the following months, Nour complained of incessant harassment by state security (*New York Times*, 19 October 2005). His dubious defeat in the opening rounds of legislative polls on 9 November further confirmed suspicions that he was the target of an organized campaign to remove him from national politics. On 24 December, Nour was convicted on the forgery charges and sentenced to five years in prison (*Reuters*, 24 December 2005). His imprisonment and the sabotage of Al Ghad (whose renegade faction won a single seat in parliament) demonstrated the Mubarak regime's boldness at dispatching its most effective critics.

While on the surface Mubarak's 26 February announcement seemed to advance Anwar Sadat's 1976 proposal for multiparty politics, its impact was severely limited. As the subsequent fate of his strongest opponent in those elections demonstrated, this measure did not bring about the "sea change" in Egyptian politics that it initially promised (*New York Times*, 27 February 2005). For elections subsequent to 2005, the amendment poses nearly insurmountable barriers to opposition participation. Much like the political parties law, it subordinates opposition activity to the discretion of the ruling party, requiring official parties to have 5 percent support from the elected MPs in each house of parliament. The threshold for independent candidates is even higher and includes local support among the country's governorates. Under these stipulations, the competitiveness of future presidential elections will depend on the preceding competitions that feed the national parliament and local councils. In a basic sense, therefore, the president remains an indirect appointee of other NDP-controlled offices. With the president still chosen and accountable only to an inner circle, the most important ramification of the 2005 election amendment was that it gave a veneer of public involvement to a decision that remained private and insular.

In January 2006, Gamal Mubarak was appointed to be one of three assistant secretary-generals of the National Democratic Party. Thus, at the time of this writing, the president's son holds the NDP's penultimate post behind Safwat Sherif, who was transferred from heading the influential Ministry of Information to preside over the Consultative Assembly. Gamal Mubarak also heads the NDP Policies Secretariat's increasingly influential

Higher Policies Council, an incubator where university intellectuals can test their ideas and set their sights on cabinet posts. The much-hailed electoral caucuses have been moved to the background, having seemingly provided a dispensable bridge over which New Guarders crossed into the Old Guard's domain. Now that they are consolidating their hold within the NDP, Gamal's confederates seem reticent to keep party reforms moving, much less level the playing field for opposition candidates.

The question of succession is arguably the principal bisector of Egypt's political forces: How much longer will a Mubarak rule? Will Mubarak the Younger soon replace Mubarak the Elder, bringing Egypt its first dynastic handover since 1936? On this issue, the opposition stands uncharacteristically united against a Gamal Mubarak presidency, but it remains trapped in the regime's net of legal maneuvers and repressive measures. The NDP leadership, divided to an extent between pro-Hosni and pro-Gamal factions, has come together in facilitating the regime's continuity. Such solidarity does not preclude the opening of a debate at the moment of a change in presidency, but as long as Hosni Mubarak remains at his post, even Gamal's adversaries within the ruling party seem content to bide their time and sustain their loyalty. Meanwhile, the president's son has gathered a coterie of academicians and businessmen who perceive him as their promoter and defender. As this technocratic cadre grows and embeds itself, the push for dynasticism gains momentum. Hence, the regime is pro-Mubarak in the broadest sense, while the opposition, although fragmented by other issues, collectively seeks to preserve some modicum of republicanism.

Recognizing that healthy party competition has taken hold in such previously unlikely locales as Ghana and Mali, it is not credible to attribute Egyptian's persistent autocracy primarily to economic, demographic, or cultural factors. Rather, the primary obstacle to competitive democracy is political: The National Democratic Party refuses to allow alternative organizations to participate fully and publicly in politics. From a comparative perspective on democratic transitions – or lack thereof – reformist elements within the NDP have withdrawn from playing the role of soft-liners who partner with nonviolent opposition movements and rotate power with them through free and fair elections. So long as the NDP continues to steer the "reform process," as it has done over nearly three decades of multiparty politics, proposals are more likely to raise new problems while postponing genuine solutions than to institute competitive democratic processes. Indeed, Hosni Mubarak's amendment providing for contested presidential elections has become a new hurdle for the opposition to clear. Yet it has also opened the door to a civilian presidency, a position Gamal Mubarak seems increasingly well positioned to occupy.

Mahathir Thwarts Reform: Malaysia, 1997–2006

When Semangat dissolved, Mahathir's control of UMNO had never been more consolidated. The premier then turned his power on his own deputy, Anwar Ibrahim. Perhaps seeing the makings of another Musa or Raza-leigh – an alternate pole for elite and mass support – Mahathir stripped Anwar of his post, pushed him from UMNO and crushed the reform movement that rallied to Anwar's defense. Malaysia's 1999 parliamentary elections offer a closing example of UMNO's imperviousness to even broad public opposition. The polls that followed in 2004 under Mahathir's chosen successor ushered in a fresh period of UMNO rule.

Decades before his plummet from UMNO's peaks, Anwar Ibrahim began his political career among the opposition as an organizer of the Malaysian Islamic Youth Movement and a supporter of PAS in 1978. In 1982, Mahathir recruited him as an UMNO candidate for parliament (Crouch 1996: 116). Anwar then rose to the position of president of UMNO Youth. Before the 1987 party elections, he stepped down from that position and threw his weight behind the Mahathir-Ghafar camp, Team A. In those same elections, he ascended into the ranks of the party's vice presidents and continued to climb after the 1990 elections (Milne and Mauzy 1999: 144). In 1993, he launched a bid for UMNO's second-highest post, Ghafar's office of party deputy president. Anwar initiated this coup by surreptitiously collecting the nominations of district heads, each worth ten votes each. By the time an internal party election was called, Anwar already held a sizable lead over Ghafar in the vote count. The election was quickly decided in Anwar's favor. Ghafar resigned from his UMNO and government positions (Milne and Mauzy 1999: 152). Anwar served the next five years as Malaysia's deputy premier and the ruling party's deputy president.

Following the 1995 parliamentary elections, Mahathir declared that party support for the leadership was an UMNO tradition and that neither he nor Anwar could be challenged. The move effectively blocked Anwar from getting closer to the party presidency. At the same time, Mahathir intimated that Anwar would eventually follow him, saying, "the successor to the president is the deputy prime minister." The implication was that the time for that succession had just not arrived (Liak Teng Kiat 1996: 231). Mahathir also banned campaigning for the highest posts in the party and used "bonus votes" and "no-contest resolutions" to prevent challenges to his leadership (Slater 2003: 90). These protracted maneuvers typified UMNO's capacity for settling leadership debates while privileging affiliation over defection. The alternative, a political showdown like that of 1987, would have meant open factionalism and an appeal to the public for the resolution of private disputes. Averting such a rift, the seventy-year-old premier confined contestation to the lower ranks of the party and locked in the status quo until he chose to retire.

Even this arrangement did not satisfy Mahathir. When Anwar began advocating reform within the party, including curbs on corruption, his mentor responded aggressively (Funston 1999: 169). In July 1998, known Anwar supporters in Malaysia's media were forced to resign their posts. Perhaps sensing the other shoe was about to drop, scores of UMNO MPs reaffirmed their loyalty to Mahathir (Funston 1999: 170). On 2 September, Mahathir struck against Anwar politically and litigiously, ousting him from his position as deputy prime minister and lobbing allegations of sexual misconduct. Two days later, UMNO's Supreme Council expelled Anwar from the party (Khoo 2000: 165). The rejected politician then went to court, facing multiple counts of corruption and sodomy. Following two highly politicized trials, he was sent to prison (Khoo 2000: 168–169).

Isolated but unrelenting, the former deputy prime minister launched a fresh battle for political change alongside the opposition PAS and the DAP. First during his trial and then from jail, Anwar called for the pluralization of Malaysia's political system beyond the UMNO-NF oligarchy (Funston 1999: 172–173). Advocating *reformasi* (reformation), he gathered sympathetic supporters, both Malay and non-Malay, to challenge the injustice of his trial and push for greater civil liberties in general. This social movement implicitly revived the long-faded dream of Dato Onn for noncommunal politics, with Malays and non-Malays working as equals. Khoo Boo Teik suggests that Anwar's Reformasi coalition was successful in attracting a broad spectrum of followers interested in putting ideas ahead of race:

Reformasi had achieved a critical cross-cultural breakthrough which created novel possibilities of multiethnic alliances.... With the opposition parties... making common cause, *Reformasi* drew into its fold "Anwarists," Islamicists, "Malaysianists," social democrats, NGO activists, women, concerned Christians, and students. Within *Reformasi*, the ethnic divide blurred. Malaysia's new or reinvented leaders of dissent became figures identified with a political standpoint, not the colour of their skin (2000: 172–173).

Reformasi's institutional umbrella was called Gerak (short for *Majlis Gerakan Keadilan Nasional*, the Council of the National Justice

Movement), and it included more than a dozen NGOs in addition to its constituent parties (Funston 1999: 173). The movement was also labeled the *Barisan Alternatif* (Alternative Front, AF) because it posed a coordinated challenge to the National Front (Khoo Boo Teik 2000: 174). Building on the electoral strategies of 1986 and 1990, the *Parti Rakyat Malaysia* (People's Party of Malaysia, PRM), PAS, and DAP agreed to field no more than one opposition candidate against each National Front representative. When Mahathir called early elections in 1999, the AF took its program to the voters (Khoo Boo Teik 2000: 173).

The Alternative Front galvanized national discontent with Mahathir's rule but faced an uphill battle against UMNO. Anwar's coalition performed better than Semangat had in 1995 but considerably worse than Razaleigh's alliance in 1990. Particularly damaging to Gerak's performance was the noticeable absence of top-level UMNO figures joining Anwar in political exile. While thousands of the party's members went over to PAS, the leadership remained steadfastly allied with Mahathir (Funston 1999: 175). Lacking defectors who could otherwise have shifted influence from the ruling party to Reformasi, Anwar was unable to leverage an insider position into an effective push for systemic change.

Once more, UMNO's advantages in the areas of media and government patronage proved decisive. During a whirlwind eight-day campaign period, ruling party leaders pledged pay raises for government bureaucrats and new support for schools and sports centers while portraying Anwar as an IMF pawn and an instigator of ethnic strife (Case 2001: 51). State media and security forces vigorously suppressed the Alternative Front while the UMNO-compliant Electoral Commission disqualified nearly half a million pro-Anwar voters to ensure the ruling party's victory (Khoo Boo Teik 2000: 179). Although UMNO lost twenty-two seats, its representation in parliament declining from 94 to 72 MPs, the National Front won 148 of 193 seats (77 percent) and easily sustained its two-thirds majority (Tan 2001: 180).

Anwar's experience vividly displayed the limits of an involuntary loss of elite position, even when the individual attracts a large following. When leaders are forcibly pushed from their party rather than exiting voluntarily with their status and influence preserved, they face obstacles similar to those encountered by activists already working from the outside. This difference matters, because ruling party leaders use sanctions as well as rewards when managing their coalitions. If rejected elites wielded the same power as elite defectors, then the decision to leave or stay would not have significant implications for a leader's subsequent fortunes. But this choice, shaped as it is by the structure of incentives in the ruling party, significantly affects later political outcomes. Having lost access and prestige, expellees are less capable than defectors at weakening the system. Consequently, Anwar suffered the same fate as Harun and Razaleigh before him.

After leading UMNO and Malaysia through five parliamentary elections, Mahathir Mohamad elected to step down from his post. In the fall of 2003, after twenty-two years as UMNO president, Mahathir passed the premiership and UMNO presidency to Abdullah Badawi, a figure much less prominent than Anwar had been. Even as Malaysia's renowned "Dr. M" began to enjoy the celebrity of retirement, the party he bequeathed to Badawi preserved the country's tradition of Malay dominance. The following elections, held on 21 March 2004, returned a 90 percent majority for the National Front. Anwar's party took only a single seat. As Reformasi seemed to go the way of Semangat, dissipating after its flash, the regime softened its stance toward Mahathir's chastened aide and released Anwar from prison. UMNO had stopped the Alternative Front and appeared ready to maintain its dominance under Mahathir's designated successor.

In this and prior chapters, I have noted the insufficiency of popular mobilization, absent the aid of elite defectors, for toppling an authoritarian regime. When democratic processes convert social backing into political authority, a campaign with extensive support in the electorate can remove incumbents. But before a dictatorship buckles, its mechanisms of control must also be subverted. Because their popularity will not deliver them victory, challenger candidates need elite allies who carry influence over the process of government. These defectors can counteract their peers' manipulation of the governing process and unfetter elections, enabling constituent support to carry the opposition into government. When Mahathir isolated his old deputy, Anwar's movement lacked such partners on the inside. Malaysia's 1999 polls provide a further instance of a strong opposition stymied by a cohesive coalition. Anwar took few UMNO leaders with him and could not neutralize Mahathir's legal and electoral subterfuge.

Conclusion

As the third wave capsized autocracies around the world, Egypt and Malaysia's regimes stayed afloat. Over the past thirty years, each country's rulers have survived eight limited multiparty elections, the very plebiscitarian ploys that allegedly destabilized peer regimes elsewhere. Exhibiting a combination of persistence and guile that Machiavelli might have envied, Mubarak and Mahathir have consistently prevented opposition activists from converting their popular bases into government power. Their success at stabilizing dictatorship during turbulent times should not be understood as a product of will, but as an effect of organizations that channeled ambition – their own interests and those of their fellow elites. Both rulers entered their positions in control of parties, and those organizations continue to lay the groundwork for what will follow them. For the past fifty years, the NDP (and its forebears) and UMNO have dominated electoral politics and kept their opponents from power. By providing opportunities for long-term personal advancement and political influence, these parties have curbed elites' incentives to exit the regimes or push for change from the outside. Motivations to defect have been dulled, if not eliminated, and public dissent from the party has been confined to localized rebellions. This capacity to frustrate even the broadly supported movements of Semangat's alliance in 1990 and Anwar's reform campaign in 1999 points to the critical role of elite defectors in destabilizing regimes and bringing electoral defeat, the subject of the next two chapters.

5

Elite Defections and Electoral Defeat

Iran during the Third Wave

The previous chapter showed the impact of parties by examining how they affected elite behaviors: When disgruntled leaders seemed to be heading toward forming a separate public faction, the ruling party provided political influence, drawing dissidents back into the coalition by guaranteeing a role in national agenda setting. Historical analysis of elite cohesion and electoral control in Egypt and Malaysia thus provides one set of evidence that ruling parties account for the two countries' shared experience with durable authoritarianism. Reinforcing this account with cases of contrast, the present and following chapter examine the record of nonparty regimes and unbounded tactical alliances in Iran and the Philippines.

Such partnerships can be potent vehicles for gaining power and eliminating common foes. They prove ineffective, however, for consolidating power and managing the conflicting interests of newly dominant leaders. Where elites lack reliable mechanisms for protecting their long-term influence, intraregime debates escalate, and distrust mushrooms. Catalyzed by the top leader's earlier abandonment of political parties, personal insecurity spreads in the ruling class. As erstwhile insiders find themselves adrift, they may seek new partners among the marginalized, moderate opposition. Thus, by eschewing any lasting institutional bonds between elites, leaders bent on monopolizing power may instead squander it, alienating the opportunists with whom they previously colluded. Conversely, these estranged elites buoy long-time activists and enable them to make new breakthroughs.

During the 1990s, Iran lacked the institutional structure that protected rulers in Egypt and Malaysia from their opponents. After Khomeini's death in 1989, the Islamic Republic found itself torn between the same clerical factions that had debated democracy after the revolution. The country's hierocracy split along ideological lines, exposing the regime to suppressed demands for genuine republican rule. Not since weathering the challenges of Shariat-Madari and Bani-Sadr had the regime been so exposed to popular calls for representative government as it was in the late 1990s. Yet that moment of opportunity was itself embedded in a context of preceding conflicts and subsequent decisions. The persistence of elite tension after regime formation in 1979–1981 had already undermined the development of a ruling party. The IRP's dissolution – ordered by its leaders – presaged the revival of open factionalism among rightist and leftist clerics.

Although institutional decline opened political opportunities for intense contestation, these opportunities were not in themselves sufficient to oust obstreperous traditionalists: Reformists had to push for regime change through a direct confrontation, and at that point they balked. Fearful of the violence and uncertainty a second revolution might bring, prodemocracy politicians who carried 70 percent of the electorate with them refrained from encouraging street demonstrations or other forms of contentious collective action. Favoring formal electoral participation over protest politics, the reform camp soon lost the capacity to conduct either. Its gradualist strategy alienated passionate supporters and provided the traditionalists with a chance to regroup and regain the governmental turf they had ceded.

Rupture in the Right: Iran, 1993–1996

In 1992, Leader Khamenei and President Rafsanjani had achieved an unprecedented feat in postrevolutionary Iran: They had ended the long-running stalemate between the right wing and the Islamic left, a balance of power that Khomeini had carefully maintained during his rule. Given the surfeit of influence that fell into their hands, Khamenei and Rafsanjani might have been expected to sustain this momentum and permanently exclude the left-wing clerics from the Islamic Republic's most important governing bodies. Instead, the policy differences between the traditionalist right and modernist right escalated during the third Islamic Assembly (1992–1996), pitting the long-time partners against one another as their factions battled over the state's resources and direction. These policy clashes then fueled a political confrontation in the legislative elections of 1996.

Purging the Islamic left in 1992 did not resolve the disagreements between Rafsanjani and his parliament. Indeed, much to the president's chagrin, the new, SCC-dominated Islamic Assembly resisted his proposals for modernization and reconstruction as obstinately as its predecessor had, particularly after his reelection in 1993. The traditionalists and the modernists differed on the proper strategy for reviving Iran's economy and rebuilding its infrastructure. Traditionalists sought to protect the *bazaar* from any state intervention, eschewed higher taxes, resisted cutbacks to the public sector, and staunchly opposed the repatriation of Iranian nationals linked to the shah's fallen regime, an act the traditionalists perceived as a betrayal of the revolution's core values (Saghafi 1996). Their stance was conservative and protectionist, maintaining Iran's isolation in foreign affairs and pursuing limited solutions to its domestic economic ills. Perhaps the only area in which they favored political reform was in their advocacy of decentralizing the national government's influence over local affairs, a move transparently intended to shift power away from President Rafsanjani and toward their own districts (Baktiari 1996: 221–223). Speaker Ali Akbar Nateq-Noori led the traditionalist right's push in these areas.

In contrast to the speaker's insular proposals, the president and his associates viewed structural adjustment and international integration as the only way of pulling Iran out of its economic slump: In order to finance reconstruction, the state would have to marshal domestic capital by collecting taxes and regulating the *bazaar*, and it would also have to draw foreign capital, first and foremost by attracting those wealthy Iranians who had fled the Islamic Republic (Ehteshami 1995: 117–118; Moslem 2002: 190, Saghafi, 1996). The modernist right's pursuit of capital focused on the country's wealthy "foundations" (*bonyads*), some of which were built with funds expropriated from Iranian capitalists after the revolution. Those funds would need to be returned if the country were to enlist the skills and investment of its exiled entrepreneurs (Ehteshami 1995: 111–114; Ansari 2003: 245–246). Civil service reform was another point of contention. Iran's state bureaucracy had grown to two million workers by Rafsanjani's second term. This vast constituency for the traditionalists resisted change and deterred foreign investors (Ehteshami 1995: 121–122).

When the president attempted to accommodate the traditionalists' program by incorporating several of their affiliates into his cabinet, Khamenei's faction remained contemptuous (Moslem 2002: 203–204).

In 1994, the leader forced Rafsanjani's brother to resign from his post as head of state broadcasting (Baktiari 1996: 233–234). The parliament, controlled by Khamenei's Society of Combatant Clergy, expelled several of Rafsanjani's ministers. Some traditionalists even intimated that the Islamic Republic should rid itself completely of its presidency and elected offices, becoming an unadulterated hierocracy (Ansari 2003: 246–247). A former minister of the interior allied with the Islamic left attributed the fissure to the same tensions that had crippled the Islamic Republican Party: "The rightist trend has a short-sighted attitude and a closed and extremely narrow party structure. It says that anyone joining our process is with us and those who do not join are against us and will be treated as the enemy.... The rightist trend left over from the IRP is behaving in the same way because the IRP contained two specific trends."[1]

Just as the traditionalist right seemed to be gaining ground against its erstwhile compatriots, parliamentary elections in spring 1996 offered the modernists a chance to rally behind their embattled chief. The hope of Rafsanjani's colleagues was not shared by many, however. Most of Iran's diverse leaders held the same perspective on the elections: The Islamic left could not seriously contest them, and the traditionalist right would therefore sweep the polls. Because the traditionalist right controlled the Council of Guardians, and through it candidate vetting, Khamenei and Karrubi's adversarial factions both expected the traditionalists would increase their share of parliament in the elections and lay the ground for Nateq-Noori to become president in 1997 (Buchta 2000: 26). Demoralized and determined not to relive the experience of 1992, the Islamic left's Association of Combatant Clerics opted to boycott the elections.

The exigencies of political survival spurred the modernist right to venture forth publicly as its own faction, distinct from the traditionalists and the Islamic leftists. When Rafsanjani's group sought a compromise that would put five of their number on the SCC's electoral list, they were harshly rebuffed (Future Alliances International 1996: 78). Pushing for total control, the SCC leaders insisted on an exclusionary dichotomy, saying there were only "two political trends in the country...the line of Velayat-e faqih and those without Velayat-e faqih."[2] This polarizing refrain signaled the traditionalist right's bid to narrow the regime's

---

[1] "Iran: Mohtashami Interviewed on Elections," *Salam*, 12 February 1996, FBIS-NES-96-039, 27 February 1996.
[2] "JRM Official Against Coalition With Other Iranian Parties," IRNA, 21 January 1996, FBIS-NES-96-016, 24 January 1996.

leadership even further than it had in 1992. Deprived of an integrated electoral list, the luminaries of the modernist right felt compelled to pursue their agenda independently. A collection of nonclerical businessmen and politicians, most of whom were members of President Rafsanjani's cabinet, organized themselves as the Executives of Reconstruction (*Kargozaran-e Sazandegi*). The group's founding membership included many of the country's foremost officials and technocrats, with Tehran mayor Gholamhossein Karbaschi, Central Bank head Mohsen Nourbakhsh, vice president of parliamentary affairs Ataollah Mohajerani, and the head of Iran's Atomic Energy Organization, Ali Amrollahi, among them (Future Alliances International 2000: 15). Four of the Executives' sixteen founding members held Ph.D.s in economics or hard sciences; eight had master's degrees in management, economics, engineering, or industry (Future Alliances International 1996: 88–89). The Executives' backgrounds and professions distinguished them from the Society of Combatant Clergy and its constituents in the bazaar.

On 18 January 1996, the Executives of Reconstruction publicly declared their membership and platform (Buchta 2000: 21, fn. 20). Their mission statement echoed the president's policy initiatives, citing the need for "[economic] development ... expansion of international relations based on the principles of the revolution, use of experts and reliance on expertise, and creation of a [domestic] environment where ideas can flourish" (Moslem 2002: 129). Their strategy was to boost Rafsanjani's structural adjustment efforts and disrupt Nateq-Noori's presidential ambitions by backing a more centrist speaker. Days after the group formed, the president recognized the Executives, thereby formalizing his faction's separation from Khamenei's SCC.[3]

The Executives' debut exposed the widening cleavage among the formerly preeminent right wing, reviving the prospect of factional rivalries that had characterized the 1980s. The *Tehran Times* editorialized that the breakup of the Khamenei-Rafsanjani coalition was rooted in the abandonment of the unifying IRP and in the traditionalists' contempt for the modernist right:

The first political party which was formed by the followers of the late Imam Khomeini was the Islamic Republican Party. ... No doubt it functioned as a loose but strong front against the enemies who were determined to overthrow the nascent Islamic system. But when the enemies were defeated, cracks began to

---

[3] "Rafsanjani Approves List of Officials to Contest Tehran," IRNA, 22 January 1996, FBIS-NES-96-014, 22 January 1996.

emerge in the ranks of the members of the party to the extent that it was compelled to stop functioning. . . . Today again we observe that the [SCC] is breaking ranks. . . . If the major Islamic groupings do not form political parties, there will be further defections.[4]

Nearly a decade after Khamenei and Rafsanjani had dismantled the IRP, the two figures generated the kind of internecine struggle they had earlier tried to resolve.

Amid the traditionalists' overconfidence and the leftists' despair, the entry of the Executives ushered in an unexpectedly competitive election. When the Council of Guardians issued its decisions on candidacies, it allowed only 3,228 of 5,359 applicants (60 percent) to run. Among this group was a slightly modified set of the Executives of Reconstruction's nominees (Moslem 2002: 238). The modernist right faction ran twenty of its members on their electoral list for Tehran.[5] The public battle playing out among the right wing's factions generated extensive popular interest: Previously uninvolved middle and upper-class Iranians participated, and for the first time the majority of voters were women. Turnout reached an unprecedented 24.9 million (71 percent of the electorate) (Future Alliances International 1996: 38). In Tehran, the initial round of voting decided only two seats, one going to the president's daughter, Faezeh Hashemi Rafsanjani, and one to Nateq-Noori (Moslem 2002: 239). The SCC's and the Executives' strongest candidates faced each other in run-off races. Recognizing that high turnout favored the modernist right's dark horses, Nateq-Noori tried to dampen voter participation. The speaker condemned the Executives as "liberals" and attempted to disqualify their candidates. His eleventh-hour mudslinging was partially successful: Turnout waned in the final round of voting and weakened the Executives' campaign for parliament (Fairbanks 1998: 23–25).

When the dust settled and the final results were tabulated, each faction could claim a limited victory: The traditionalist right still controlled parliament (with 120 seats of its own, plus the support of 50 independent MPs), and Nateq-Noori survived as speaker, but the Executives entered

---

[4] "Absence of Parties Said to Endanger Iranian Political System," *Tehran Times*, 23 January 1996, FBIS-NES-96-018, 26 January 1996.

[5] Through an arrangement enabled by Iran's open list system, in which candidates may appear on multiple electoral slates, the Executives' list also included Nateq-Noori and nine other members of the SCC. Yet Executives candidates were still competing against the SCC's *full* list, and the group advertised primarily for its 20 genuine candidates. "Iran: Reconstruction Group Lists Tehran Candidates," *IRNA*, 28 February 1996, FBIS-NES-96-040, 28 February 1996; Future Alliances International (1996: 38).

the Islamic Assembly with a substantial bloc of 60 seats and allied themselves with leftist MPs. Most important, the Executives' performance bolstered Rafsanjani's position and prevented the SCC from monopolizing the republican tier of government (Future Alliances International 2000: 16). By curbing the traditionalist right's bid for hegemony, the modernist right signaled that elections remained a tool for rallying popular support and challenging the Islamic Republic's most rigid leaders.

The subject of debate between Iran's elite factions mattered less than the institutional context of those clashes. In its political program, Iran's modernist right resembled Egypt's New Guard: Both groups sought to restructure the state and hence threatened powerful constituencies that benefited from government protections, both hoped to expand their existing influence within the regime, and both were amenable to working with those vested traditional interests who resisted change. There is no indication that elite cleavages in Iran were more serious than those in Egypt; the policy disagreements between Rafsanjani and Khamenei were divisive but not inherently explosive. The Egyptian case shows that such debates could have been resolved without one side decisively trumping the other if elite behavior had been restrained and channeled through a party organization. The path of reconciliation, however, was a road Iran's elites would not take: Even when the modernists sought compromise, traditionalist leaders brokered no political accord. In rejecting calls for cooperation, the traditionalists eroded the authority they fought to fortify, pushing the modernist right into allying with the marginalized Islamic left.

The Left's Revival: Iran, 1997–2000

As the end of Rafsanjani's second term approached, Iran faced a three-way fight between the traditionalist right of the SCC, the modernist right of the Executives of Reconstruction, and the Islamic left of the ACC. When members of the Executives failed to amend the constitution to enable Rafsanjani to serve a third consecutive four-year term (the limit was two consecutive terms), the group opted to support the Islamic left's nominee for the position, former minister of culture and Islamic guidance Seyyed Mohammed Khatami. Citing the modernist right's successes in 1996, Khatami had urged his colleagues to abandon their cynicism and recognize that the ballot box could still be a weapon for their cause. Khatami's candidacy – along with the candidacy of Nateq-Noori and two other contestants – was approved by the Council of Guardians (Buchta 2000: 31). An alternative had emerged, one that promised to continue the pragmatic modernization programs of Rafsanjani while infusing them with the left's program of cultural and political liberalization (Moslem 2002: 246–247).

The Islamic left's electoral reentry was the result of a calculated concession by its foes in the traditionalist right. In post-revolutionary Iran, presidential elections had come to function as plebiscites of approval for the system; in the uncompetitive races, turnout was the priority.[6] To the SCC's chagrin, levels of participation in the presidential polls had been declining, hitting a record low in 1993 (Buchta 2000: 35). Plummeting public interest reflected poorly on the traditionalist right and its dominion over the regime's highest posts. The SCC therefore sought a contest that would rouse the electorate while still delivering victory to its candidate. Attracting voters to turn out and elect Nateq-Noori required that their candidate face a credible competitor (Bakhash 1998: 88–89). Khatami seemed a safe choice.

The traditionalists controlled the regime's clerical institutions, while their opponents cultivated glassroots support. All major branches of the state endorsed Nateq-Noori: The leader, a majority of parliament, the Council of Guardians, clerics around the country, and even the minister of intelligence publicly supported the speaker's candidacy (Bakhash 1998: 81). Yet his status as regime favorite did little to help Nateq-Noori's chances against the increasingly popular Khatami. As the affable cleric spoke of developing civil society and promoting a "dialogue between civilizations," Khatami brought hope to millions of despondent voters (Menashri 2001: 83; Moslem 2002: 246). The traditionalists had underestimated the potential for celebrity of the soft-spoken Khatami, who campaigned "entirely under the slogans of culture and democracy" (Buchta 2000: 29). Iranians saw Khatami's campaign as a way to weaken the traditionalists and awaken a moribund regime with a message of change. In this context, Nateq-Noori's slew of high-level endorsements backfired, widening the gulf between the speaker's conservative defense of the status quo and the public's yearning for reform (Buchta 2000: 31).

As the anointed fall guy became an insurgent frontrunner, the prospect of defeat dawned on the traditionalists. Reacting crudely to this reversal of fortune, Khamenei's faction began using thuggery and fraud to halt

---

[6] In all presidential elections since 1981, negotiations within the regime had produced a leading candidate whom the public then elected overwhelmingly: Khamenei had been the regime's choice in 1981 and 1985, Rafsanjani in 1989 and 1993. Even before campaigning began, Nateq-Noori was the presumptive victor for 1997 (Saghafi 2002: 17–19).

Khatami's advance. In the last weeks of the campaign, the newspapers of the traditional right vilified Khatami's movement. Acting even more aggressively, *hizbollahis*, with the tacit permission of the Ministry of the Interior, assaulted the candidate's campaign offices. Rumors circulated that further force would be deployed by the Islamic Revolutionary Guards and the *baseej* if Nateq-Noori were to lose.[7] Defying these acts and threats of coercion, ACC leader Karrubi warned Khamenei that Khatami would withdraw his candidacy – and thus deprive the regime of a legitimating election – if the Leader did not ensure civility during the final days of campaigning. Khamenei complied (Buchta 2000: 33).

Even more grave than the ominous attacks on Khatami's supporters, in the week prior to the elections, a new rumor emerged that the counting of ballots would be rigged against the reformist candidate (Buchta 2000: 32; Moslem 2002: 250). As this possibility grew and elections approached, Rafsanjani intervened. In 1992, the president had supported the regime's exclusion of ACC candidates and assured voters that the leftists had been lawfully disqualified; in 1997, by contrast, he protected the ACC's standard-bearer and ensured that Khatami had a genuine chance of victory. The Friday before the election, Rafsanjani delivered a sermon criticizing the traditionalists' suspected plot to intervene. From the pulpit, he condemned electoral fraud: "The worst crime I know of is manipulating the will of the electorate; it is an unpardonable sin" (Buchta 2000: 32). By exposing the schemes of electoral manipulation, Rafsanjani cornered Khamenei into addressing the problem. Though he had been prominently connected to Nateq-Noori's candidacy, the leader was now forced to vow that the elections would be clean and fair. As Mehdi Moslem argues, the last-minute push for transparency was critical to Khatami's chances: "This reassured people that their vote would actually count and made any wrongdoing that might have been planned impossible given the atmosphere that had developed after the assertions of the president and the leader" (2002: 250–251). Thanks to Rafsanjani's intercession, Khatami's upstart campaign moved ahead to the polls unimpeded.

When the election took place on 23 May 1997 (2 Khordad 1376 in the Iranian calendar), the hopes of Khatami's partisans and the fears of Nateq-Noori's were confirmed. Record turnout of 80 percent brought the reform

---

[7] With regard to the Islamic Revolutionary Guards, the threat may have been exaggerated. Seventy-three percent of the Revolutionary Guard's personnel are reported to have voted for Khatami. In contrast, support for the traditionalists has tended to be stronger in the country's paramilitary forces, the *hizbollahis* and *baseej* (Buchta 2000: 125).

advocate a speedy and decisive victory with 20 million votes (70 percent of those cast).[8] Women and youth formed the bulk of Khatami voters (Buchta 2000: 38–39). His movement attracted voters with a diverse socioeconomic profile, drawing supporters from both Iran's upper-middle-class "intelligentsia" and its impoverished underclass (Kazemi 2003: 90–91). Their 1992 rout long behind them, elites from the Association for Combatant Clerics had returned to the center of Iranian politics, this time steering a new and expansive reform movement. Solidifying their upset victory against the traditionalist camp, the left's newly formed Islamic Iran Participation Front (IIPF) joined with the Executives of Reconstruction to create the Twenty-Third of May Front (Rajaee 2004: 163).

While Nateq-Noori had quickly conceded to his opponent, he also managed to retain his post as speaker the following month (Buchta 2000: 33). In the wake of 23 May, it became apparent that the traditionalists would employ violence to undercut President Khatami's mandate and neutralize his movement. Although the Islamic Assembly approved all of Khatami's initial cabinet nominees, the honeymoon of cordial presidential-legislative relations was over by the next year. Unable to assail the president directly, the traditionalists took aim at Khatami's most influential associates, beginning with Tehran's modernist mayor, Gholamhossein Karbaschi. A longtime ally of Rafsanjani, Karbaschi had openly favored Khatami's candidacy, providing financial and logistical support in the capital. The traditionalists retaliated against Karbaschi through their allies in the country's judiciary, headed by the conservative Ayatollah Mohammad Yazdi. Charged with embezzlement and corruption, the popular Karbaschi was eventually sentenced to two years' imprisonment, forced to pay a heavy fine, and barred from political office for ten years (Moslem 2002: 259–260). That summer, the traditionalist bloc in parliament also impeached Khatami's minister of the interior, Abdollah Nuri, claiming that Nuri had failed to quell public controversy instigated by Hossein-Ali Montazeri about Khamenei's credentials for the leadership (Moslem 2002: 260–261). In fact, Nuri's well-known loyalty to the fallen Montazeri had prompted Khamenei to retain personal control over the state's law enforcement forces (the conventional province of the Ministry

---

[8] Daniel Brumberg has proposed an alternative interpretation, that Nateq-Noori's defeat was a strategic concession by Khamenei and his allies to perpetuate their hold on power (2000: 130). Such an account leaves unexplained the SCC's failed subterfuge against Khatami, as well as the regime's violent retaliation against Khatami's supporters in the years that followed. Had Khatami's victory fit seamlessly in the traditionalists' strategy, one would expect to observe a more accommodating approach by the leader and his minions.

of the Interior). Hence, in one of the more paradoxical attacks of the traditionalist right, Nuri was punished for not deploying policemen he had
never controlled (Buchta 2000: 142).

After successfully challenging Karbaschi and Nuri, the traditionalists
went after Khatami's reform-minded minister of culture, 'Ata'ollah Mohajerani. Mohajerani had overseen a renaissance in Iran's print media, lifting censorship restrictions and allowing reformist newspapers to proliferate. In summer 1998, judiciary head Yazdi began to roll back these
advances for free expression, closing *Jame'eh*, a pro-Khatami newspaper
that reached more than three hundred thousand readers (Buchta 2000:
144). Other critical publications were similarly shut down, often reopening under new names shortly after their closure (Moslem 2002: 263;
Rajaee 2004: 164). But the leader and Islamic Assembly went further
still, pressuring Mohajerani to adopt a more conservative posture toward
the print media and assume the duties being performed by the judiciary.
Wary of suffering the same fate as Nuri, Mohajerani retreated from his
progressive stance and agreed to heed the traditionalists' wishes (Buchta
2000: 145). Even this concession did not protect him, though. In January
1999, *hizbollahis* physically assaulted both Mohajerani and the ousted
Nuri (Moslem 2002: 263). A special clerical court later sentenced Nuri to
five years' imprisonment (Arjomand 2005: 509).

Escalating attacks on Khatami's allies revealed the obstacles that
remained in the path of the Twenty-Third of May Front, as well as the
urgency of its mission.[9] Elections provided the most immediate avenue of
action. In 1998, Iranians took part in elections for the eighty-six-member
Assembly of Experts, which was charged with selecting a successor to
Leader Khamenei or, if warranted, removing him. Members of the assembly served for eight-year terms and were predominantly from the clergy.
This pattern held in 1998, when the Council of Guardians excluded all
lay and female candidates. In a blatant expression of the traditionalists'
continued hold over the vetting process, the final list of 146 approved
candidates included only 10 persons supportive of Khatami's program
(Buchta 2000: 149). Even more striking, Rafsanjani flipped his support
back to the traditionalist right, taking the Executives with him and leaving
the Islamic left in the lurch. Aside from Rafsanjani's own ambition to join

---

[9] The vulnerability of Khatami's defenders grew in proportion to their institutional distance
from the president. While members of the Khatami administration suffered political isolation and physical intimidation, intellectuals outside of government faced even harsher
retribution. In fall 1998, five prominent figures from Iran's resurgent community of writ-
ers and academics were murdered or died under suspicious circumstances rumored to be
linked to the traditionalist right's most violent members (Moslem 2002: 264).

the Assembly of Experts, the shift may have been driven by the modernist right's wish to alleviate the pressure on Karbaschi and save its other members from a similar fate. The former president's realignment confirmed the tactical and transitory nature of the 1997 partnership between his and Khatami's factions. But his capricious gamble did not pay off: The elections produced a fresh majority for traditionalists in the Assembly of Experts; flushed with success, they felt no need to reciprocate the modern right's assistance (Buchta 2000: 150–153). Demonstrating his inimitable skills as a political survivor, Rafsanjani won election to the assembly but was denied its chairmanship and had to settle for the deputy post.[10]

The lopsided elections had provoked vociferous protests from the ACC's Karrubi and drawn less than half the electorate to the polls (Buchta 2000: 151). The Islamic left did not have to wait long for another chance to translate popular support into political gains. In February 1999, Khatami enacted a long-dormant section of the constitution calling for the local election of city and municipal councils rather than their centralized appointment (Ehsani 2000). Unlike the elections for the Assembly of Experts, Iran's first municipal elections were open to nonclergy, thus enabling the Twenty-Third of May Front to bring its thousands of supporters into the Islamic Republic's base. The Front won an overwhelming landslide, capturing an estimated 80 percent of votes in competition for some two hundred thousand posts (Abdo 1999; Tajbakhsh 2000: 377). The victory demonstrated the reformists' continued public endorsement despite the traditionalists' political and violent attacks against them. But Khamenei's faction had also showed its resolve not to back down.

The reform movement now approached an impasse: If elections proved insufficient to deliver on the promise of democracy, would Khatami and his peers confront the regime in other ways? Khatami's own actions soon answered this question in the negative. In early July 1999, thousands of University of Tehran students poured into the streets and called for the release of political prisoners and the reopening of opposition newspapers (MERIP Special Correspondent 1999; Vaziri 1999). They beseeched Khatami for help in accomplishing these goals, but the president turned on them and urged calm (Brumberg 2001a: 393–394). With Khatami

---

[10] The 1998 Assembly of Experts elections encapsulate the volatility of Iran's unbounded factions and partyless politics. Having tipped the last presidential election in Khatami's favor, Rafsanjani oscillated back toward the traditionalist right. Successful mainly at alienating reformists, the opportunistic Rafsanjani found himself rebuffed (once again) by the traditionalists. Within the span of a few months, a fresh tactical alliance (between the modernist right and traditionalist right) had burgeoned and burst.

advocating order over free expression, domestic security forces violently dispersed the vulnerable demonstrators (Future Alliances International 2000: 18).

The gulf between reformists' support in Iranian society and their lack of control over the Iranian state – most dramatically, their failure to curb official violence – persisted through the parliamentary elections of 2000. Because elections to the sixth session of the Islamic Assembly offered the prospect of a reformist lock on Iran's republican institutions, early politicking over the electoral rules and candidate selections was especially fraught. Well aware that the tide of public opinion had turned against them, Nateq-Noori and his fellow traditionalist MPs fought to save their political careers by rigging the electoral rules against reformist candidates. The SCC proposed changing the elections to a "single-stage" system without runoffs. They hoped that the shift to speedy plurality voting would benefit incumbents while disadvantaging their more numerous reform-inclined opponents.[11] Representatives from the Executives of Reconstruction thwarted the measure by staging a walkout that broke the legislature's quorum.[12] The next day, parliament defeated the bill (113–110) and passed alternate legislation: Candidates would need a 25 percent share to win a first-round victory and a relative majority for victory in a runoff.[13] Stymied in the legislature, Nateq-Noori and his associates turned to the Council of Guardians, imploring the screening body to disqualify the most viable challengers of the SCC. The council largely complied, ignoring calls by President Khatami and the opposition press that it not abuse its power. Outspoken newspaper editor Abbas Abdi and former minister of the interior Nuri were among the council's most prominent victims (Afrasiabi 2000: 13; Boroumand and Boroumand 2000: 118–119). But the Twenty-Third of May Front flooded the council with thousands of nominees and thereby avoided having all of its candidates washed out. In all, the Council of Guardians turned down approximately 11 percent of the applications, a relatively low share in comparison to eight years earlier (Maloney 2000: 60).

For his part, Nateq-Noori opted not to run rather than face certain defeat by the reformists. His pessimism was not misplaced. In the first

---

[11] "Iranian Press: MPs Comment on Majles Walk-Out," *Iran News* (Internet version), FBIS-NES-2000-0103, 3 January 2000.

[12] "Majles Deputies Protest Election Procedure," *IRIB Television First Program Network*, FBIS-NES-2000-0102, 2 January 2000.

[13] "Iran: Majles Rejects 'Single Stage' Election Bill," *IRIB Television First Program Network*, FBIS-NES-2000-0103, 3 January 2000.

round of voting alone, the Twenty-Third of May Front took a 160-seat majority of 290 contested seats. By that point, several of the most well-known SCC leaders (Hassan Rowhani, Mohammad Reza Bahonar, and Javad Larijani, for example) had already lost (Maloney 2000: 61; Future Alliances International 2000: 30). With reformist victories outpacing the traditionalists' wins by a ratio of four to one, the Council of Guardians began intervening midway through the elections to undercut the movement and roll back its gains. The council was responsible for "monitoring" elections by certifying election results; by gross extension, its members also wielded the power to annul victories. When reformists took an additional forty-six seats in the second round, the council froze the verification of Tehran's vote and threatened to invalidate all of the city's thirty seats. The Ministry of the Interior, staffed by Khatami appointees and responsible for the logistics of vote counting, resisted the council's move. The ministry's objections were joined by public outrage over the manipulation of results: The Council of Guardians had provoked rioting, the kind of public confrontation Khatami had condemned the prior summer (Boroumand and Boroumand 2000: 118). In a rare concession to public opinion, the traditionalists gave in: With the country verging on widespread domestic turmoil, Khamenei ordered the count concluded without further delay (Maloney 2000: 63). The Twenty-Third of May Front lost ten seats to the council's manipulation but succeeded in sending 189 of its candidates to parliament (a 65 percent majority) (Boroumand and Boroumand 2000: 114).

By summer 2000, the conjunction of election victories and state violence divided the Islamic Republic between ascendant reformists and entrenched hierocrats. In the span of three years, the Islamic left, energized by an influx of young cadres, had revived its place in national politics. Presidential, local, and parliamentary elections propelled the movement from the margins of Iranian politics back into its core. There, Khatami and his fellow reformists rekindled the nation's debate about democracy, arguing for limits on clerical rule and expansion of popular sovereignty. Yet the recalcitrant traditionalists still obstructed these plans. Even their climactic victory in the 2000 elections confirmed the reformists' dilemma: Except under conditions of duress, the leader and Council of Guardians would disregard public opinion before abiding by it; even genuine election victories – and the leaders they produced – would be ignored unless determined protests reinforced them. And the Twenty-Third of May Front had already shown its reluctance to adopt confrontational tactics or respond to state repression with contentious collective action. When public clashes occurred, both Khamenei and Khatami stood together, calling for stability and calm – an arrangement that contained the reformists' mass constituencies and emboldened the traditionalists' agents (Brumberg 2001a: 393–394). The reform movement was popular enough that its exclusion from government triggered mass discontent, but once it had won control of the presidency and parliament, how much further could it advance? To Khatami and other prodemocracy leaders, the path ahead appeared perilous.

The Traditionalists Retaliate: Iran, 2000–2006

After the 2000 elections the reform movement's struggle revived the tension of earlier factional politics. Once again, the Islamic left commanded the republican (lower) levels of government; Mehdi Karrubi even regained his post as speaker of parliament. And once more, the traditionalist right controlled the leadership, Council of Guardians, and Assembly of Experts. In this situation of dual sovereignty, the leftists and traditionalists battled for control, with the reformists hoping to enhance the regime's democratic aspects and their opponents seeking to entrench hierocratic dominance.[14] The opposition's election victories in 1997, 1999, and 2000 posed anew the revolution's most basic questions: Who would rule, and on what basis? Did power reside with the people or the Shi'i religious hierarchy? In their attempt to resolve this debate, the advocates of popular sovereignty pursued a gradualist strategy, hoping that Khamenei and his associates would voluntarily accede to the groundswell of discontent and surrender some of their powers to the elected president and parliament. This posture, adopted out of fear of a second revolution or of mass bloodshed, eventually alienated the elected reformists from their constituencies, costing them what political power they had gained (Arjomand 2005: 509).

Reformist electoral victories did little to slow the traditionalists' campaign against civil society luminaries and prodemocracy newspapers (Ansari 2003: 62). On the contrary, each loss they suffered seemed only to make the traditionalists more vicious. By late 2000, nearly a hundred intellectuals and activists had been abducted and murdered by the *baseej*, *hizbollahis*, and other agents of domestic repression (Mudara 2000; Rajaee 2004: 164). Although their supporters in society bravely

---

[14] On the political arc of Iran's reform movement from 2000 to 2005, see, among other works, Boroumand and Boroumand (2000), Khosrokhavar (2004), Saghafi (2004), Semati (2004), McFaul and Milani (2004).

endured threats on their very lives, the Twenty-Third of May Front's officeholders pursued a parliamentary solution to the factional logjam. By 2001, an electorate that had been wildly enthusiastic about the reform movement was clearly standing out in front while its leaders bided their time. At a Khatami reelection rally led by the president's brother, MP Mohammed Reza Khatami, one student gave voice to a general concern among his compatriots. Observers recounted: "He asserted passionately that while the students support Khatami, their support is not without criticism. While the past four years may have called for quiet leadership, he continued, the reformist students now needed a leader who would more aggressively move reform forward." The student received a standing ovation from the crowd (Sohrabi and Keshavarzian 2001). His remarks reflected the distance between Khatami and his original constituents. During his first four years in office, the president had drifted away from the engaging rhetoric of his initial campaign, replacing dynamism with conservatism as he accommodated Khamenei and the traditionalists. In 2001 Khatami won a second term easily, but his candidacy no longer incited the enthusiasm and promise of his first run. Whereas his first candidacy had upset the system of having a designated front-runner, his reelection in the absence of a serious traditionalist challenger conformed to that earlier tradition. The upstart democracy advocate of 23 May 1997 had become the establishment choice (Saghafi 2002).

Even with a fresh mandate for change and a parliament loyal to his cause, the president proved unable to deliver on his initial promises to advance democracy and human rights in the country. Legislative proposals to redistribute power foundered against the unflinching Council of Guardians. Halfway through their term, the reformists in the Islamic Assembly passed two pieces of legislation designed to shift power to the regime's elected bodies: One bill increased the president's ability to prosecute violators of the constitution, whereas the other stripped away the Council of Guardians' ability to veto candidates in elections (Rezaei 2003: 45; Arjomand 2005: 514). Jointly, they would have augured an unprecedented codification of popular sovereignty, but their final passage depended on approval by the legislation's very target, the Council of Guardians itself. Having essentially banked on the council's members having a democratic epiphany or, at the very least, a certain modesty about openly rejecting democratic change, reform-minded MPs were chastened by the council's rejection of both measures (Ansari 2003: 62; *Financial Times*, 7 March 2003). Khatami then compounded this setback by reneging on his own promise to resign if the measures were not approved

(Akbarzadeh 2005: 31). As the traditionalists relished the confrontations their opponents eschewed, the reformists attempted to salvage their fading credibility, belatedly discussing a direct appeal to the people in the form of a referendum on the regime. It would be another year until they made any such move.

Local election results on 28 February 2003 signaled the costs of this strategy. Parliament, and not the Council of Guardians, oversaw candidate selection for the first time, allowing many previously barred leftist politicians to compete. Even after the reform camp entered the races in force, however, their candidates performed poorly in influential urban districts. Turnout in the larger cities averaged less than a third of the electorate, and, in a devastating reversal for the reformist camp, Tehran's entire municipal council went to affiliates of Khamenei. Voters in the capital chose as their new mayor a little-known former member of the Revolutionary Guards named Mahmoud Ahmadinejad (Arjomand 2005: 511–512). The reformists had become estranged from the students who had previously propelled their victories. When these same constituents protested publicly in the summer of 2003, the MPs "disowned" them (Arjomand 2005: 512). Iran's fledgling democratic movement had begun to fragment.

While the reformists hesitated, their opponents regrouped. In 2003, observers were already describing the situation as a political impasse: "[F]actional gridlock within the ruling clergy shows little sign of ending any time soon. For now, the Islamic Republic's leaders have calculated that stalemate is less costly than a decisive victory by one faction over the other. Khatami's camp cannot afford to quicken the pace of reform and the conservatives want to avoid resorting to repression on a massive scale that may incite civil war" (Baktiari and Vaziri 2003: 39). It seemed that Khatami and the Twenty-Third of May movement had morphed into the junior partners of their foes, perpetually subordinate to Leader Khamenei and the Council of Guardians. Another, slightly more hopeful, view was that the traditionalists' power was "primarily negative," and that they were best at "clog[ging] the system's arteries" (Ehsani 2004).

Even this obstructionist capacity could be used offensively, as the traditionalists again demonstrated in 2004. The reformist MPs' failure to effect significant change rebounded on them when the council rejected some 3,600 of 8,200 applicants (44 percent) for candidacy in the upcoming election, including 80 incumbents from the Twenty-Third of May Front (Ehsani 2004; Rajaee 2004: 164; Arjomand 2005: 503). With their political posts jeopardized, the MPs staged a sit-in within parliament to protest the Council of Guardians' decisions. Driven by the urgency of political survival, the reformists implored their supporters to rally (Saghafi 2004). The student movement, earlier abandoned by the same leaders who now clamored for help, was indifferent to the reformists' pleas, issuing statements but not moving to act (Arjomand 2005: 503). As Morad Saghafi put it, "Even the supportive communiqué pointed out that the deputies themselves were primarily to blame for their predicament, as they had failed the 27 million voters who had elevated them to power by having compromised repeatedly with the unelected conservatives" (2004). Stranded in a lame-duck legislature with no hope of reelection, the leaders of the Twenty-Third of May Front resigned their posts in one final protest and then stood aside. Simultaneously, Khatami capitulated to Khamenei and agreed that his minister of the interior would hold the elections on schedule (Arjomand 2005: 503).

Despite the reformists' exclusion from the 2004 elections, 24 million voters (over 50 percent of the electorate) turned out, and the tradition-alists won a supermajority in the Islamic Assembly (Saghafi 2004). The results recapitulated the lopsided outcome of 1992, with the Islamic left again purged from parliament, though this time their fate was largely of their own making. After a series of propitious victories in the late 1990s, the reform movement failed because its leaders overestimated the will-ingness of powerholders to relinquish their control voluntarily. Unwilling to risk public conflict and hopeful that Khamenei's group would sim-ply accept democratization, Khatami's partisans demurred from mobiliz-ing their base against the traditionalists. As Mohammed Reza Khatami described it, Iran's moderate democrats had chosen to outlast their rulers rather than oust them:

Some people say the only means left is violence and revolution, but we don't agree. If we organize ourselves and our supporters better, [hard-liners] will slowly give up. Something like the Spain model, where Franco ruled like a dictator until his last day. But after his death the society transformed so much that reform took root and the system became democratic – without any bloodshed. We need to look at such models and work toward them (*Newsweek International*, 1 March 2004).

Given the reformists' aversion to sudden change, it is little surprise that the discontented masses who had earlier delivered the electoral triumphs of 1997 and 2000 ultimately outpaced the supposed vanguards of their movement. Mohammed Reza Khatami's remarks allude to the calcula-tions behind this abortive strategy, a preference for accommodation over confrontation that cost Iran's reformists an opportunity for democratiza-tion.

While the Twenty-Third of May Front was clearly more diffident than its eager supporters, what could be precipitously judged a lack of courage may also be seen as an abundance of prudence. Given that Iranians may vote as early as age fifteen and more than half the population was born after the revolution, many of the reform movement's supporters have no memory of the regime's formative tribulations or, for that matter, its protracted conflict with Iraq (Kazemi 2003: 90). Those same historic experiences ingrained a deep skepticism and fear about the risks of radical, rapid change and violent conflict in the politicians elected in 2000.[15] Urged on by their followers, these leaders were uncertain what outcome might follow a complete upheaval of the system. With postrevolutionary demagoguery and instability in mind, they took an approach that was conservative in the most literal sense: They tried to curb autocracy while preserving the system.

Presidential elections in June 2005 brought the dismal sequel to the reformists' ejection from parliament the prior year. Khatami, already discredited by his failure to deliver on the pledges of his earlier campaigns, was constitutionally limited to two consecutive terms and thus could not make a new electoral bid. The contours of the historically competitive race for his successor signaled that public opinion had sufficiently shifted away from the reformists' position that even a renewed partnership between Khatami's movement and the ubiquitous Rafsanjani could not keep the presidency from the traditionalist right (*New York Times*, 20 June 2005). Amid a diverse field of eight contenders (one of whom dropped out), the five leading candidates spanned the spectrum of Iran's factions (Keshavarzian 2005). Karrubi represented the Islamic left currently organized in the Association of Combatant Clerics, but reformist Mostafa Moin also ran on the left. Providing a nonclerical voice for reform, Moin carried the mantle of the Islamic Iran Participation Front, the umbrella political group that sprang from the Twenty-Third of May Front. Thus, two Khatami supporters were running against each other. The traditionalist right also fielded two candidates: Police general Mohammad Baqir Qalibaf and Tehran mayor Ahmadinejad. In this politically bifurcated field, Rafsanjani positioned himself as a compromise candidate for pragmatic development.

To the surprise of many, his centrism proved uncompelling to the electorate. Results from the first round of voting on 17 June eliminated both

---

[15] Interview with Morad Saghafi, 20 August 2002, Tehran; Interview with Amir Ali Nourbaksh, 27 August 2002, Tehran.

reformist candidates and put second-place finisher Ahmadinejad, with 19 percent of the vote, in an unexpected run-off against Rafsanjani, who garnered 21 percent. Driven by immediate economic necessities, working-class voters flocked to the plainspoken Ahmadinejad and the unpretentious Karrubi, who came in a close third with 17 percent of the vote.[16] The reformist majorities of 1997 and 2000 had shattered.[17] Voters in the cities and countryside defied calls by some on the left for a boycott and turned out in strong numbers (turnout was 61 percent), but they did not rally behind a single reformist candidate. Neither did they oscillate to the traditionalist right, whose expected frontrunner, Qalibaf, captured only 15 percent of the vote (Ehsani 2005). It was candidates' economic positions that determined their fate. Populism, not democracy, swayed Iran's voters in 2005: Appeals to the lower classes and pledges of government relief for the unemployed and indigent resonated far more profoundly than debates over political reform. In this context Ahmadinejad excelled by using simplistic social justice slogans that sidestepped the tough economic decisions facing Iranian policy-makers. In the 24 June run-off Ahmadinejad defeated the veteran Rafsanjani. Victory by the uncouth but popular Ahmadinejad (he won with 61 percent of the vote) carried significant political repercussions, as it concluded the traditionalist right's takeover of Iran's republican institutions (*Newshour*, 27 June 2005).

The traditionalists' comeback in 2003–2005 was largely a by-product of their opponents' failure to effect change. Khamenei's faction had made inroads into cultivating a popular following: Ahmadinejad's populist rhetoric presents one facet of this appeal for support. But the traditionalists' primary constituents are still found in the *bazaar* and the *bonyads* (*New York Times*, 3 July 2005). Protecting both from state intervention necessitates secreting away revenue needed to develop social safety nets for the most needy portions of the population. Given these constraints, it is unlikely that Khamenei's faction will deliver on the new president's campaign promises (Arjomand 2005: 517). With no serious

---

[16] After losing a spot in the runoff by less than one million votes, Karrubi cried foul, claiming that the Council of Guardians and Revolutionary Guards has manipulated the vote in Ahmadinejad's favor. Moin's campaign staff launched similar accusations, saying they had observed affiliates of the Council of Guardians intervening in the tally in some areas (*New York Times*, 19 June 2005).

[17] The reform movement had previously depended on four constituencies: the urban-based intelligentsia, students, women, and the poor (Kazemi 2003: 90–91). Many lower-income voters, women among them, backed Ahmadinejad, thus depriving the Islamic left of a large mass of prior supporters.

domestic economic reform program on their agenda, they are more likely to continue relying on international sources of legitimacy, framing themselves as the defenders of Iranian self-determination in the face of Western aggression.

The reformists' retreat had occurred amid tempestuous relations between Iran and the United States. In fall 2001, Iran's leaders expressed sympathy for the 9/11 victims, supported the American-led overthrow of the Taliban regime (long a thorn in Tehran's side), and supported relief and rescue operations. The two nations continued cooperating through early January 2002, when the Iranian government pledged $560 million for Afghan reconstruction at an international donors conference (Akbarzadeh 2005: 34). Yet this tacit alliance was abruptly curtailed when President Bush capitalize distanced the United States from Iran in his State of the Union address on the twenty-ninth of that same month. The president famously placed Iran, along with North Korea and Iraq, among the primary dangers to international security, referring obliquely to the Islamic Republic's then-covert nuclear program: "Iran aggressively pursues these weapons [of mass destruction] and exports terror, while an unelected few repress the Iranian people's hope for freedom.... States like these, and their terrorist allies, constitute an axis of evil, arming to threaten the peace of the world.... In any of these cases, the price of indifference would be catastrophic (Bush 2002)."In 2002, while the implications of this speech for U.S. foreign policy were unclear, some in Iran embraced the idea of an American-led invasion that would overthrow the clerical autocrats as the Taliban had been ousted in Afghanistan. The prospect briefly held the promise of squeezing the traditionalists out of power. (Among the political elite, though, Bush's talk of imposed regime change stirred dread of the kind of mass chaos that nearly all of Iran's factions have sought to avoid.) In any event, that possibility soon disappeared. As the Bush administration's crosshairs settled on Iraq in fall 2002, Khamenei and his colleagues could rest assured that the United States did not constitute an immediate military threat. The invasion of Iraq and commitment of some 130,000 U.S. troops in March 2003 proved the traditionalists had dodged the regime change bullet. Between autumn 2001 and spring 2003, the United States committed its military to removing two of Iran's historic nemeses while leaving the Islamic Republic's regime unscathed.

In February 2003, President Khatami announced that the government had uranium enrichment plants in Natanz and several other cities. Khatami invited the head of the International Atomic Energy Agency

(IAEA), Dr. Mohammed El Baradei, to visit these sites (Sahimi 2003). El Baradei's team inspected Iran's plants in late February 2003, and that fall the IAEA called on Iran to disclose all information about its nuclear energy program. In subsequent years, the Iranian regime has selectively permitted monitoring and inspection of its facilities, which all of its leaders maintain are for domestic, civilian purposes. Meanwhile, the United States, joined by Israel and some members of the European Union, has accused Iran of pursuing a nuclear weapons program and called for a halt to further uranium enrichment activities. Under international scrutiny but confident they face no serious military threat, Khamenei and the traditionalist leadership began practicing a kind of low-scale brinkmanship on the nuclear issue, stoking American hostility to boost their flagging legitimacy with the Iranian people (Rezaei 2003: 42). Because the overwhelming majority of Iranians regard nuclear power, if not nuclear weapons, as a national right, the advancement of Iran's nuclear program is one area where even the most rigid leaders are aligned with public opinion (Gheissari and Nasr 2005: 186–187).

The axis of evil speech, the occupation of Iraq, and heightened Western scrutiny on the nuclear issue all benefited the opponents of democratic reform in Iran. By concentrating Iranians' minds on pressing matters of national security, they further weakened the already feeble position of Khatami and his confederates. With their country flanked by two vivid examples of state failure and social turmoil, Iranians became anxious about the prospect of catastrophic domestic instability, whether from a foreign invasion or an indigenous uprising. This anxiety undermined the Twenty-Third of May Front's social support base while exacerbating its leaders' own hesitancy (Rajaee 2004: 169). Thus, an array of national security concerns made mass mobilization, already far from the reformists' agenda, nearly inconceivable. America's axis of evil posture did not throw Iran's nascent democracy movement off course; rather, U.S. policies toward Iran and its neighbors further confined reformists to the course of moderate, evolutionary change that they had been timidly treading for years. The current policies of President Ahmadinejad present the culmination of the traditionalists' strategy to obscure domestic policy failures with international defiance.

Conclusion

Given the setbacks Iranian democrats have suffered during the past years, the regime of Khamenei and Ahmadinejad might appear at first glance an invulnerable monolith. The bellicose posture of traditionalist Iranian leaders toward the United States and the pursuit of a nuclear program reinforce this interpretation, particularly when they are received by Western audiences often entirely unaware of the criticisms those leaders face inside Iran. Yet such a reading of Iranian politics minimizes the substantial levels of public elite and mass competition that the country has experienced in the previous decade. The Iranian regime is one of the most repressive in the Middle East, but it is also the only authoritarian regime in the region that presently faces a viable alternative alliance of elites and constituents. Iran's reform movement has demonstrated its strength not only through elections under disadvantageous conditions but also through the defiance of its authors, intellectuals, and politicians. As analyst Kaveh Ehsani remarked after the reformists' early defeat in the 2005 presidential elections: "[N]o single political trend enjoys hegemony.... Barring a disastrous foreign military intervention, the path of democracy in Iran will continue to be tortuous, but real" (2005).

In contrast to the durable dictatorships of Egypt and Malaysia, Iran's regime has been both more contested and more repressive – politically more vulnerable to its opponents, who have periodically entered the halls of power, yet precisely for that reason more openly hostile toward its own populace. The array of specialized terms attached to the Iranian regime attests to the ongoing tug-of-war between competing factions, a seemingly unending struggle that distinguishes the Islamic Republic from more consolidated autocracies: "[D]issonant institutionalization" (Brumberg 2001b), "suspended equilibrium" (Kamrava and Hassan-Yari 2004), "dual sovereignty,"[18] and similar terms evoke the tension in and irresolution of Iran's political regime.

Viewed in broad comparative terms, the period of reformist-led government constituted a "democratizing moment" (Yashar 1997: 17–18) or, as I have contended, an opportunity for democratization that appears to have passed but may recur. Although traditionalists presently hold the upper hand, neither the advocates nor the opponents of hierocracy have decisively defeated the other. Moreover, Khamenei again seems bent on concentrating power among a narrow clique of personal supporters rather than investing in an organization that could transform current alliances into sustainable partnerships (Arjomand 2005: 516). These conditions open up the prospect of a viable indigenous push for democratization the next time discontented ruling elites realign. Such factionalism would

---

[18] Interview with Hadi Semati, 6 October 2002, Tehran.

be the natural continuation of a long-standing trend of public leadership disputes and polarization.

Ongoing elite factionalism in Iran is a direct descendant of postrevolutionary debates about the regime's accountability to the public: When those disputes persisted after the regime had defeated its nonclerical opponents, they undermined the possibility that the regime would be able to build a cohesive elite. Given the inherently contentious nature of politics in a regime's highest echelon, organizations like ruling parties are an essential means for preventing policy debates from escalating into political disputes; correspondingly, the absence of political mechanisms for resolving elite conflict is sufficient to drive elite defections. In the absence of organizations like ruling parties, elite relations take on a factionalized quality, with self-interested politicians realigning based on the exigencies of the moment instead of holding together collectively as members of a long-term coalition. These realignments make the conventional boundary between insiders and oppositionists vulnerable to challenge: Erstwhile loyalists may seek new tactical partners among excluded activists. Such was the case in Iran in the mid- to late 1990s. The Islamic left–modernist right alliance provided an opportunity for galvanizing the public and challenging the traditionalist right. While this opportunity was a structural opening – largely absent in durable dictatorships like Egypt or Malaysia – its ultimate effect depended on the attitude of would-be democratizers toward exploiting the opening and overturning the system. Hence, the absence of parties is sufficient for elite defections but insufficient for democratization.

When counteralliances confront the regime directly using the mobilized constituencies that earlier propelled their electoral victory, they may finally translate popular support into political power. Success depends on the opposition's readiness to clash with the regime and revisit foundational questions about its composition and function. Iranian reformists were not so bold, and in their hesitancy they suffered a dismal retreat. That experience imparts a general lesson about the prospects of democratization in the context of weak ruling institutions: So long as a regime's foes confine their struggle to the strictures of conventional politics, they risk squandering the opportunity presented by elite defections and counteralliances. Hovering in a limbo between tactical electoral successes and programmatic political failure, the Iranian reform movement soon lost the institutional terrain it had captured and the popular support that had enabled its revival.

Although the window of opportunity for political reform seems to have closed, if it reopens in the near future it will likely be by virtue of the same internal discord that has challenged the regime since its founding. Early signs of internal tension suggest that the traditionalists' dominance has not brought an end to factionalism and elite conflict. Just as the elections returned the Islamic left to the marginal position they had held after the 1992 polls, they also positioned the right wing for a fresh round of internecine conflict unbridled by any unifying organization. Thus, the reentrenchment of Khamenei and the traditionalist right adds another chapter to Iran's saga of weak institutions and elite factionalism. If the reformists or their political successors are to succeed, their success will depend on the very kinds of open confrontation they earlier avoided: the mobilization of popular support to challenge incumbent autocrats and strip them of power. Chapter 6 returns to the Philippine case and analyzes the course not yet taken by Iran's gradualist democrats.

6

Confrontation and Democratization

The Philippines during the Third Wave

In contrast to durable authoritarianism in Egypt and Malaysia and a squandered opportunity for democratization in Iran, the Philippines provides a case of authoritarian breakdown and democratization. The movement to end Marcos's dictatorship combined elites and mass support in an inspiring push to restore representative government. As in the three cases already examined, this dramatic outcome was one effect of an extended process whose roots long predated the third wave. Marcos suffered from the same institutional deficit that plagued prior generations of Philippine leaders: The nation's political groups did not provide a stable home for elite coalitions. Indeed, Marcos's own successful jump from the Liberal Party to the Nacionalista Party in pursuit of a 1965 presidential nomination epitomized the elite disunity that plagued the Philippines. Once he controlled the country, Marcos let his coalitional ties atrophy as he concentrated power among a much smaller set of clients drawn from his friends, family, and home region. It is in this context – the freezing of the Nacionalista Party, the privileging of personalism over political affiliation, and the subversion of accepted hierarchies for advancement – that one must situate any understanding of Marcos's regime and its eventual downfall.

The tale of elite defections and counteralliances in the Philippines adds another layer to our understanding of the role of moderation in democratization. The country's pivotal elites, those political leaders whose counterparts in Egypt and Malaysia continued to support the rulers, assembled apart from Marcos years before the president's final election in 1986 (Bermeo 1997: 315–316). The counteralliance of elites and oppositionists was therefore out in front, publicly criticizing the regime ahead of the violent anti-Marcos campaign of the New People's Army (NPA). In this way, the NPA's radicalism pushed the centrist alliance toward power rather than frightening its members back into the regime. Moderation was also critical to the counteralliance's emergence and growth in the wake of the 1978 elections: Its moderate political stance positioned the group as a viable alternative to Marcos, friendly to both domestic capitalists and U.S. interests. That posture proved compatible with contentious collective action. Whereas Iranian democrats balked at public protest, the anti-Marcos movement mobilized its millions of supporters into the streets of the capital, overwhelming Marcos's military forces and seizing power from him.

Opportunists become Oppositionists: The Philippines, 1979–1984

Marcos's New Society Movement (KBL) followed the NP's demise much as the Society of Combatant Clergy succeeded Iran's IRP: It was a faction grouped around the ruler in the wake of a defunct party. By tightening his patronage network and overturning established political hierarchies, Marcos showed that he favored narrow factional solidarity over coalitional breadth. The former assistant to the KBL secretary-general described party caucuses as managed affairs: "A lot of those meetings were sort of scripted.... The meetings or caucuses ran in the direction that Marcos wanted."[1] A long-time opposition leader described the climate as "dictatorial," adding, "Marcos did not brook dissent."[2] Defense minister Enrile recounted the president's seemingly deliberate divisiveness: "As a practical politician what [Marcos] did was to organize a party represented by people who were more or less sympathetic to him and to his political thinking and policies. In effect he said, 'Let's draw the line. Those who are with me, let them come and join this new political group. Those who are against [me], let them stay out.'"[3] This style alienated career politicians who would otherwise have remained loyal to the regime. Leaders like the Laurel brothers, who found themselves at odds with the ruler, feared perpetual marginalization. Enrile depicted the Laurels' dispute with Marcos as one of "personal relations": "The Laurels felt that they were the Mr. Nacionalistas and here is a newcomer from another party, who happened to become president of the country,

---

[1] Interview with Gabriel Claudio, 26 May 2003, Manila.
[2] Interview with Aquilino Pimentel, 21 May 2003, Manila.
[3] Interview with Juan Ponce Enrile, 28 May 2003, Manila.

lording it over them. And so they did not like that."[4] Jose Laurel Jr. may have reflected the feeling of many disgruntled elites with his comment: "I am fighting Marcos because I have an investment in him. I was hoping to collect but I have waited long enough" (Thompson 1995: 103).

The Laurels and their peers reaped a poor return on their investment in Marcos because the president directed his attention to a much smaller circle of friends, close relatives, and compatriots from his home province of Ilocos Norte (Overholt 1986: 1147). The Philippine political system had never been institutionalized around policy programs or an organizing ideology, but it had provided a disorderly system for elites to jockey for the top patronage opportunities of the capital. Two parties and regular presidential elections offered advancement opportunities through the clientelism that linked traditional national elites to local networks. This rowdy incarnation of presidentialism had managed to diffuse power around the country among the archipelago nation's seventy-eight provinces and thirteen regions. When a region was excluded from power, presidents often faced violent uprisings. During Marcos's regime, though, political exclusion became a major concern. Not since the time of Quezon had the presidency been controlled by elites from a single area for so long; no two consecutive presidents had been from the same region, let alone the same province (see Table 6.1).

Marcos not only favored Ilocos Norte and a few other strategic areas such as the capital, he also targeted his opponents by neglecting or abusing their bases of power, as William Overholt describes: "The Visayas, home of Marcos's former rival, Vice President Lopez, and of major political competitor [Sergio] Osmeña [III], were neglected by the regime and ruthlessly exploited by the sugar monopoly. . . . The provinces and regions or other political competitors were also systematically starved" (1986: 1147). Whereas a national ruling party could have ameliorated this bias, Marcos's New Society Movement compounded it, promoting Ilocanos at the expense of career politicians from critical areas such as Cebu and Batangas. Aggravating personalization with unprecedented regionalization, the president alienated hordes of potential supporters.

The opportunistic elites whom Marcos distanced were not natural opponents of his rule. Defectors who gathered around Salvador Laurel were more worried about political self-preservation than democratization. Nonetheless, they pragmatically promoted change to protect their interests. Their concerns broadly resembled the criticisms Team B lodged

[4] Interview with Enrile, 28 May 2003, Manila.

TABLE 6.1. *Regional Backgrounds of Philippine Presidents*

Name	Term of Office	Party	Region of Origin	Province of Origin
Manuel Quezon	1935–1944	NP	Central Luzon (III)	Tayabas
Sergio Osmeña	1944–1946	NP	Central Visayas (VII)	Cebu
Jose P. Laurel*	1943–1945	NP	Southern Tagalog (IV)	Batangas
Manuel Roxas	1946–1948	LP	Western Visayas (VI)	Capiz
Elpidio Quirino	1948–1953	LP	Ilocos Region (I)	Ilocos Sur
Ramon Magsaysay	1953–1957	NP	Central Luzon (III)	Zambales
Carlos Garcia	1957–1961	NP	Central Visayas (VII)	Bohol
Diosdado Macapagal	1961–1965	LP	Central Luzon (III)	Pambanga
Ferdinand Marcos	1965–1986	NP	Ilocos Region (I)	Ilocos Norte

* Served as president under Japanese occupation during Quezon and Osmeña's presidencies-in-exile.
Source: http://www.gov.ph/aboutphil/presidents.asp;
http://www.philippinecentral.com/presidents.html. Accessed on 2 August 2006.

against Mahathir in Malaysia; however, unlike Musa, Laurel could not use a party organization to redress his group's grievances. Instead, the group turned directly to the public arena of elections, its traditional area of experience.

A veteran party leader himself, Laurel had stuck with Marcos after the declaration of martial law and took a seat in the interim legislature as a KBL candidate in 1978. But the KBL functioned as Marcos's instrument for winning elections, and Laurel saw Marcos favoring close friends and relatives over seasoned politicians. Such behavior followed Quezon and Osmeña's tradition of using loyal followers to fend off more senior rivals who could pose a leadership challenge (McCoy 1988: 117, 132). Dissatisfied, Laurel began reorienting in 1980, first by supporting a local-level anti-Marcos campaign and then by formally breaking with the KBL.

Like Musa's group in Johor, Laurel and his associates soon demonstrated the power of elite defectors to make electoral breakthroughs. In January 1980, Marcos called local elections on short notice, allowing for a constricted three-week campaign period. Salvador Laurel's nephew, Joey Laurel, ran for and won the governorship of their family's home province, Batangas, defeating a KBL partisan in the process. Salvador Laurel credited his nephew's eventual triumph amid disadvantageous conditions to a combination of grassroots engagement and high-level negotiations (Joacquin 1985: 270–271). David Wurfel similarly notes the power of the Laurels' political machine in accomplishing the "spectacular opposition success" in Batangas (Wurfel 1988: 209).

This episode proved a local harbinger of how Marcos's disgruntled defectors could undermine the regime's control and accomplish what Aquino had failed to do in Manila in 1978. In one village, Laurel recounts, voters physically obstructed soldiers who attempted to drive off with the ballot boxes (Joaquin 1985: 268). Refusing to be disfranchised, the crowd even began to stone the soldiers. The elder Laurel contacted defense minister Enrile and warned that the conflict could escalate if the ballot boxes were not returned. Without further interference, the boxes were then transported to the counting station, where they delivered a substantial victory to the anti-KBL candidates, including Joey Laurel. In other areas of the country, such as the southern island of Mindanao, opposition success was similarly hard-fought. Only two anti-Marcos candidates won mayoral elections in Mindanao, one of whom, Aquilino Pimentel, recalled: "We manned the precincts, personally and physically.... [We] prepared [our supporters] beforehand with flashlights and even sticks to hit the heads of the fraudulent manipulators of elections."[5]

To Salvador Laurel, the election marked a watershed: Foes of Marcos could gain ground in elections if they could neutralize the regime's intervention. He reasoned, "If we had not resisted, we would have been trampled on; we would have been cheated, as the voters in Manila were cheated in 1978" (Joaquin 1985: 270). Encouraged by his nephew's win, Laurel began to build a political alliance. In February 1980, he resigned from all of his commitments in the New Society Movement and affiliated with the legislature's non-KBL bloc. He declared: "Henceforth, I shall take my place in the ranks of the Opposition into which the Nacionalista Party and other political groups not affiliated with the KBL have been converted. If, as reported, the KBL has been accredited as a political party, it is necessary for me to sever all relations therewith, and to resume exclusive representation of the Nacionalista Party" (Joaquin 1985: 274). The senator joined a collection of anti-Marcos figures intent on ending the dictatorship. He recalled: "At the meeting the Liberals and Nacionalistas agreed to join forces. We formed a council of leaders under the co-chairmanship of the two party presidents and composed of the heads of the various opposition groups" (Joaquin 1985: 271). Laurel and his fellows from the NP soon gained recognition as forming a "major part of the opposition" (Wurfel 1988: 209).

5 Interview with Pimentel, 21 May 2003, Manila.

The incipient counteralliance of former Marcos partisans and long-time regime opponents formalized its organization on 29 August 1980. Eight organizations, including the Laurels' Nacionalista Party faction, issued a "Covenant for Freedom" that called for the "termination of the Marcos dictatorship" and the "dismantling of martial rule," declaring, "Never in our history have so many Filipinos been arbitrarily arrested, detained and tortured – many of them vanishing without a trace – than during this repressive and repugnant regime."[6] In addition to the Laurel brothers and other Nacionalistas, signatories included former president Diosdado Macapagal of the Liberal Party and prominent Liberal leader Gerardo Roxas, son of the late Manuel Roxas (Wurfel 1988: 209). Benigno Aquino endorsed the declaration from his hospital bed in the United States, where he was recuperating after heart surgery.[7] The collected leaders called for national elections to "establish a truly democratic and representative system of government."[8] The declaration created a common political program for a range of anti-Marcos organizers. In all, twelve opposition groups seeking to restore constitutional democracy joined together as the United Democratic Opposition (Unido).

Unido gave outcasts from Marcos's personalistic autocracy a channel for their discontent. Later defectors from the regime included former governor Rene Espina and former congressman Antonio Cuenco, who ran for office in 1978 under the KBL banner but lost due to lack of support from Marcos (Thompson 1995: 208, fn. 30). For Cuenco, the Laurels' break from Marcos encouraged others to realign and oppose the president: "We were disorganized in the beginning. . . . We thought everything was hopeless until some brave souls, like Jerry Roxas, the Laurels, who regretted their association with Marcos very much . . . became very active."[9] Another belated oppositionist was ex–Marcos cabinet member Ernesto Maceda. Maceda viewed electoral challenge as the only viable path to change and discounted the support behind more radical resistance movements working outside the system (Goodno 1991: 84). Many others shared this view, and in its formative stage Unido benefited from its explicitly moderate approach to change. "We [could not] support Marcos;

---

[6] "Opposition Party Leaders Issue Joint 'Manifesto,'" *AFP*, 29 August 1980, FBIS-APA-80-170, 29 August 1980.

[7] "Endorsed by Aquino," *AFP*, 29 August 1980, FBIS-APA-80-170, 29 August 1980.

[8] "Opposition Party Leaders Issue Joint 'Manifesto,'" *AFP*, 29 August 1980, FBIS-APA-80-170, 29 August 1980.

[9] Interview with Antonio Cuenco, 20 May 2003, Manila.

[nor could] we support a violent upheaval in the country," oppositionist Pimentel reflected, "so we tried to provide a third [option] – an alternative to forces that were banging against each other."[10]

Unido's initial progress was slow. Much like the Executives of Reconstruction in Iran, the movement gradually built momentum as it strategically engaged in elections and expanded its base. Marcos formally ended martial law soon after Ronald Reagan's inauguration as U.S. president in January 1981, but he made no major concessions to Unido's demands. His primary audience was the American government. Working to maintain the democratic ruse he had begun in 1978, Marcos held a national referendum on expanding his own powers and proposed a contested presidential election. These superficial measures won the accolades of the U.S. House of Representatives, which passed a resolution praising Marcos for ending martial law, and from Vice President George Bush, who toasted to Marcos, "We love your adherence to democratic principle and to the democratic processes" (Bonner 1987: 308–309).

Less sanguine than Marcos's foreign patrons, Unido leaders saw Marcos's proposals as a transparent bid to bolster his already extensive powers and even position his wife, Imelda, to assume the presidency if he were incapacitated. After unanimously boycotting the April plebiscite on constitutional changes, they debated how to approach the presidential elections (Wurfel 1988: 210). Laurel favored participating because even a losing run would position him ahead of rivals in a future, post-Marcos race (Thompson 1995: 107). Conditions for the presidential election of June 1981 were too restrictive, however, for even the ambitious Laurel. When Marcos trimmed the allotted campaigning time from two months to a matter of weeks, Laurel and Aquino agreed that Unido should boycott, as the abridged preelection period was too brief for any serious attempt at recruitment or awareness-raising (Joaquin 1985: 278). In comparison to the 1990 opposition boycott in Egypt and the Iranian left's 1996 boycott, Unido's decision yielded the intended effect: Marcos's main "challenger" was a regime affiliate, Alejo Santos. Denied the chance to steal victory from a real opponent, Marcos won reelection with a declared 88 percent share of the vote but gained only the thinnest layer of legitimacy in the process (Hartmann, Hassall, and Santos 2001: 228).

Marcos would need to concede more to his challengers before they would return to the electoral field. In fact, many of Marcos's critics on the left completely disdained the idea of electoral competition and non-revolutionary change. During the post-1972 period, the number of armed

---

[10] Interview with Pimentel, 21 May 2003, Manila.

communists in the Philippines grew from an estimated eight hundred people in a small portion of the countryside – the miniscule force on the basis of which Marcos had originally justified martial law – to become the 20,000 strong New People's Army (Overholt 1986: 1140; Thompson 1996: 184). After a decade of living under martial law, many Filipinos had begun to see the NPA and other revolutionary movements as capable challengers to Marcos's rule, and the country's Communist Party grew to become "the largest nongoverning Communist party in Southeast Asia" (Wurfel 1988: 223). The centrist Unido clarified the choices before the country: Maintenance of the dictatorship, violent overthrow by the communist army, or a middle course in which the leader would be removed while the overall system remained intact.

In the two years after the presidential election, Laurel and Aquino struggled to weaken Marcos while competing with the radical Left for popular support. Political channels were severely constricted, but the movement indirectly benefited from the worldwide recession, which hit the Philippines especially hard and brought fence-sitting businessmen over to the anti-Marcos movement (Overholt 1986: 1142). After living in exile in America for years, Aquino opted to return to Manila in August 1983. On arrival, he was shot and killed on the tarmac by an assassin linked to President Marcos. Already widely respected for his early opposition to Marcos, Aquino's stature reached mythic proportions after his death. Attendance at his funeral was unprecedented, greater than "at the Pope's visit, MacArthur's sentimental return [at the end of World War II], and Magsaysay's funeral," according to Overholt (1986: 1157). The assassination was an "eye opener" for Filipinos, concentrating attention on the regime's deterioration and brutality (DeGuzman and Tancangco 1986: 134; Overholt 1986: 1156).[11] "It jarred the sensibilities of the people," reflected former defense minister Enrile. "Many people felt that the country was no longer safe, that nobody was safe."[12] Marcos's opponent soon turned Aquino's fate into a rallying cry: "After the death of Ninoy we were able to galvanize the opposition.... We used that as a campaign issue. 'Justice for Ninoy.'"[13]

Unido's political influence grew as discontent with Marcos rose. The group began to leverage its position as opposition vanguard to improve its electoral chances. Professing a program of nonviolent reform from within the system, Unido provided a moderate alternative to the torpid

[11] Interview with Rudolph Albano, 26 May 2003, Manila.
[12] Interview with Enrile, 28 May 2003, Manila.
[13] Interview with Salvador Laurel, 30 May 2003, Manila.

KBL, on the one hand, and the violent radicals, on the other. This centrism had attracted numerous domestic politicians to Unido's cause, and it soon influenced the opposition's relations internationally. The Laurels cultivated an image of gradualism and moderation in communications with the U.S. Central Intelligence Agency. Marcos had already been diagnosed with a fatal form of lupus. If the CIA saw the president as weakening, the agency might encourage Marcos to cede power to a viable alternative group or at least push him to allow the opposition a greater opportunity to participate within the system (Thompson 1995: 107).

This strategy paid off when the Marcos regime recognized Unido as the Philippines' dominant opposition party, thereby granting the movement an official capacity to observe elections. In April 1984, three members of the regime-allied Commission on Elections (COMELEC) determined that Unido had "gained the widest public...[and had] the capability of a political organization to wage a bona fide nationwide campaign as shown...by the number of political parties which have joined forces with them, with candidates in all regions known and identified with the opposition."[14] The formal designation granted Unido personnel who could attend the vote counting and certification process, an advance that enabled Laurel and his partners to compete in parliamentary elections in 1984 in a way LABAN could not in 1978 (Tancangco 1988: 101, 105).

At the same time that Unido was developing as a political counteralliance, Philippine military leaders were gathering against Marcos. General Fidel Ramos and defense minister Enrile balked at Marcos's penchant for deprofessionalizing the country's military, historically a much more stable and respected institution than the parties. Marcos had corrupted the military by appointing Ilocanos and family friends to top posts, passing over Western-trained career military men like Ramos (Overholt 1986: 1149, 1152). Chafing at the president's nepotism, Ramos and Enrile began planning to retake the military and overthrow the regime. Their organization, RAM (Reform the Armed forces Movement), would eventually depend on the opposition into accomplishing its goal.

Election Monitors and Political Momentum: The Philippines, 1984

Like the Iranian leaders who craved high electoral turnouts to validate their own power, Marcos judged that elections against his opponents

---

[14] "Unido Viewed as Dominant Opposition Party," *Bulletin Today*, 15 April 1984, FBIS-APA-84-075, 17 April 1984.

would help sustain his "new constitutional order": By going through the motions of democracy, the president hoped to ward off political and economic ruin (Wurfel 1988: 233). Aquino's assassination had left American officials concerned and foreign investors anxious. As Enrile remarks, the escalation of political criticism drove economic difficulties far beyond manageable levels. On their own, capital flight and mounting deficits were "nothing," but *"because* of the assassination of Ninoy Aquino," Enrile explained, these problems were "exacerbated."[15] In March 1984, President Reagan referred obliquely to the tragedy, cautioning Marcos that "continued movement toward fully functioning democratic institutions appropriate to the Philippines is the key to the rebuilding of both economic and political confidence after the difficulties of the last months" (Munro 1984: 176). Marcos responded by holding parliamentary elections, which offered a reinvigorated Unido a fresh chance to challenge the dictator.

Once more, the radical anti-Marcos opposition perceived the elections as a tool for the regime's rejuvenation, not its reform. But Laurel thought the pressures on Marcos made these elections a good opportunity for competition and political change (Wurfel 1988: 284). Unido's decision to participate distanced it further from the communist forces in the eyes of the United States, which was wary of a communist takeover in the Philippines. The promise of a contest mobilized the public, and large numbers turned out to vote. James Goodno has observed: "[E]lections held a fascination for most Filipinos. They provided the sporting core of Philippine political culture" (1991: 85). That interest drove millions to participate despite the fraud of 1978 and 1981 and the high probability it would be repeated. For the first time, however, Unido fielded monitors on the ground. Allied with the National Citizens Movement for Free Elections (Namfrel), a domestic group affiliated with the Asia Foundation, an American NGO, Unido fought to neutralize Marcos's manipulation.

The success of Unido in the election, in which it contested nearly all of the available 183 seats, justified Laurel's hopes. Where Unido activists thwarted the regime's attempts to rig the voting, opposition candidates tended to win; as in 1980, they were most successful in the home areas of their own leaders. Unido and Namfrel exposed electoral fraud in urban centers and much of the countryside. In metropolitan Manila, the site of the 1978 "shutout," the United Democratic Opposition won 15 of the city's 22 seats by invoking Aquino's memory. "Our campaign line [was] 'If you want to punish the administration for what it did to Ninoy

---

[15] Interview with Enrile, 28 May 2003, Manila.

[Benigno Aquino], vote for the Opposition!'" recalled Laurel. It helped that Corazon Aquino, Benigno Aquino's widow, and her children campaigned for Unido. Election monitoring also contributed to Unido's success: "Namfrel was really effective in Metro Manila and it played a major role in keeping the elections in the city fairly clean" (Joaquin 1985: 310). Raul De Guzman and Luzviminda Tancangco's exhaustive report describes the Manila election:

> The lackluster performance of the KBL in Metro Manila came despite the 'overkill campaign strategy' launched with the full backing of the president and the First Lady. The political machinery was highly organized and well-oiled but it did not effectively run.... NAMFREL provided the organizational machinery for the electorate themselves to get involved in the electoral process and to protect the sanctity of the ballot so that the people's collective will could prevail over election frauds, intimidation and other dirty tactics (1986: 26).

The correlation of fraud prevention and opposition success held across the country, such that "[l]imits on the ruling party's cheating were a necessary condition for the opposition's victory in a particular city, province, or region" (Thompson 1995: 130). Through its own monitors, Unido even succeeded in areas not covered by Namfrel: In the five areas for which Unido fielded its own inspectors (metropolitan Manila, Cebu City, and Regions 3–5), the party took a majority of seats (DeGuzman and Tancangco 1986: 105–106). Of those races, only Region 5 had an "unacceptable" electoral quality, as reported by De Guzman and Tancangco. These victories included nineteen of twenty-one seats in the home provinces of the opposition's leadership; three of the four seats in the Laurels' Batangas province went to Unido candidates (Thompson 1995: 129).

Where the monitors were absent, however, Marcos's KBL dominated. Laurel's observations about what happened in Cebu province, where Unido could not field observers, illustrate how the regime controlled election outcomes when not constrained by observers during the voting: "In Cebu province, the count was at first 6–0 in our favor but on May 19, five days after the polls, they were still counting the ballots and the count became 4–2 in *their* favor.... So, at 2:30 in the afternoon we were marching with placards, about ten thousand strong, and all the UNIDO candidates were there. We marched around the capitol, all its doors were closed" (Joaquin 1985: 308). The protest did not shift the result for Unido and the KBL eventually claimed 5 of the province's seats.

In addition to its manipulation of opposition strongholds, Marcos's group had its own bastions of support. The president's political machine could overwhelm the opposition in certain areas of the country through mass support rather than fraud. In those regions, the opposition was unable to field candidates who could compete against Marcos's partisans in the KBL. In the president's home region of Ilocos Norte (Region 1), for example, visible opponents to the regime were few, and some residents said that there were "no elections in the province," by which they meant that their outcome was a foregone conclusion (De Guzman and Tancangco 1986: 102). The KBL took twelve of the sixteen available seats for the region. Although it did make use of "vote buying and flying voters," the 75 percent regime victory in Ilocos Norte "seemed to approximate the will of the people in this region" (De Guzman and Tancangco 1986: 102).

Final results gave Unido 60 seats out of 183 contested (parliament included an additional 17 MPs appointed by the president) (Hartmann, Hassall, and Santos 2001: 222). With just under one-third of the seats in parliament, the coalition of moderates lacked the numbers to pass an impeachment motion against the president, but it had proven that even under authoritarianism elections could become tools for promoting pluralism. Success had vindicated pragmatism: The elections gave Unido a parliamentary presence and a leading position in the field of anti-Marcos movements.

Mass Mobilization: The Philippines, 1985–1986

In accordance with constitutional changes made in 1981, Marcos's six-year term as president would expire in 1987. He was then expected to seek reelection or designate a close ally as his successor. Neither scenario took place, because Marcos moved the election up to 1986. Raymond Bonner records how President Marcos announced to an American audience that the early election would dispel questions about his authority:

On [*This Week with David Brinkley,*] [George] Will asked: "President Marcos, there is a perception here that your problems derive from the fact that your mandate is gone, whatever it once was. . . . And there are some people here who wonder if it is not possible and if you would not be willing to move up the election date, the better to renew your mandate soon, say, within the next eight months or so. Is that possible, that you could have an election earlier than scheduled?" Marcos leaned into the pitch he had been waiting for. "Well, I understand the opposition has been asking for an election. In answer to their request I announce that I am ready to call a snap election perhaps earlier than eight months, perhaps in three months or less than that" (1987: 392)

When Sam Donaldson pressed Marcos to guarantee a fair voting process, including "outside observers," the president replied, "You are all invited to come, and we will invite members of the American Congress to please come and just see what is happening here" (Bonner 1987: 392).

Marcos's announcement brought the opposition's long-awaited victory within reach. By the time of Marcos's American television appearance, the Philippine opposition had long been debating who would top its ticket. The forces of Salvador Laurel and Corazon Aquino, standard-bearer for her late husband, realized that only a united front could challenge Marcos in such a crucial contest. Although Laurel had been pursuing the presidency for years, his previous affiliation with Marcos impaired his ability to lead a countrywide campaign against the dictator. As Thompson explains, "Opposition newspapers... often questioned Laurel's credentials as an oppositionist because he had not spoken out against early martial law and had run as a KBL candidate in the 1978 legislative elections, breaking with the Philippine president only in late 1979" (1995: 133). In contrast, Corazon Aquino symbolized the loss many Filipinos had suffered and stood in the stead of her late husband, one of the original opponents of martial law and the most prominent casualty of Marcos's regime. The opposition thus nominated Aquino as their presidential candidate and Laurel as her vice presidential running mate. The memory of the fallen Ninoy Aquino helped activate their supporters.[16] When supporters gathered, they chanted "Cor-y! Cor-y!" and made the "L" sign, thumb and outstretched forefinger, for LABAN, the People Power movement (Goodno 1991: 90).

On 7 February 1986, election day, Marcos responded to the outpouring of support for the Aquino-Laurel ticket with extensive cheating, including the removal of millions of voters from the polling stations' lists (Steinberg 1994: 146). This time, however, his electoral malfeasance evoked a powerful outcry at home and abroad. First and foremost, Namfrel operatives and U.S. observers witnessed the fraud and condemned it. The National Movement for Free Elections estimated that 4.89 million votes were affected by regime-sponsored disenfranchisement. It judged procedural conditions in more than half of the precincts "abusive" or "intolerable." Subnational variations in fraud reflected the patterns established in 1980 and 1984: Marcos's home region remained a KBL stronghold, while the Laurels' region and metropolitan Manila were fiercely contested (Namfrel 1986: 3–4). Visiting U.S. senator Richard Lugar supported Namfrel's accusations that counting by the official Commission on Elections was

---

[16] Interview with Laurel, 30 May 2003, Manila.

manipulated to favor Marcos: "[T]he results of the count of Friday night [7 February] were managed and the results aborted by government officials," he announced (Namfrel 1986: 74).

Meanwhile, Namfrel conducted its own "quick count," tallying votes from the 74 percent of precincts it was able to cover. The following day, Namfrel declared Aquino had won with 51.7 percent, or 7.91 million votes to Marcos's 7.38 million (Namfrel 1986: 3). But the KBL-controlled National Assembly soon announced Marcos the victor with 53.7 percent, or 10.8 million votes to Aquino's 9.3 million. COMELEC and media tallies supported the assembly's results, which came from 97 percent of precincts, an area much larger than that of Namfrel's quick count. Yet the limitations on Namfrel coverage were themselves a product of regime interference, and Marcos made statistically incredible gains in his own bailiwicks, conceivably building a "reservoir" of votes to compensate for his weak showing elsewhere (De Guzman and Tancangco 1986: 153; Namfrel 1986: 74). Although the actual result may not be determinable, the closeness of the race in the presence of extensive and well-documented attempts by Marcos's agents to steal the election tipped it decisively in Aquino's favor. Namfrel officials designated Aquino as the rightful victor. Despite what it acknowledged as "spurious results" in some areas, Namfrel concluded that its quick count provided "a more accurate reflection of the will of the people" than the assembly's count (Namfrel 1986: 4). Cardinal Jaime Sin also endorsed the opposition's results, declaring: "The people have spoken or have tried to. Despite the obstacles thrown in the way of speaking freely, we, the bishops, believe that on the basis on our assessment as pastors of the recently conducted polls, what they attempted to say is clear enough" (Goodno 1991: 97).

As the idea that the opposition had rightfully won the election took hold among the populace, the contest moved to the streets. LABAN first announced its victory on 8 February 1986. Ramos and Enrile then broke away from the president, only to find themselves under siege by the military's remaining loyalist factions. Even at this late stage in the election process, the United States remained officially neutral in the brewing domestic altercation. Four days after the polls closed, Reagan had responded noncommittally to the accusations of electoral tampering made by fellow Republicans, including Lugar, saying, "Well, I think that we are concerned about the violence that was evident there and the possibility of fraud, although it could have been that all of that was occurring on both sides" (Goodno 1991: 97). Enrile claims that the U.S. Embassy stood aside and provided no assistance to this troubled revolt against Marcos.[17] Thus, it was the domestic opposition rather than foreign support that tipped the balance. Eventually, Aquino's supporters came to the aid of the RAM leaders, dampening continued military support for Marcos and extricating the would-be coup leaders. The repressive agents deployed to disperse the crowds gradually joined them instead (Overholt 1986: 1162). Belatedly, the American administration promoted the opposition. Not until the dust had settled on 24 February, more than two weeks after LABAN had announced its victory, did President Reagan agree that Marcos had to go (Goodno 1991: 102). International influences were perceptible mainly in the final act of the 1986 push for democratization: On the evening of 25 February, Marcos flew into exile aboard a U.S. helicopter, saying as he departed, "I am so very, very disappointed" (Bonner 1987: 445).

Unido and LABAN had aggressively pushed to end the Marcos regime, enforcing their political agenda with the mass support of millions who had backed them in the elections. Although it is not easy to account for the willingness of millions of people to stand before a dictatorship and demand its surrender, the memory of Benigno Aquino's assassination appears to have played a critical role in enabling the opposition to seize the opportunity for democratization. Whereas Iranian reformists withdrew when the regime attacked their most prominent supporters, Philippine democracy activists advanced. Recent experiences with the dictatorship drove politicians at the head of the democratization movement to adopt confrontation rather than compromise as their strategy. In fact, at the culmination of the regime change campaign, the quality and form of the opposition's posture mattered more than the quantity of its supporters: From 1997 to 2000, Khatami's movement commanded 70 percent support in the electorate, but even the most favorable estimates give Aquino a bare majority.

Consoled but Unconsolidated: The Philippines, 1987–2006

When opposition movements remove an autocratic ruler, the regime may change a great deal or hardly at all. Newcomers to political authority may find themselves replicating the very abuses and excesses they deplored while out of power. The prospects for the new regime depend in part on the extent to which elites resolve foundational conflicts and build durable

---

[17] Interview with Enrile, 28 May 2003, Manila.

institutions. In this regard, the Philippine experience from 1986 onward reveals the continuation of a regime rather than a new start. By reestablishing the basis of government in the electorate, Aquino and Laurel's victory broke the fourteen-year hold of one man and his personal network. While this rupture delivered relief from the repression and arbitrary practices of Marcos, it also returned the Philippines to an earlier system – troubled yet sustainable – of weak parties and rampant clientelism. As a consequence, elected Philippine leaders have faced much the same difficulties that dogged their predecessors from 1946 to 1972; paradoxically, three of the country's four recent presidents have been accused of abusing power that they have barely been able to retain.

The challenge of restraining partisanship and channeling both elite and mass discontent has persisted from the beginning of Aquino's term through the present embattled administration of Gloria Macapagal Arroyo. LABAN's belated ally at the downfall of the Marcos regime, Fidel Ramos, insulated Aquino from early ejection from office by defusing coup plots from within the military. Enrile and his RAM faction were the source of one such threat. Enrile contended that his group was the rightful heir of the People Power movement. Only by nurturing Ramos's allegiance did Aquino escape the intrigue of Enrile and his supporters (Thompson 1996: 187–188). While Ramos's intercessions helped the post-Marcos democracy survive a rocky start (and positioned him for his own subsequent presidential bid), they did not remedy the underlying sources of instability: fragile parties, corruption, and limited policy linkages between government and society. The period of relative calm during the second half of Aquino's term and the duration of Ramos's tenure appears to have been the consequence of Ramos's personal stature. Governmental authority remained weak, and individuals continued to supercede institutions.

Neither Aquino nor Ramos built a party. Aquino explicitly refused even to join a party. While she gave modest support to PDP-LABAN (Philippine Democratic Party-LABAN), she also allowed her brother to recruit old Marcos supporters into the organization and thereby transform this vehicle of opposition into another grouping of clients like the LP and NP before it (Rocamora 1998: 11). Even more telling was Aquino's abandonment of the PDP-LABAN at the time of the 1992 elections. Rather than support the PDP, the outgoing president pivoted to promote Ramos and his Lakas-NUCD (*Lakas ñg Sambayanan* [Strength of People's Power]-National Union of Christian Democrats). Reincarnating the pendulum swings of pre–martial law politics, members of parliament then broke from the majority bloc and affiliated with Ramos's party

(Rocamora 1998: 11–12). Beneath the vicissitudes of such turncoatism lay a familiar, enduring structure of oligarchic domination by influential families and their clients. The predominant features of the country's new elected elites were incumbency and a familial political tradition: 66.5 percent of the legislature had prior electoral experience, and 16.5 percent were "relatives of 'old faces' in politics or belonged to traditional political families" (Gutierrez, Torrente and Narca 1992: 162). A study by the Philippine Institute for Popular Democracy concluded, "At best, most parties that exist today are...loose alliances of politicians, coalitions of different local elite interests, or personal campaign machineries of individual personalities" (Gutierrez, Torrente and Narca 1992: 166).

Since institutions could not curb personalistic competition even after Marcos had lost power, successive administrations failed to establish political authority that extended beyond their immediate tenture. One of the few positive side effects of this partyless clientelism is that even the periodic strongman is unable to sustain his dominance. Quezon confronted this problem, as did Marcos; most recently, Ramos's supporters were stymied by the factionalism that undermines party building. During the Ramos administration, newcomers flocked to Lakas-NUCD, and the party commanded more than 60 percent of seats in the House of Representatives (Rocamora 1998:11; Hartmann, Hassall, and Santos 2001: 222–223). The party's leaders schemed to convert this ascendancy into lasting control, as evinced by a draft constitution proposing the creation of an "authoritarian parliamentary system" similar to those of Malaysia and Singapore. Joel Rocamora explains: "All indications show[ed] that Lakas leaders want[ed] to change the political system in such a way as to enable it to become the ruling party in a quasi-parliamentary one-party state." But prominent leaders, including Aquino and key figures from the Catholic Church, blocked this attempt (Rocamora 1998: 28).

The country's two presidents since Ramos, Joseph Estrada (r. 1998–2000) and Arroyo (r. 2000-present), have struggled to fend off rivals and remain in office.[18] The Philippine Senate nearly impeached the populist Estrada on corruption charges in 2000 but held back from reviewing all the evidence. The implication that Estrada, a known affiliate of Marcos's old allies, had apparently bought off his "jury" provoked thousands in Manila to rally for his removal. This movement gained the name "People

---

[18] The following discussion of recent events is drawn primarily from Country Watch's *Country Report: The Philippines* (2005).

Power 2." Because of popular pressure, the president agreed to leave office, although he did not formally resign, and Vice President Arroyo was sworn in. Controversy immediately surrounded Arroyo's succession, however, because the Supreme Court that installed her had sidestepped the constitution by unilaterally declaring Estrada unable to fulfill the duties of his office (Paguia 2003). In April 2001, Estrada unsuccessfully appealed to the Supreme Court, arguing that Arroyo was only serving in a temporary capacity and that he was still president. The failure of this appeal officially stripped Estrada of his position and his parliamentary immunity, exposing him to criminal prosecution. He was arrested on 25 April and charged with having taken in more than $80 million in bribes and other illegal funds during his presidency. Six days later, his supporters rioted at the presidential palace, claiming that Arroyo had unlawfully usurped the presidency. The protest ("People Power 3") was the largest since 1986; several demonstrators during the siege on Malancanang, against which Arroyo was prepared to reinforce conventional police forces by deploying the army. Yet the new president survived this inauspicious beginning to her term. Mid-May elections strengthened Arroyo's hold with a slim Senate majority in her favor.

In the years since Arroyo's first inaguration, the Philippines has faced several further destabilizing episodes. Although she reached a ceasefire with the Moro Islamic Liberation Front, Arroyo continued to battle the Abu Sayyaf splinter movement in the south of the country. In July 2003, three hundred soldiers mutinied against the president and called unsuccessfully for Arroyo's resignation. In May 2004, a year after declaring she would not seek reelection, President Arroyo won a new six-year term in an election criticized domestically for irregularities. That victory soon fed another outburst of public protest against Arroyo's presidency. In summer 2005, Arroyo acknowledged that she had been in contact with election officials in charge of the 2004 vote count. Her admission triggered urban protests, which she attempted to channel into a formal impeachment trial – one that she was confident she could survive, given her level of support in the Senate.

Elite sentiment also began to run against the president, with Aquino, Catholic bishops, and much of her own cabinet calling for her to resign. Ironically for an executive carried to office by mass protests and extraordinary circumstances, Arroyo called for order: "This is democracy that's held together by the Constitution and the rule of law," she declared. "The Philippines has fallen into a dangerous pattern where the answer to every crisis is to subvert due process rather than work within the system. This must stop." The following spring, Arroyo took drastic steps to ensure her political survival, declaring a state of emergency and jailing three of her critics even as the country prepared to celebrate the People Power anniversary (*Los Angeles Times*, 25 February 2006; *Associated Press*, 26 February 2006). The president justified her actions as security measures in the wake of a foiled coup plot timed to coincide with commemoration of Marcos's ouster (*New York Times*, 26 February 2006). Although tens of thousands of Filipinos, rallied at times by former president Aquino, turned out to protest, Arroyo neither stepped down nor was removed from office. As the duration of her presidency eclipses those of her elected predecessors, uncertainty hovers over the Arroyo administration and the fate of the Philippines' unruly democracy (*New York Times*, 6 March 2006).

Conclusion

At times, Philippine democracy seems ready to revert to authoritarianism, but the unbridled pluralism of the post-Marcos era casts a hopeful light on what may lie beyond Iran's reform impasse. When elites constrain electoral outcomes, even heavy opposition participation may fail to effect change. Political transformation depends on incumbent forces subverting the regime's control over election processes. Elite assistance was pivotal in the elections won by Iranian and Philippine oppositionists. After institutional decline exacerbated elite rivalries, defectors qualitatively improved elections in order to defeat their former associates. Their pragmatic partnership with the opposition in turn allowed committed activists to vie for government posts previously denied to them. Rulers became political casualties of the very elections they had chosen to hold and previously controlled. But this is not the end of the story: To explain why the Philippines succeeded in establishing meaningful multiparty competition while Iran did not, the foregoing account highlights the readiness of moderate oppositionists to spearhead a public confrontation with the regime's ruler and security forces. The specter of revolution in Iran deterred reformists from pressing their popular mandate in a showdown against the clerical institutions. In the Philippines, on the other hand, Benigno Aquino's murder galvanized dissent, and opposition leaders invoked his cause in a fateful push for change.

Whereas the defeat of reformists in Iran may carry seeds of hope, the victory of prodemocracy forces in the Philippines brought cause for concern. Both regimes suffer from continued factionalism among their most influential leaders, placing the two countries on opposite sides of the divide between challenged dictatorship and struggling democracy. That border marks the political frontier for dozens of countries in the developing world today. Figuring out what conditions will help countries like Egypt and Malaysia reach it – and help states like Iran and the Philippines cross it – remains a principal problem for researchers and policymakers grappling with the mixed record of authoritarianism and recent democratization.

7

Conclusions

Over the preceding chapters, I have developed a historical-institutional explanation for the variation between durable authoritarianism and opportunities for democratization. In this account, the institutional legacies of early elite conflict are the parameters that circumscribe subsequent political actors' contests for power. Weak organizational bonds and the corresponding defection of disgruntled elites are the wellspring of viable opposition alliances, although not the only determinant of their success. This theory of ruling parties and regime persistence builds on an array of existing arguments about regime change and authoritarianism, even as it offers a novel alternative to these accounts. Through a cross-regional comparison that covers an average of half a century's history in each of four countries, I have sought to broaden the generality of my findings.

Findings

This study yields seven main conclusions that expand our understanding of authoritarianism and which I will discuss in turn:

(1) The maintenance and collapse of authoritarian regimes depends on more than just the unrestrained and arbitrary use of power by capricious individuals. Indeed, the reverse is more accurately the case: Organizational restraints prolong and expand power.

(2) The structural opportunities that enable opposition movements to redistribute power and democratize a regime are not caused by mass protest alone, but rather by the intersection of elite defections and opposition activism. In some instances, public elite rifts may

energize a beleaguered opposition, but vigorous challenges by the "outs" do not directly disrupt the cohesion of the "ins."

(3) Some institutions matter more than others. By managing elite conflict, ruling parties shape the interface of other institutions, such as elections, with society. Elections alone do not capsize regimes; rather, discord among regime elites capsizes elections.

(4) Opposition movements must surmount or subvert the state's means of violent reprisal before they can achieve power, but the strength of a regime's repressive apparatus depends on the solidity of its political apparatus.

(5) The influence of U.S. pressure and support has been secondary to the domestic dynamic by which regimes cohere or fragment. The formation of viable alliances between elite defectors and embattled activists has generally preceded U.S. involvement rather than springing from it.

(6) Social cleavages are mediated by the institutional context of ruling parties, through which differently positioned self-interested elites debate and compete. Parties do not merely transmit societal concerns: They create an arena in which those perspectives are renegotiated and reconciled.

(7) By generating political power – influence over the national agenda – ruling parties do not simply constrain the options of leaders or satisfy their material needs through patronage. They also bind together otherwise fractious elites in durable coalitions that enable individual advancement amid collective security.

The Limits of Leadership

This book opened with a passage from Machiavelli's *The Prince*, a classic of political philosophy that still reads today like a handbook for dictators. Indeed, many recent autocrats, including Nasser, are alleged to have read Machiavelli's work multiple times. Are long-lived authoritarian regimes such as that of Egypt the by-product of guileful leaders' applying the lessons of earlier students of politics? This comparison of Egypt and three other recent regimes suggests not: Political stability is not simply the result of masterful individual leaders. The coalitions that sustain regimes depend on more than an individual bent to become a modern-day "Prince." They require institutions that enable the kinds of conflict mediation and resolution Machiavelli discussed – organizations that transcend the capacity of any single figure and thereby curb the tendency of even the most gifted leaders toward prolonged excess or the type of arbitrary action that embitters valued allies toward him.

In any authoritarian regime, the leader may overshadow the organizations and myriad factions that he supervises. In Egypt and Malaysia, Mubarak and Mahathir are clear examples. Generally speaking, when we begin to associate a regime with an individual leader's name, this signals the onset of "personalistic rule," also known as "patrimonial rule" or "sultanism," and a corresponding departure from institutions.[1] But both rulers succeeded in sustaining the kinds of political coalitions that their counterparts in Iran and the Philippines destroyed, and not because they were honest, transparent, or pluralist leaders. The point is that the label of "personalism" tells us only part of the story – and, I would contend, the less novel part. Comparison between the two pairs of cases suggests that whereas the desire for a ruler to remain in power and even to concentrate power around himself is nearly omnipresent, this intention does not translate into capacity without the appropriate institutions – institutions that, paradoxically enough, provide for some checks and impose some routines on the ruler's influence. Such boundaries do not make state-society relations or intraelite politics egalitarian. Mahathir, for example, was unquestionably the ultimate decision maker and proved willing to strike back viciously against those who impeded his plans. But the structure of ruling parties curbs and ameliorates factional disputes, containing conflicts that might otherwise burst into the public sphere. The tendency toward personalism is common but generally less stable than the combination of personalism with ruling parties.[2]

If institutions were less critical and personalistic rule sufficient to sustain political coalitions, we would expect to observe partyless leaders like Khamenei and Marcos mending the kinds of cleavages that Mubarak and Mahathir addressed. Instead, elite conflicts in Iran and the Philippines escalated rapidly following the dissolution of parties in each country. When Khamenei and Marcos attempted to channel power into their own personal cliques, they instead diminished it, driving erstwhile partners toward the opposition. Unbridled personal ambition became the midwife of counteralliances and viable threats to both rulers. A series of orderly successions in Egypt and Malaysia further evince the importance

---

[1] On personalism, see Chehabi and Linz (1998b). For approaches to Egyptian and Malaysian politics that emphasize the executive's role as chief patron, consult Kassem (1999) and Hwang (2003).

[2] For a lucid discussion of the interaction between parties and personalism in Malaysia, see Slater (2003).

of parties. Parties provided the bridge in these countries from one leader to the next, revealing that regime persistence hinged not on one figure's preternatural political acumen but on the continual organizational infrastructure in which all were embedded.

The contrast between durable authoritarianism in Egypt and Malaysia and opportunities for democratization in Iran and the Philippines demonstrates why institutions gird autocracies and prevent the drift toward exclusionary personalism. Other works, most notably Geddes's statistical analysis of authoritarian breakdown, have noted the tendency for regimes with parties to outlast their less institutionalized counterparts. The cases of this book illustrate why that is the case in terms of underlying mechanisms and processes. Any leader may read *The Prince*, but applying Machiavelli's maxims requires a ruling party organization to regulate the ambitions of political rivals and bind them to the ruler.

Elite Insecurity and Opposition Challenges

When assessing the impact of opposition movements, the comparative democratization literature has oscillated between two perspectives. The first posits that political change depends on mutual guarantees that secure the long-term interest of rulers while responding to the demands of oppositionists (Dahl 1971: 16). In this view, elites will not relinquish power when their backs are against the wall; only when change comes with insurance of their continued livelihood and influence will they accept it. It follows that the key to opposition success lies in moderating demands and reducing the sense of threat felt by incumbent leaders. This assumption pervades the project on transitions from authoritarianism in Latin America and Southern Europe, which concluded that the most common path away from dictatorship was a conservative regime change that guaranteed the property and influence of business elites (O'Donnell and Schmitter 1986: 69). Subsequent scholars have similarly emphasized the importance of mutual security and the pacts in which such agreements are reached (Karl 1990: 9; Cook 2006: 66). These studies portray democratization as a process of negotiation and gradual concession by elites to oppositionists with whom they can coexist. The driving force is the dampening of opposition demands, which will then nudge rulers to step down from power. Other scholars have responded with a second view, revising the original accounts of transitions to stress the role of opposition protest in compelling rulers to step down. Democratization, they argue, is not delivered "from above" by comfortable elites but won "from below" by mass mobilization and direct challenge (Wood 2001: 863).

In their most basic form, neither approach to democratization finds support in these cases. If mutual guarantees and the presence of a moderate opposition movement were sufficient inducements for rulers to step down, then the Egyptian and Malaysian regimes should have ceded power to their opponents long ago. Each regime faces conventional moderate opposition movements that eschew violence and participate in elections. Twice, in 1990 and 1999, Mahathir's party was even challenged by an explicitly pan-Malaysian coalition, a functional alternative to the ruling National Front that could have introduced a two-coalition system to Malaysia's stilted parliament. The limits of moderation are just as stark in Iran and the Philippines, particularly given the Islamic Republic's retreat from reformist government in 2000–2004.

The cases similarly disprove the inverse claim that strong opposition movements can simply push elites out of power. In this regard, the experiences of the Philippines and Malaysia are especially instructive. The downfall of Marcos is often treated as a pure product of People Power and hence one of the most famous examples of democratization through mass mobilization (for example, Huntington 1991: 146). But the success of Corazon Aquino's movement in 1986 was the culmination of a longer process of mobilization that began with the inauspicious rout of her husband's party in the 1978 Manila elections. With airtight control over election results, the Marcoses shut out Benigno Aquino and his fellow candidates, completely overriding the wishes of the throngs that had clamored for change in a citywide noise barrage. Only after Marcos's own regime began to drive elites like Salvador Laurel to join the opposition were these controls overcome and the regime exposed to the discontented masses arrayed against it. As shown by Malaysian premier Mahathir's survival of the *reformasi* movement in 1999, moreover, mass protest can be contained and deflected so long as a regime's political coalition coheres.

Explanations that begin with elite decisions or mass protest become more informative when connected to the institutional variables that regulate elite conflict. In the presence of a ruling party, neither is sufficient to bring about change; in the absence of a party, both are necessary. Consider the resilience of the power of the NDP and UMNO in the Mubarak and Mahathir eras. So long as elites have remained confident that their long-term influence rests within the party, they have been content, even determined, to throw their support behind the regime. The result is stability, not transition, and there is no reason to expect this calculus will change in the immediate future. Insulated from their opponents, regime elites need not engage in pacts nor heed protests.

By contrast, in regimes without parties, where political coalitions are not maintained and elites are left to fend for themselves, both elite defections and mass protests are critical for regime change. Elite realignments create opportunities for democratization that activists must exploit through public contestation, pushing incumbents to relinquish their posts. Yet a crucial precondition for elite realignments is the availability of moderate allies with whom elite defectors may affiliate. Such potential allies are not rare, but they are critical. Rafsanjani would have been much less likely to reach out to the outlawed Mojahedin or Iran Freedom Movement than to the religious leftists with whom he shared a certain background and outlook. Likewise, Laurel and other veteran politicians looked not to the communist movement but to their mainstream rivals when forming the United Democratic Opposition. Once in place, these counteralliances then depended on the mobilization of mass support, a tactic adopted by the Philippine opposition but rejected by Iranian reformists. At that point, the performance of the two movements diverged, largely for the very reason scholars of democratization-from-below propose: As a regime fights for its very survival, power will not be given to the opposition. It must be taken.

To summarize, the four cases complicate but advance the continuing debate over the elite or mass origins of democratization. Once we take into account the institutional context in which elites conceptualize their interests, we find that both approaches find support, and both variables are crucial elements in the collapse of regimes that have abandoned ruling parties.

Rulers and Electoral Rules

Institutions matter, but different institutions influence different outcomes. This study has given close attention to the institution of elections under authoritarian regimes, one of the most common features of nondemocratic rule today. The statistical tests of Chapter 1 and subsequent case studies show that these elections in themselves do not account for variations in regime outcomes over time. Given the ubiquity of limited elections, this finding should not be that surprising: When nearly all regimes are holding elections but a much smaller portion are losing power, some other factor must be deciding their fates. Although seemingly intuitive from a global perspective, this point has been minimized in works that treat dictators' elections as inherently destabilizing. At the same time, the opposite proposition – that elections uniformly strengthen autocracies – is also dubious, given the dramatic defeats of leaders like Marcos in the Philippines.

Resolving when and why elections impair or bolster regimes requires that we turn to other institutions, the core institutions that mediate elite relationships and buttress coalitions. Elections do not cripple regimes; regimes that have fragmented their coalitions cripple themselves. Their debility manifests itself in elite defections and electoral defeats. The direction of this causal argument suggests an additional implication about the role of formal rules in the maintenance or downfall of authoritarian regimes: So long as the ruler sustains a political coalition, such institutions are subordinate to the elite's proclivities for manipulating them to their own advantage. What occurs within the authoritarian regime matters more than its formal structure.

In the literature on democratization and democratic consolidation, a large set of arguments focuses on the formal institutions of government, such as electoral laws and the executive-legislative system (presidential or parliamentary) (Linz 1993; Horowitz 1993). The approach of this project is to move further back in the chain of explanation to the strategies and techniques of rulers and oppositionists coping with and manipulating these rules. Because authoritarian leaders exercise the will and capacity to circumvent or undermine the official laws governing political competition, such rules should be incorporated into the analysis as part of the process in which regimes continue or collapse. It would be inaccurate, for example, to expect that Mahathir Mohamad had a harder time staying in power because he was a prime minister than Hosni Mubarak, a president. Both leaders had to practice coalition management in order to retain their hold on power. Additionally, although elections directly threatened the chief executive's office in Malaysia and the Philippines but reached only subordinate positions in Egypt (the parliament but not the presidency before 2005) and Iran (the presidency and legislature but not the Council of Guardians and Supreme Leadership), leaders in all four countries were intent on retaining as much power as possible and preventing the opposition from winning any influence in government. Their effectiveness in achieving that goal depended on the coalitions they maintained. Differences in the allotment of formal authority therefore do not account for the observed contrasts in the ability of rulers to retain authority. This point applies to elections: Allegedly disadvantageous electoral laws and districting rules do not necessarily lead to the defeat of incumbents.

The contrast between sustained electoral dominance in Egypt and Malaysia and the rise of electoral contestation in Iran and the Philippines eludes explanation in terms of formal rules. Whereas Gary Cox, for instance, posits that long-term opposition weakness in the Japanese case derives from the single, nontransferrable vote in multimember districts (1997: 100–102, 238–239), none of the present four cases share this characteristic. Egyptian and Malaysian ruling party candidates have succeeded in single-member (or dual-member in Egypt) plurality voting districts. Meanwhile, Iranian and Philippine opposition candidates first lost and then won in multiple-vote, multimember districts. Challengers to the regime overcame their "coordination problems" despite disadvantageous conditions, while opposition parties in Egypt and Malaysia have failed even though they operated in much smaller districts (Cox 1997: 249).

T. J. Pempel's volume on the dominant party democracies of Israel, Italy, Japan, and Sweden concluded that the chosen cases shared a political pattern characterized by proportional representation, a "cycle of dominance," and a tendency for government control to beget further influence through the manipulation of the national political agenda (1990b: 336). Such findings leave unanswered the question of why so many regimes with plurality voting remain in power. Although Pempel and his contributors did not find the persistence of authoritarian dominant party regimes puzzling, a look beyond their original cases provides new variation in their central explanatory variable (1990a: 5). With the exception of two elections in Egypt (1984, 1987), the four regimes of this project all involve plurality, not proportional, voting procedures. Plurality voting per se cannot be invoked as an explanation of Iranian or Philippine elites' electoral losses any more that it can be treated as a source of Egyptian and Malaysian hegemony. When Egypt switched from majoritarian districting to proportional voting, the regime recalibrated its intervention in the elections, but neither set of laws provoked a structural redistribution of power (Posusney 2002).

To explain variations in electoral success, then, comparativists need to decouple our expectation about political outcomes from the formal rules governing elections. For rulers such as Marcos and Mahathir, who enjoyed broad discretion over election processes, extant institutions only set the initial parameters in which they attempted to retain power. Formal institutions did not push these rulers down a path to defeat or dominance. Rather, each responded to the existing system, exploiting those rules that advantaged them and circumventing those that were hindrances. It is these variations in degree of control – above, beyond, and often in direct violation of the formal electoral rules – that must be explained if we are to understand electoral outcomes.

The Political Infrastructure of Repression

Just as party institutions shaped the outcome of each regime's electioneering, the organization of elite conflict also affected the state's ability to use violence against the political opposition. Theda Skocpol concluded that revolutions only occur where the state loses the capacity to repress its foes (1979: 285). One might therefore expect that regime change hinges not on parties but on armies and state security forces. The process that brought regime durability to Egypt and Malaysia challenges this premise. Whereas Egypt's regime has been enmeshed in military rule since the coup that brought Nasser to power, Malaysia's political system has been comparatively soft, led by professional politicians, not officers. The political apparatus and the repressive apparatus overlap relatively little in Malaysia, yet the state has remained in control despite the periodic rise of popular challengers – Malay figures such as Razaleigh and Anwar who could have won the military's support had they succeeded politically.

Corazon Aquino's success against Marcos demonstrates how such a goal can be achieved. In the Philippines, General Ramos and Defense Secretary Enrile turned against Marcos and joined the surging People Power movement. Their realignment followed the emergence of a countercoalition made up of elite defectors and moderate opposition politicians. When the movement challenged Marcos, Ramos and Enrile's group followed, and the repressive apparatus fragmented. Thus, the seeds of state collapse in the Skocpolian sense were planted in the institutional void that drove elite defections and electoral defeats.

In Egypt and Malaysia, ruling parties provided the political infrastructure through which the regime maintained control over the repressive apparatus. Marcos had undermined that same infrastructure. So had Khamenei in Iran. There, though, the reformists shrank from confrontation and thus avoided the public clash that would have brought the Iranian equivalents of Enrile and Ramos to their side. Indeed, it was the very fear of such an open-ended confrontation that drove Khatami's movement to choose accommodation over confrontation.

With regard to the Middle East cases of Iran and Egypt, the causal primacy of ruling parties means that the resilience of each regime cannot be assessed by looking at its public visage. Although the Iranian government has embarked on a renewed program of domestic repression, deployment of *baseejis* and *hizbollahis* does not resolve the political dilemma of unmediated and incessant elite conflict. From the opposite perspective, even if Egypt were to be led by a civilian president, such a shift would not inherently presage instability or democratization. So long as the ruling party continued to maintain a political coalition encompassing domestic policymakers, the military, and security services, it could emulate the civilian autocracy that has ruled Malaysia for five decades.

Foreign Patrons, Local Contestants

Whether they are allies or adversaries of the regime, external powers may constrain or buttress the domestic control of autocratic leaders. This line of argument is developed in a number of works, including most recently studies of durable authoritarianism in the Middle East (Brownlee 2002c; Bellin 2004). Therefore, one might expect U.S. foreign policy to have influenced the downfall of Ferdinand Marcos, a long-time American client, and the endurance of Hosni Mubarak, an ally in the U.S.-led "war on terrorism." The crossregional perspective of the present comparison, though, provides an additional vantage point on this problem and points to the tendency of foreign powers, principally the United States, to affect domestic politics reactively.

As shown by the processes behind the two regimes' very different fates, American involvement followed events rather than propelling them. In both the Philippines and Egypt, U.S. administrations took a wait-and-see stance, opting not to engage until a viable opposition movement arose against the country's ruler. The result in Egypt has been that successive U.S. administrations have favored the Mubarak regime and eschewed vigorous advocacy of structural reforms that would empower the opposition (Gerges 1999; Carothers 2000). The Philippines illustrates the conditions that may erode this status quo bias. In one of the more striking reversals of causal direction, domestic politics in the Philippines drove U.S. foreign policy rather than the reverse. Although Republican politicians had expressed ambivalence toward Marcos much earlier, not until the People Power movement declared and established its electoral victory did the Reagan administration openly call for and abet Marcos's departure. It follows that favorable ties to the United States such as Marcos enjoyed through February 1986 cannot be regarded as an automatic guarantor of regime stability, since supportive relationships are dependent on the domestic dynamic within the country, particularly the success of local opposition movements with whom U.S. officials feel comfortable dealing. The mutability of U.S. support may have been missed in the earlier-cited studies of Middle East cases primarily because such variation is lacking. Yet this lack may actually stem from the problem its authors seek to diagnose – durable authoritarianism – rather than causing it. One can envision – if not expect – an Egyptian equivalent of People Power composed of NDP defectors and moderate oppositionists like Ayman Nour that spurs rethinking in Washington, D.C., and a foreign policy shift that ratifies the move toward democratization on the ground.

Economic Cleavages and Political Linkages

Some skeptics of institutional arguments question whether parties influence social and economic cleavages or simply reflect them (Lipset and Rokkan 1967). As sources of livelihood vary, so will perspectives on what is good for a country and, more precisely, on what policies and approaches will help elites maintain their status as power holders. Consequently, actors' political economy interests play an important role in shaping elite preferences and strategies, influencing the fault lines and forms of debate (Kaufman 1986: 90–91; Milner 1988: 360). Leaders negotiate over which projects the state should pursue and, by implication, which individuals will benefit from the translation of political influence into economic power. Those leaders unhappy with the distribution of economic benefits may, in pursuing their own interests, disrupt the imbalance of political power between insiders and the opposition.

The case studies have taken these arguments seriously, but they have also challenged them. Material and personal interests fundamentally shape behavior, but actors engage each other in a setting where such basic concerns acquire a political aspect that is not derivable from interests alone. Institutions do not merely aggregate and sort prior, materially based interests, they also influence preferences and actions. The impact of economic rifts or other cleavages cannot be divorced from the political context in which they are articulated and acted on. Similar debates in Egypt and Iran over economic reform in the 1990s prompted very different responses depending on the availability of a ruling party organization for reconciling modernist and traditionalist factions. Concerns over corruption and nepotism in Malaysia and the Philippines yielded contrasting political behaviors based on whether party institutions could curb leaders' excesses. Hence, although theories of social and class conflict are informative, they are also incomplete. Elite behavior takes form at the *intersection* of economic preferences and political institutions. Stances in the political economy do not drive regime outcomes in a vacuum: They join with and are influenced by the institutional context in which leaders weigh their options for defending those interests. The societal constituencies on which elites depend for support matter for our understanding of elite behavior and regime outcomes, but they do not foreclose the possibility of compromise.

This finding informs recent discussions of democratization, particularly Eva Bellin's study of so-called contingent democrats. Leaders' support bases in different sectors of the economy should be considered in conjunction with their involvement in party institutions. The threat they may perceive from other groups is structured by the institutional opportunities for rivals to coexist in a positive-sum fashion. In all six countries where Bellin observes labor or capitalist "diffidence" toward democratization, for example, a ruling party had been in place for decades (Egypt, Indonesia, Mexico, Singapore, Syria, Tunisia). Her cases also support the logical inverse claim: The lack of a ruling party means more support for change. A ruling party was present in only one (Zambia) of the four cases where one of these sectors had been an "enthusiastic champion of democratization." The other three (Brazil, Chile, and South Korea) were military regimes (Bellin 2000: 177–178). Hence, there is good reason to believe that the institutional context played a major role in shaping how different sectors – labor and capitalists – viewed the risks and rewards of regime change. Even as scholars have pushed the field forward by endogenizing institutional variables through the exploration of their origins in social conflict and elite negotiations, we must also treat material interests in the institutional arena where they become actions.

Additionally, variables of elite conflict based on material concerns must reckon with the ways political institutions can exacerbate or allay elite fears. For comparativists to do so, concepts like David Waldner's useful variable of "high-intensity elite conflict" must be measured independent of the outcomes that ensue (1999: 29). The cases of Egypt, Iran, Malaysia, and the Philippines show that it is the extent to which party institutions defuse conflict that determines the way in which material interests are manifested in political actions. If political economy differences were reflected in subsequent regime outcomes, we would expect to find regimes that face easier issues to be more durable than those attempting to cope with less tractable problems. So, for instance, the Marcos and Mahathir regimes might have been resilient because they "only" coped with problems of top-level nepotism, whereas the Egyptian and Iranian regimes debated major structural adjustment that pitted externally oriented businessmen against state-dependent bureaucrats. Instead, we find variations in regime durability cutting across political economy differences. Ruling party regimes in Egypt and Malaysia had different class compositions yet fared equally well at controlling elections. Those regimes that abandoned a ruling party performed poorly, even though they differed in the structure of their coalitions and the policy decisions they faced. The Iranian regime was torn between making concessions to the bazaar on the one hand and rationalizing the economy to promote privatization and fiscal conservatism on the other. In the Philippines, political leaders watched Marcos attend to his personal network of relatives and crony capitalists rather than distribute state perks across the political ruling class. Policy stances do not operate independently; they interact with the context in which they are pursued. Institutions shape the resulting conflicts and their consequences, particularly the decisions of leaders to break away or remain loyal.

In the cases of Egypt, Iran, Malaysia, and the Philippines, we find similar sources of elite competition (economic reform perspectives in Egypt and Iran, clashing networks of favoritism in Malaysia and the Philippines) but differences in whether those issues polarized elites. The institutional arena in which debates were resolved affected whether conflicts became intense. When top leaders in Iran and the Philippines politically asphyxiated unwanted coalition members, barring them from electoral lists and running candidates against them, elite conflict was "high-intensity." That outcome occurred after parties had been discarded. In Egypt and Malaysia, party institutions were a critical anchor of elite security. Conflict ultimately sustained elite status, thanks to the allocation of party appointments. Hence, political institutions or the lack of them shaped the stakes of conflict, determining whether leadership rivalries would become life-or-death battles. The severity of elite conflict was an effect of elite politics as structured by party institutions.

The Political Role of Parties

The final and overarching conclusion of this work follows from the prior point: Ruling parties play a political role in generating and mediating elite influence. This dimension transcends the purely material formulation of parties as clientelist distribution networks. By exposing the political impact of ruling parties in maintaining coalitions in Egypt, Iran, Malaysia, and the Philippines, this study fills a significant lacuna in the recent literature on parties and patronage. Many of the latest works on ruling parties frame clientelism – dyadic ties between rulers and ruled – as the linchpin of regime longevity. Clientelistic parties, it is argued, eschew broad programmatic platforms in favor of targeted patronage, or "side payments," to specific sets of voters (Kitschelt 2000; Estevez, Magaloni and Diaz-Cayeros 2002; Medina and Stokes 2002). Voters support the incumbent party in the expectation of receiving continuing material benefits, and thus regime durability becomes a function of distribution and exchange.

Such scholarship tends to minimize the ways in which parties create power and agenda-setting influence, exerting an influence on elite behavior far beyond material distribution and exchange. A major limitation of clientelism as an explanation is that clientelism prevails among both durable and fragile regimes. As one of the seminal works on clientelism noted, "this type of relationship must indeed be regarded as a generic trait of political systems regardless of their stages of development" (Lemarchand and Legg 1972: 149). Rene Lemarchand and Keith Legg concluded that clientelism "cannot be evaluated independently of other variables in the social and political systems" (1972: 172). Thus, the ubiquity of clientelism returns us to the question of why some clientelist governments fall while others survive. All four of the regimes studied here have practiced some form of clientelism, yet two suffered serious elite defections, whereas two did not. Why? The coalition-maintaining aspect of ruling parties rather than their operation as patronage networks explains elite cohesion within the regime and electoral control at the polls.

This argument continues to hold when we consider variations in access to resources and levels of state development. The use of state resources is a basic feature of clientelist arguments. Perhaps the more durable authoritarian regimes had more access to resources and could satisfy clients in ways their counterparts could not. Whether parties are distributing patronage or offering agenda-setting power, they depend on access to the state. Martin Shefter argues that patronage-based parties arise when democratization (expansion of the electorate) precedes bureaucratization (the development of a meritocratic civil service) (1994: 14–15). Instead of making broad programmatic appeals for support, these parties will raid the state and establish clientelist networks. Only if their core constituencies favor bureaucratic autonomy and the strengthening of state institutions will parties with the option of practicing machine politics undertake the hard work of building a genuine mass political party (Shefter 1994: 25–31). Whereas state weakness enabled local patronage parties in America, state strength and centralization drove national clientelism in Japan. According to Ethan Scheiner's study of the Liberal Democratic Party, Japan's "centralized financial structure" encouraged loyalty to the center and undermined the prospects of local politicians challenging the party (2006). Shefter's and Scheiner's works reveal a tension that the present cases further demonstrate: Parties may exploit the state regardless of whether the civil service is weak or strong.

Yet the long-term sustainability of party dominance depends on more than flush clientelist networks. As in the early American and Japanese

TABLE 7.1. *Comparative State Strength on the Weberianness Scale*

Country	Score
Egypt	7.80
Iran	n.a.
Malaysia	10.50
Philippines	6.00

Note: Lowest scores coded were Kenya 1.00 and the Dominican Republic 2.00. Highest scores coded were South Korea 13.00 and Singapore 13.50.
Source: Evans and Rauch (1999: 763).

examples, variations in bureaucratic development across Egypt, Iran, Malaysia, and the Philippines do not show a trend in terms of regime stability. Those who have quantified the extent to which a state approaches the Weberian ideal of a rational-legal order rank Malaysia as a more effective and less personalistic state than Egypt and the Philippines (Table 7.1). (Iran was not coded.) Malaysia benefits from a highly skilled civil service, but Egypt has experienced a similar tenure of regime durability despite having a weaker state. As regards the extent of programmatic appeals, parties in Egypt and the Philippines quickly became patronage-oriented, while parties in Iran and Malaysia offered some form of collective benefit to broader constituencies. In Egypt, Nasser drew support to the Liberation Rally by decrying the old system of the monarchy. Philippine leaders mobilized support to join the system established by their American colonizers, but also to challenge that arrangement and push for independence. In both countries, political declarations soon receded before material relationships between patrons and clients. Yet the long-term political trajectory of the parties diverged dramatically, with Egypt's ruling party dominating national politics through three presidents and the Philippine NP barely holding power for more than one electoral cycle at a time.

Programmatic parties in Iran and Malaysia, moreover, did not guarantee party dominance. The Islamic Republican Party promised a vague agenda of revolutionary reform that resonated with many young and underprivileged Iranians. UMNO pledged to protect Malays' privileges relative to the Chinese and Indian minorities. While the IRP and UMNO may have practiced machine politics to a lesser degree than the Liberation Rally and National Party, they were not similarly successful as political organizations: The IRP crumbled, and UMNO ascended. The net impression of these cases reinforces the contrast between Shefter's and Scheiner's subjects. The timing and extent of state development may heavily influence the manner in which parties operate, but they do not explain patterns of party dominance or weakness in contrasting cases.

The Landscape of Contemporary Democratization

In many parts of the world, the halfway house of liberalized authoritarianism has become an enduring fortress: Ruling parties have shielded incumbents and excluded the opposition, in some cases for generations. The persistence of undemocratic rule in a putative era of widening political emancipation poses a serious challenge for scholars and policymakers. As Mark Lilla has commented: "From Zimbabwe to Libya, from Algeria to Iraq...we discover nations that are neither totalitarian nor democratic, nations where the prospects of building durable democracies in the near future are limited or nil. The democratic West does not face an 'axis of evil' today, it faces the geography of a new age of tyranny....As yet, we have no geographers of this new terrain" (2002).

Just when it seemed like democracy would sweep the globe, we notice that the most recalcitrant dictators stand unshaken and unrepentant. Although much has been made of post-9/11 shifts in U.S. foreign policy and the ferment for change in the Middle East, the record of long-lived authoritarian regimes cautions us not to expect tectonic shifts overnight. In this book, I have presented a pattern of durable autocracy that originated long before the third wave of democratization in the foundational struggles that produced a cohesive elite bound together through a ruling party. I have shown that the base and basis of persistent authoritarianism lies beneath the surface of a regime's rhetoric and its public interactions with the opposition. Accurate analysis of these root causes must be critical and penetrative, piercing the fog of faux liberalization to expose how leaders preclude meaningful participation by so many. Effective policy prescriptions must contend with the core structures of regime maintenance – the ways decisions are made and enacted – and assess how, to what extent, and at what pace political power may be redistributed.

The democracy promotion discourse often emphasizes the need for incremental mobilization from below anchored in a strong civil society and vibrant associational life, but the mechanisms by which such an activated society can convert its virtuous aspirations into political accomplishments are often unclear. Presumably, the process would follow something like the conventional story we have about Poland: Demands percolate up and eventually cause powerholders to cede authority to unrepresented sectors. Like the liberalization arguments discussed earlier, this formula for democratization has not proven viable beyond its source cases. The Mubaraks and Mahathirs of the developing world have shown themselves to be ready and willing to constrain societal and political activities, suppressing their foes and foiling bottom-up mobilization strategies. Even when large numbers turn out against the regime – for example, in the Philippines in 1978 and Malaysia in 1990 and 1999 – some mass mobilizations have proven insufficient for defeating regime candidates through the electoral process. The tendency instead has been for regimes to hold power in the face of societal mobilization so long as significant rifts do not divide the ruling house against itself.

Precisely because this conclusion may initially discourage some democracy promoters, it merits sustained discussion and attention. A candid assessment of the obstacles to democratization should not be dismissed as unhelpful pessimism. Rather, it should be seen as the first step toward effective mobilization and engagement. False optimism, after all, makes for bad strategy. Recognizing that civil society is not always the midwife for democratic change means that democracy promoters may choose to encourage the building of a viable countercoalition by activists and insiders. Rather than focusing resources and attention on civic education and neighborhood associations, advocates of political reform might consider ways of enlisting elites to publicly commit to leveling the field between regimists and opposition figures. Such measures – once they are endorsed by regime leaders willing to try a fairer kind of politics – could include independently supervised elections, the lifting of restrictions on party formation and campaigning, and a national convention to discuss changes to the constitution and greater checks on the executive. These ideas may seem grandiose and unobtainable in conditions of entrenched autocracy, but the foregoing comparisons show they promise to have greater impact than grassroots programs.

Party institutions provide valuable tools for democratic consolidation (Mainwaring and Scully 1995b; Diamond 1999: 96–98). The cases of Egypt and Malaysia, however, suggest that parties can also facilitate the consolidation of nondemocratic regimes.[3] In light of these accounts,

---

[3] This "parallelism" suggests the effects of some variables may have been undergeneralized: Certain factors may bring similar results – for stability and breakdown – in both democratic and authoritarian regimes. For instance, consensus among elites was judged a supportive variable for regime durability in democratic systems but also in authoritarian Mexico under the PRI (Burton, Gunther and Higley 1992b, Knight 1992a). Public elite rifts and the formation of new alternative coalitions have challenged authoritarian

parties appear to be double-edged instruments for inculcating durable democracy: They restrain factionalism, curbing the chaos that accompanies partyless politics, but they also maintain autocratic coalitions, diffusing the pressures that would prompt new coalitions and rotation of power. This characteristic is a stumbling block for democratic change, as the very organizations that deliver manageable political competition may also be used to suppress pluralism. In much of Latin America and Southern Europe, military leaders essentially handed power from one set of institutions – their own – to civilian leaders of political parties. Democratization in Egypt and Malaysia would likely require a party-to-party transfer of power, which would be more complicated, since party operatives, unlike soldiers, cannot withdraw from politics and continue operating successfully. Beyond the elite cohesion of Egypt and Malaysia and the divisiveness of Iran and the Philippines lies the potential for multiple groups' competing peacefully through institutionalized parties, but the path to this point is not a straight one, and the risks of institutional reengineering are substantial: Both democracy *and* stability may be lost as interventionists try to improve either.

Ongoing conflict in post-Saddam Hussein Iraq corroborates Huntington's cautionary words of four decades ago that neither force nor charisma can ensure prolonged stability – only political organization can (1968: 461). The present civil war defies early expectations that appropriate intervention could democratize Iraq with minimal costs to human life. Analysts of the war and occupation have pointed out that the decision to dismantle Hussein's Baath Party fueled a Sunni uprising (Diamond 2005: 322). The Baath Party's disintegration also denied the Coalitional Provisional Authority the very instruments it needed to govern the country following the initial invasion. Iraq's slide from durable dictatorship into state failure cautions us of the trade-offs involved in disbanding local institutions: Even authoritarian ruling parties may have a role in democratization. By organizing elite politics and linking the regime to society, parties sustain regimes and regulate competing demands. Although they may stabilize democracies, they also insulate incumbents. Therefore, the dilemma of institutional reengineering entails maintaining the effect of

---

and democratic regimes alike (Yashar 1997; Bermeo 2003). Finally, institutional decay has been a problem for new democracies as well as for personalistic rulers concentrating power in their own hands (Mainwaring and Scully 1995b; Chehabi and Linz 1998b). The potential of integrative approaches to democratization is best explored through projects that study dictatorships and democracies side by side and test the null hypothesis that analogous causal patterns cross regime types.

parties as social ballast without entrenching powerholders. As this study demonstrates, the two often come in tandem.

If Iraq, pre- and post-2003, evinces the extremes of nondemocratic outcomes – brutal, enduring authoritarianism under Saddam Hussein and conflict-ridden chaos after his fall – the cases of Egypt, Iran, Malaysia, and the Philippines offer modal examples of regime variation. Buttressed by ruling parties, the Egyptian and Malaysian autocracies have enjoyed fifty years of rule without a coup, revolution, or democratic rotation of power. In Egypt, relative domestic stability has come despite early and repeated wars. In Malaysia, continuity has trumped intercommunal conflict and the threat of antiminority riots. Quietude and a lack of widespread violence have accompanied authoritarian durability. The NDP and UMNO have helped rulers organize politics, thereby providing a self-serving stability quite different from the contested pluralism of Iran and the Philippines. Open elite dissent in the latter countries has brought significant opportunities for democratization. Indeed, in the Philippines, leadership changes are almost a constant. Less than half as old as Egypt's republic, the Islamic Republic of Iran has already witnessed the rise of a potent reform movement, and major intraelite fissures remain active. These two cases of factionalism without party-bound coalitions manifest a milder version of the turmoil that follows weak institutions than does Iraq. There lies the promise and problem of unmanaged factionalism: Limited institutionalization and limited entrenchment by rulers are accompanied by great potential for violent oscillations in national politics. Accordingly, the challenges for democratic development are quite different in the two pairs of countries: Egypt and Malaysia would need to disperse power into multiple competing parties or coalitions, while Iran and the Philippines would need to consolidate their rival factions within distinct organizations that can rotate power peacefully.

The diversity of these problems complicates traditional Huntingtonian notions that power must be accumulated before it can be shared. The only functioning democracy among the four countries is the Philippines, where no single group has succeeded in monopolizing political influence for a prolonged period. Meanwhile, in Egypt and Malaysia, where leaders have achieved dominance, incumbents have not magnanimously offered their opponents the opportunity to partner with them in governance. By reinforcing rather than reforming the politics of durable authoritarianism, UMNO and the NDP invert Huntington and Clement Henry's expectation that parties are a necessary but insufficient condition for democratization (Huntington and Moore 1970: 513): For decades, ruling parties have been a sufficient cause for *preventing* democratization, and their decline has been a necessary but insufficient component of democratic development. Only in the cases where parties were abandoned (Iran and the Philippines) did an autocratic regime weaken and start to give way to the opposition.

Returning to the dilemma that this relationship between parties and political stability poses for democracy promotion, we must ask, If strong institutions can sustain authoritarianism while weak institutions are associated with unconsolidated regimes or, at best, precarious democracy, under what conditions can a durable dictatorship become a durable democracy? Does weakening the ruling coalition require undermining its institutions, which in turn bequeaths a poor legacy for democratic development? For activists hoping to break the NDP's control in Egypt or UMNO's dominance in Malaysia, is the ruling party's destruction the only way elite defectors will come forward to open the opportunity for electoral contestation? If so, what kind of regime would follow – a weakly institutionalized pluralist system with fluid party organizations along the lines of the Philippine model? Must opposition victory come at the cost of a regularized polity free of periodic authority crises?

Because the stabilizing influence of institutions on political behavior develops over time, it may be axiomatic that durable authoritarianism cannot be replaced by institutionalized, competitive multiparty democracy without a significant period of weak political structures and contingent political conflict. A rare alternative may obtain when a ruling party fragments after a long period of dominance and incumbent elites then become the loyal opposition. Such cases, like those of Taiwan and Mexico after 2000, seemingly vindicate Huntington's intuition that "the transition from [ruling party regimes] is likely to be more difficult than the transition from a military regime to democracy, but it is also likely to be more permanent" (1991: 120). Both countries also support the causal argument of this study, for the ruling parties – Mexico's PRI (r. 1929–2000) and Taiwan's KMT (r. 1950–2000) – split prior to each regime's electoral defeat.[4] These are precisely the kinds of public rifts Mubarak and Mahathir avoided in the 1990s. Hence, we should not expect oppositionists to gain ground in Egypt and Malaysia absent the formation of a lasting elite-based counterparty akin to Mexico's Party of the Democratic

---

[4] For a pre-regime change analysis of the PRI and KMT, see Haggard and Kaufman (1995: 267–306). For analysis of the parties' ruptures and their implications for electoral dominance, see Solinger (2001) and Langston (2006).

Revolution (founded 1989) or Taiwan's New Party (f. 1993) and People's First Party (f. 2000).

Institutions for mediating elite conflict predated the third wave era and have enabled many autocrats to survive it. The causal connection between parties and regime stability presents a catch-22 in resilient dictatorships: Ruling parties offer valuable institutions for consolidating political authority in a future democratic system, but they also shield incumbents from pressure to reform. To avoid the fate of the Philippines, in which institutional weakness threatened a dictator and his elected successors, rulers in places such as Egypt and Malaysia must relinquish their hegemony while retaining their organizations.

References

Interviews Cited
Biographical information is from 2004

Albano, Rudolph, former KBL member of parliament, 26 May 2003, Manila.
Amin, Nasser, director of the Arab Center for the Independence of the Judiciary and the Legal Profession, 2 June 2002, Cairo.
Badrawi, Hossam, NDP member of parliament (2000-2005), 19 July 1999, 20 April 2002, Cairo.
Claudio, Gabriel, former assistant to the secretary-general of the KBL, 26 May 2003, Manila.
Cuenco, Antonio, former UNIDO member, 20 May 2003, Manila.
Din, Gamal Essam El-, journalist, 17 April 2002, Cairo.
Enrile, Juan Ponce, former minister of defense, 28 May 2003, Manila.
Gomez, Edmund Terence, professor of economics at the University of Malaya, 6 June 2003, Kuala Lumpur.
Laurel, Salvador (1928–2004), former senator, former president of UNIDO, former vice president of the Philippines, 30 May 2003, Manila.
Marcos, Imee, daughter of Ferdinand Marcos, congresswoman, 21 May 2003, Manila.
Tan Sri Musa Hitam, former deputy prime minister and deputy president of UMNO, 11 June 2003, Kuala Lumpur.
Nourbakhsh, Amir Ali, political analyst, 27 August 2002, Tehran.
Pimentel, Aquilino, opposition candidate under martial law, senator, 21 May 2003, Manila.
Rageb, Mohammed, NDP member of Consultative Assembly, 4 April 2002, Cairo.
Saghafi, Morad, editor and journalist, 20 August 2002, Tehran.
Said, Rifaat al-, assistant secretary-general of NPUP, 22 June 2002, Cairo.
Semati, Hadi, professor of political science, University of Tehran, 6 October 2002, Tehran.

Shamseddin, Ali, former NDP deputy secretary of youth for Cairo, 30 April 2002, Cairo.
Wali, Sherif, NDP member of Consultative Assembly, 25 April 2002, Cairo.

Books, Articles, and Chapters

Abdel-Malek, Anouar. 1968. *Egypt: Military Society*. New York: Random House.
Abdel Maguid, Wahid. 2001. "Al-Mustaqillun: Ahamm zawahir intikhabat 2000." *Al-Dimuqratiyya 1* (1) (Winter): 97–103.
Abdo, Geneive. 1999. "Electoral Politics in Iran." *Middle East Policy 6* (4) (June): 128–137.
Abu Rida, Mohammed. 2001. "Al-binya al-siyasiyya wa al-ijtima'iyya li majlis al-sh'ab 2000." *Al-Dimuqratiyya 1* (1) (Winter): 72–81.
Afrasiabi, K. L. 2000. "Iran's Majlis Election." *Middle East Insight 15* (3): 12–14.
Aidi, Hisham. 2003. "*State Withdrawal and Political Change: Corporatism, Capacity and Coalitional Politics in Egypt and Mexico*." Ph.D. Dissertation, Columbia University.
Akbarzadeh, Shahram. 2005. "Where is the Islamic Republic of Iran heading?" *Australian Journal of International Affairs 59* (1) (March): 25–38.
Alawi, Mustafa, ed. 2000. *Intikhabat Majlis al-Sh'ab 2000*. Cairo: Konrad Adenauer Stiftung.
Aldrich, John H. 1995. *Why Parties? The Origin and Transformation of Political Parties in America*. Chicago: University of Chicago Press.
Allardt, Erik, and Yrgo Littunen, eds. 1964. *Cleavages, Ideologies, and Party Systems: Contributions to Comparative Political Sociology*. Transactions of the Westermarck Society 10.
Anderson, Benedict. 1988. "Cacique Democracy in the Philippines: Origins and Dr eams." *New Left Review* 169 (May–June): 3–31.
Ansari, Ali M. 2003. "Continuous Regime Change from Within." *The Washington Quarterly 26* (4) (Autumn): 53–67.
———. 2003. *Modern Iran Since 1921: The Pahlavis and After*. London: Pearson Education.
Ansari, Hamied. 1986. *Egypt: The Stalled Society*. Albany: State University of New York Press.
Arjomand, Said Amir. 1988. *The Turban for the Crown: The Islamic Revolution in Iran*. New York: Oxford University Press.
———. 2005. "The Rise and Fall of President Khatami and the Reform Movement in Iran." *Constellations 12* (4) (December): 502–520.
Armony, Ariel and Hector Schamis. 2005. "Babel in Democratization Studies." *The Journal of Democracy 16* (4) (October): 113–128.
Ayubi, Nazih N. 1995. *Over-Stating the Arab State: Politics and Society in the Middle East*. London: I.B. Tauris.
Bakhash, Shaul. 1990. *The Reign of the Ayatollahs: Iran and the Islamic Revolution*. New York: Basic Books.
———. 1998. "Iran's Remarkable Election." *Journal of Democracy 9* (1) (January): 80–94.

Baktiari, Bahman. 1996. *Parliamentary Politics in Revolutionary Iran: The Institutionalization of Factional Politics.* Gainesville: University Press of Florida, 1996.

Baktiari, Bahman and Haleh Vaziri. 2003. "Iran: Doubting Reform?" *Current History* 102 (660) (January): 36–39.

Banlaoi, Rommel C. and Clarita R. Carlos. 1996. *Political Parties in the Philippines from 1900 to the Present.* Makati City: Konrad-Adenauer-Stiftung.

Banuazizi, Ali. 1994. "Iran's Revolutionary Impasse: Political Factionalism and Societal Resistance." *Middle East Report* 191 (November–December): 2–8.

Barkey, Henri J., ed. 1992. *The Politics of Economic Reform in the Middle East.* New York: St. Martin's Press.

Beattie, Kirk J. 1994. *Egypt During the Nasser Years: Ideology, Politics, and Civil Society.* Boulder, Colo.: Westview Press.

_____. 2000. *Egypt During the Sadat Years.* New York: Palgrave.

Beck, Thorsten, George Clarke, Alberto Groff, Philip Keefer, and Patrick Walsh. 2001. "New Tools in Comparative Political Economy: The Database of Political Institutions." *World Bank Economic Review* 15 (1): 165–176.

Beeman, William O. "Iran's Religious Regime: What Makes It Tick? Will It Ever Run Down?" 1986. *Annals of the American Academy of Political and Social Science* 483 (January): 73–83.

Bellin, Eva. 2000. "Contingent Democrats – Industrialists, Labor, and Democratization in Late-Developing Countries." *World Politics* 52 (2) (January): 175–205.

_____. 2004. "The Robustness of Authoritarianism in the Middle East." *Comparative Politics* 36 (2) (January): 139–157.

Bermeo, Nancy. 1990. "Rethinking Regime Change." *Comparative Politics* 22 (3) (April): 359–377.

_____. 1997. "Myths of Moderation: Confrontation and Conflict During Democratic Transitions." *Comparative Politics* 29 (3) (April) 1997: 305–322.

_____. 2003. *Ordinary People in Extraordinary Times: The Citizenry and the Breakdown of Democracy.* Princeton, N.J.: Princeton University Press.

Binder, Leonard. 1966. "Political Recruitment and Participation in Egypt," in Joseph LaPalombara and Myron Weiner, eds., *Political Parties and Political Development,* 217–240. Princeton, N.J.: Princeton University Press.

Bishri, Tareq al-. 1991. *Al-Dimuqratiyyah wa-Nizam 23 Yuliyu 1952–1970.* Cairo: Dar Al-Hilal.

Bonner, Raymond. 1987. *Waltzing with a Dictator: The Marcoses and the Making of American Policy.* New York: Times Books.

Boroumand, Ladan and Roya Boroumand. 2000. "Reform at an Impasse." *Journal of Democracy* 11 (4) (October): 114–128.

Bratton, Michael and Nicolas van de Walle. 1997. *Democratic Experiments in Africa: Regime Transitions in Comparative Perspective.* New York: Cambridge University Press.

Brownlee, Jason M. 2002a. "Low tide after the Third Wave: Exploring Politics under Authoritarianism." *Comparative Politics* 34 (4) (July): 477–498.

_____. 2002b "The Decline of Pluralism in Mubarak's Egypt." *Journal of Democracy* 13 (4) (October): 6–15.

———. 2002c "... And Yet They Persist: Explaining Survival and Transition in Neopatrimonial Regimes." *Studies in Comparative International Development* 37 (3) (November): 35–63.

Brumberg, Daniel. 1992. "Survival Strategies vs. Democratic Bargains: The Politics of Economic Reform in Contemporary Egypt." In Henri Barkey, ed., *The Politics of Economic Reform in the Middle East*, 73–104. New York: St. Martin's Press.

———. 2000. "A Comparativist's Perspective." *Journal of Democracy*, 11 (4) (October): 129–134.

———. 2001a. "Dissonant Politics in Iran and Indonesia." *Political Science Quarterly* 116 (3) (Fall): 381–411.

———. 2001b. *Reinventing Khomeini: The Struggle for Reform in Iran*. Chicago: University of Chicago Press.

Brzezinski, Zbigniew. 1989. *The Grand Failure: The Birth and Death of Communism in the Twentieth Century*. New York: Charles Scribner's Sons.

Buchta, Wilfried. 2000. *Who Rules Iran? The Structure of Power in the Islamic Republic*. Washington, D.C.: Washington Institute for Near East Policy, 2000.

Bunce, Valerie. 1999. *Subversive Institutions: The Design and the Destruction of Socialism and the State*. New York: Cambridge University Press.

———. 2003. "Rethinking Recent Democratization: Lessons from the Postcommunist Experience." *World Politics* 55 (2) (January): 167–192.

Burns, Gene. 1996. "Ideology, Culture, and Ambiguity: The Revolutionary Process in Iran." *Theory and Society* 25 (3) (June): 349–388.

Burton, Michael, Richard Gunther, and John Higley. 1992a. "Introduction: Elite Transformations and Democratic Regimes." In John Higley and Richard Gunther, eds., *Elites and Democratic Consolidation in Latin America and Southern Europe*, 1–37. New York: Cambridge University Press.

Burton, Michael, Richard Gunther, and John Higley. 1992b. "Elites and Democratic Consolidation in Latin America and Southern Europe: An Overview." In John Higley and Richard Gunther, eds., *Elites and Democratic Consolidation in Latin America and Southern Europe*, 323–348. New York: Cambridge University Press.

Bush, George W. 2002. *The President's State of the Union Address*. United States Capitol, Washington, D.C., 29 January.

Carothers, Thomas. 2000. "Clinton Record on Democracy Promotion." *Carnegie Paper No. 16*. Washington, D.C.: Carnegie Endowment for International Peace, (September) 2000.

———. 2002. "The End of the Transition Paradigm." *Journal of Democracy 13* (1) (January): 15–21.

Case, William F. 1996a. Elites *and Regimes in Malaysia: Revisiting a Consociational Democracy*. Clayton, Victolie, Australia: Monash Asia Institute.

———. 1996b. "Can the 'Halfway House' Stand? Semidemocracy and Elite Theory in Three Southeast Asian Countries." *Comparative Politics 28* (4), July: 437–464.

———. 2001. "Malaysia's Resilient Pseudodemocracy." *Journal of Democracy 12* (1) (January): 43–57.

Chaudhry, Kiren Aziz. 1997. *The Price of Wealth: Economies and Institutions in the Middle East*. Ithaca, N.Y.: Cornell University Press, 1997.

Cheah Boon Keng. 1998. "The Erosion of Ideological Hegemony and Royal Power and The Rise of Postwar Malay Nationalism, 1945–1946." *Journal of Southeast Asian Studies* 19 (1) (March): 1–27.

Chehabi, H. E. and Juan J. Linz, eds. 1998a. *Sultanistic Regimes*. Baltimore: Johns Hopkins University Press.

Chehabi, H. E. and Juan J. Linz. 1998b. "A Theory of Sultanism 1: A Type of Nondemocratic Rule." In Chehabi and Linz, eds. *Sultanistic Regimes*: 3–25.

Collier, David, ed. 1979. *The New Authoritarianism in Latin America*. Princeton, N.J.: Princeton University Press.

Collier, David and Steven Levitsky. 1997. "Democracy with Adjectives." *World Politics* 49(3) (April): 430–452.

Collier, Ruth Berins. 1999. *Paths Toward Democracy: The Working Class and Elites in Western Europe and South America*. Cambridge: Cambridge University Press.

Collier, Ruth Berins and David Collier. 1991. *Shaping the Political Arena: Critical Junctures, the Labor Movement, and Regime Dynamics in Latin America*. Princeton, N.J.: Princeton University Press.

Cook, Steven A. 2006. "The Promise of Pacts." *Journal of Democracy* 17 (1) (January): 63–74.

Coppedge, Michael. 1999. "Thickening Thin Concepts and Theories – Combining Large N and Small in Comparative Politics." *Comparative Politics* 31 (4) (July): 465–476.

Cox, Gary W. 1997. *Making Votes Count: Strategic Coordination in the World's Electoral Systems*. Cambridge: Cambridge University Press.

Crouch, Harold. 1992. "Authoritarian Trends, the UMNO Split and the Limits of State Power." In Joel S. Kahn and Francis Loh Kok Wah, eds., *Fragmented Vision: Culture and Politics in Contemporary Malaysia*, 21–43. Honolulu: University of Hawaii Press.

———. 1996. *Government and Society in Malaysia*. Ithaca, N.Y.: Cornell University Press.

Crystal, Jill. 1994. "Authoritarianism and its Adversaries in the Arab World." *World Politics* 46 (2) (January): 262–290.

Cullinane, Michael. 1988. "The Rise of Sergio Osmeña, 1898–1907." In Ruby Paredes, ed., *Philippine Colonial Democracy*, 70–113. New Haven: Yale Southeast Asia Studies.

Dahl, Robert Alan. 1971. *Polyarchy: Participation and Opposition*. New Haven: Yale University Press.

De Guzman, Raul P. and Luzviminda G. Tancangco. 1986. *An Assessment of the May 1984 Batasang Pambansa Elections: A Summary of Findings*. Manila: University of the Philippines.

De Guzman, R. and M. Reforma, eds. 1988. *Government and Politics in the Philippines*. Singapore: Oxford University Press.

Dekmejian, R. Hrair. 1971. *Egypt Under Nasir: A Study in Political Dynamics*. Albany: State University of New York Press.

Delury, George E., ed. 1987. *World Encyclopedia of Political Systems and Parties*. New York: Facts On File.

Diamond, Larry Jay. 1999. *Developing Democracy: Toward Consolidation*. Baltimore: Johns Hopkins University Press.

———. 2002. "Thinking about Hybrid Regimes." *Journal of Democracy* 13 (2) (April): 21–35.

———. 2005. *Squandered Victory: The American Occupation and the Bungled Effort to Bring Democracy to Iraq*. New York: Times Books.

Diamond, Larry, Juan J. Linz, and Seymour Martin Lipset, eds. 1988. *Democracy in Developing Countries*. Boulder, Colo.: Lynne Rienner.

Dimond, Larry, and Marc Platter, eds. 1993. *The Global Ressurgence of Democracy*. Baltimore: Johns Hopkins University Press.

Di Palma, Giuseppe. 1990. *To Craft Democracies: An Essay on Democratic Transitions*. Berkeley: University of California Press.

Duverger, Maurice. 1954. *Political Parties, Their Organization and Activity in the Modern State*. New York: Wiley.

Egyptian National Committee. 1995. *Taqrir li al-lajna al-wataniyya li mutaba'a al-intikhabat al-barlamaniyya 1995*. Cairo: Ibn Khaldun Center for Development Studies.

Egyptian Organization for Human Rights. 2000. *Report on 2000 Parliamentary Elections*. Cairo, Egypt.

Ehsani, Kaveh. 1999. "Do-e Khordad and the Specter of Democracy." *Middle East Report Online* 212 (Fall).

———. 2000. "Existing Political Vessels Cannot Contain the Reform Movement: A Conversation with Sai'id Hajjarian." *Middle East Report Online* (13 March).

———. 2004. "Round 12 for Iran's Reformists." *Middle East Report Online* (29 January).

———. 2005. "Iran's Presidential Race: The Long View." *Middle East Report Online* (24 June).

Ehteshami, Anoushiravan. 1995. *After Khomeini: the Iranian Second Republic*. London: Routledge.

El-Amrani, Issandr. 2005. "Controlled Reform in Egypt: Neither Reformist Nor Controlled." *Middle East Report Online* (15 December).

Esfandiari, Haleh, and Andrea Bertone, eds. 2002. *An Assessment of the Iranian Presidential Elections*. Woodrow Wilson International Center for Scholars.

Estevez, Federico, Beatriz Magaloni, and Alberto Diaz-Cayeros. 2002. "The Erosion of One-Party Rule: Clientelism, Portfolio Diversification and Electoral Strategy." Paper presented at the Annual Meeting of the American Political Science Association, Boston, Mass., 29 August–1 September.

Evans, Peter B., Dietrich Rueschemeyer, and Theda Skocpol, eds. 1985. *Bringing the State Back In*. Cambridge: Cambridge University Press.

Evans, Peter B. and James E. Rauch. 1999. "Bureaucracy and Growth: A Cross-National Analysis of the Effects of "Weberian" State Structures on Economic Growth." *American Sociological Review* 64 (5): 748–765.

Fairbanks, Stephen C. 1998. "Theocracy Versus Democracy: Iran Considers Political Parties." *Middle East Journal* 52 (1) (Winter): 17–31.

Fearon, James D. and David D. Laitin. 2004. "Neotrusteeship and the Problem of Weak States." *International Security* 28 (4) (Spring): 5–43.

Franco, Jennifer Conroy. 2000a. *Campaigning for Democracy: Grassroots Citizenship Movements, Less-Than-Democratic Elections, and Regime Transition in the Philippines.* Quezon City: Institute for Popular Democracy.
————. 2000b. *Elections and Democratization in the Philippines.* New York: Routledge.
Freedom House. 2004. *Freedom in the World-2004.* Washington, D.C.: Freedom House.
————. *Freedom In the World 2006: Selected Data from Freedom House's Annual Global Survey of Political Rights and Civil Liberties.* Washington, D.C., 2006. http://www.freedomhouse.org/uploads/pdf/Charts2006.pdf
Friend, Theodore. 1965. *Between Two Empires: The Ordeal of the Philippines, 1929–1946.* New Haven: Yale University Press.
Fukuyama, Francis. 1989. "The End of History?" *The National Interest* 16 (Summer).
Funston, John. 1980. Malay *Politics in Malaysia: A Study of the United Malays National Organization and Party Islam.* Kuala Lumpur: Heinemann Educational Books.
Funston, John. 1999. "Malaysia: A Fateful September." *Southeast Asian Affairs*, 165–184.
Future Alliances International Country Intelligence Unit. 1996. *"Special Report on Majles Elections."* Tehran: Menas Associates and Future Alliances International.
————. 2000. *"Special Report on Iran's 6th Majles Elections: Events, Analysis and Policy Prospects."* Tehran: Menas Associates and Future Alliances International.
Gamblin, Sandrine, ed., 1997. *Contours et Détours du Politique en Égypte: Les Elections Législatives de 1995.* Cairo: CEDEJ.
Geddes, Barbara. 1999a. "Authoritarian Breakdown: Empirical Test of a Game Theoretic Argument". Atlanta: Annual Meeting of the American Political Science Association. Paper presented at the annual meeting of the American Political Science Association, Atlanta, Ga., 2–5 September.
————. 1999b. "What do we know about democratization after twenty years?" *Annual Review of Political Science* 2: 115–144.
————. 2003. *Paradigms and Sand Castles: Theory Building and Research Design in Comparative Politics.* Ann Arbor: University of Michigan Press, 2003.
Gerges, Fawaz. 1999. *America and Political Islam: Clash of Cultures or Clash of Interests?* Cambridge: Cambridge University Press, 1999.
Gheissari, Ali and Vali Nasr. 2005. "The Conservative Consolidation in Iran." *Survival* 47 (2) (Summer): 175–190.
Gomez, Edmund Terence and Jomo Kwame Sundaram. 1999. *Malaysia's Political Economy: Politics, Patronage and Profits.* New York: Cambridge University Press.
————. 1999. "Malaysia." In Ian Marsh, Jean Blondel, and Takashi Inoguchi, eds., *Democracy, Governance, and Economic Performance: East and Southeast Asia,* 230–260. New York: United Nations University Press.
Goodno, James B. 1991. *The Philippines: Land of Broken Promises.* London: Zed Books.

Goodwin, Jeffrey. 2001. *No Other Way Out: States and Revolutionary Movements*. Cambridge: Cambridge University Press.

Gordon, Joel. 1992. *Nasser's Blessed Movement*. New York: Oxford University Press.

Greenstein, Fred I. and Nelson W. Polsby, eds. 1975. *Handbook of Political Science, Vol. 3 Macropolitical Theory*. Reading, Mass.: Addison-Wesley.

Gutierrez, Eric U., Ildefonso C. Torrente, and Noli G. Narca. 1992. *All in the Family: A Study of Elites and Power Relations in the Philippines*. Quezon City: Institute for Popular Democracy.

Haggard, Stephan and Robert R. Kaufman. 1995. *The Political Economy of Democratic Transitions*. Princeton, N.J.: Princeton University Press.

Halpern, Manfred. 1963. *The Politics of Social Change in the Middle East and North Africa*. Princeton, N.J.: Princeton University Press.

Hamrush, Ahmad. 1993. *Thawrat 23 Yulyu al-Juz al-Thalith*. Cairo: Al-Hi'a al-Misriyya al-'Ama li al-Kitab.

Harik, Ilya. 1973. "The Single Party as a Subordinate Movement: The Case of Egypt." *World Politics* 26 (1) (October): 80–105.

Harik, Iliya and Denis J. Sullivan, eds. 1992. *Privatization and Liberalization in the Middle East*. Bloomington: Indiana University Press.

Hartmann, Christof, Ghaham Hassall, and Soliman M. Santos Jr. 2001. "Philippines." In In Dieter Nohlen, Florian Grotz, and Christof Hartmann, eds., *Elections in Asia and the Pacific: A Data Handbook: Volume 2*, 185–238. Oxford: Oxford University Press.

Hartmann Christof, Dieter Nohlen, and Florian Grotz, eds. 2001. *Elections in Asia and the Pacific: A Data Handbook: Volume 2*. Oxford: Oxford University Press.

Herb, Michael. 1999. *All in the Family: Absolutism, Revolution, and Democracy in the Middle Eastern Monarchies*. Albany: State University of New York Press.

Herbst, Jeffrey. 2001. "Political Liberalization in Africa After Ten Years." *Comparative Politics* 33 (3) (April): 357–375.

Hermet, Guy. 1978. "State-Controlled Elections: A Framework. In Guy Hermet, Richard Rose, and Alain Rouquie, eds., *Elections Without Choice*, 1–18. New York: Macmillan.

Hermet, Guy, Richard Rose, and Alain Rouquie, eds. 1978. *Elections Without Choice*. New York: Macmillan.

Heydemann, Steven. 1999. *Authoritarianism in Syria: Institutions and Social Conflict, 1946–1970*. Ithaca, N.Y.: Cornell University Press.

_____, ed. 2000. *War, Institutions, and Social Change in the Middle East*. Berkeley: University of California Press.

_____. 2000. "War, Institutions, and Social Change in the Middle East." In Steven Heydemann ed., *War, Institutions, and Social Change in the Middle East*, 2000, 1–30. Berkeley: University of California Press.

Higley, John, Michael G. Burton, and G. Lowell Field. 1990. "In Defense of Elite Theory: a Reply to Cammack." *American Sociological Review* 55 (3) (June): 421–426.

Higley, John and Richard Gunther. 1992. *Elites and Democratic Consolidation in Latin America and Southern Europe*. Cambridge: Cambridge University Press.

Hinnebusch, Raymond A. 1985. *Egyptian Politics Under Sadat: The Post-Populist Development of an Authoritarian-Modernizing State.* Cambridge: Cambridge University Press.

Hooglund, Eric. 1984. "The Gulf War and the Islamic Republic." *MERIP Reports* 125/126 (July–September): 31–37.

Hopwood, Derek. 1985. *Egypt, Politics and Society, 1945–1984.* Boston: Allen & Unwin.

Horowitz, Donald H. 1993. "Comparing Democratic Systems." In Larry Diamond and Marc F. Plattner, eds., *The Global Resurgence of Democracy,* 127–133. Baltimore: Johns Hopkins University Press.

Huber, Evelyne. 2003. "The Role of Cross-Regional Comparison." *APSA-CP: Newsletter of the APSA Organized Section in Comparative Politics* 14 (2): 1–6.

Hudson, Michael. 1977. *Arab Politics: The Search for Legitimacy.* New Haven: Yale University Press.

———. 1991. "After the Gulf War: Prospects for Democratization in the Arab World." *Middle East Journal* 45 (3) (Summer): 407–427.

Huntington, Samuel P. 1968. *Political Order in Changing Societies.* New Haven: Yale University Press.

———. 1970. "Social and Institutional Dynamics of One-Party Systems." In Samuel P. Huntington and Clement H. Moore, eds., *Authoritarian Politics in Modern Society: The Dynamics of Established One-Party Systems,* 3–47. New York: Basic Books.

———. 1984. "Will More Countries Become Democratic?" *Political Science Quarterly* 99 (2) (Summer): 193–218.

———. 1991. *The Third Wave: Democratization in the Late Twentieth Century.* Norman: University of Oklahoma Press.

Huntington, Samuel P. and Clement H. Moore. 1970. "Authoritarianism, Democracy, and One-Party Politics." In Samuel P. Huntington and Clement H. Moore, eds., *Authoritarian Politics in Modern Society: The Dynamics of Established One-Party Systems,* 509–517. New York: Basic Books.

———, eds. 1970. *Authoritarian Politics in Modern Society: The Dynamics of Established One-Party Systems.* New York: Basic Books.

Hutchcroft, Paul D. 2000. "Colonial Masters, National Politicos, and Provincial Lords: Central Authority and Local Autonomy in the American Philippines, 1900–1913." *Journal of Asian Studies* 59 (2) (May): 277–310.

Hwang In-Won. 2003. *Personalized Politics: The Malaysian State Under Mahathir.* Singapore: Institute of Southeast Asian Studies.

Ikenberry, John G. 2001. *After Victory: Institutions, Strategic Restraint, and the Rebuilding of Order After Major Wars.* Princeton, N.J.: Princeton University Press.

International Crisis Group. 2000. *Burma/Myanmar: How Strong is the Military Regime?* Asia Report 11.

———. 2005. *Reforming Egypt: In Search of a Strategy.* Middle East Report 46.

Ishak bin Tadin. 1960. "Dato Onn, 1946–1951." *Journal of Southeast Asian History* 1 (1) (March): 62–99.

Joaquin, Nick. 1985. *Doy Laurel in Profile: A Philippine Political Odyssey.* Manila: Makati Trade Times Publishing.

Jomo K. S. 1986. *Development Policy and Income Inequality in Peninsular Malaysia*. Kuala Lumpur: Institute of Advanced Studies.

Jones Luong, Pauline. 2002. *Institutional Change and Political Continuity in Post-Soviet Central Asia: Power, Perceptions, and Pacts*. Cambridge: Cambridge University Press.

Joseph, Richard. 1997. "Democratization in Africa after 1989 – Comparative and Theoretical Perspectives." *Comparative Politics* 29 (3) (April): 363–383.

Kalyvas, Stathis N. 1999. "The Decay and Breakdown of Communist One-Party Systems." *Annual Review of Political Science* 2 (1): 323–343.

Kamrava, Mehran and Houchang Hassan-Yari. 2004. "Suspended Equilibrium in Iran's Political System." *The Muslim World* 94 (4) (October): 495–524.

Kahn, Joel S., and Francis Loh Kok Wah, eds. 1992. *Fragmented Vision: Culture and Politics in Contemporary Malaysia*. Honolulu: University of Hawaii Press.

Karl, Terry Lynn. 1990. "Dilemmas of Democratization in Latin America." *Comparative Politics* 23 (1) (October): 1–21.

———. 1997. *The Paradox of Plenty: Oil Booms and Petro-States*. Berkeley: University of California Press.

Karl, Terry Lynn and Philippe C. Schmitter. 1991. "Modes of Transition in Latin-America, Southern and Eastern-Europe." *International Social Science Journal* 43 (2) (May): 269–284.

Karnow, Stanely. 1989. *In Our Image: America's Empire in the Philippines*. New York: Random House.

Karvonen, Lauri and Carsten Anckar. 2002. "Party Systems and Democratization: A Comparative Study of the Third World." *Democratization* 9 (3) (Autumn): 11–29.

Kassem, Maye. 1999. *In the Guise of Democracy: Governance in Contemporary Egypt*. Reading, MA: Ithaca Press.

Kasza, Gregory James. 1995. *The Conscription Society: Administered Mass Organizations*. New Haven: Yale University Press.

Katouzian, Homa. 1988. "The Pahlavi Regime in Iran." In H. E. Chehabi and Juan J. Linz, eds., *Sultanistic Regimes*, 182–205. Baltimore: Johns Hopkins University Press.

Katznelson, Ira. 1997. "Structure and Configuration in Comparative Politics." In Mark Irving Lichbach and Alan S. Zuckerman, eds., *Comparative Politics: Rationality, Culture and Structure*, 81–112. New York: Cambridge University Press.

Kauz, Ralph, Hamid Khosravi Sharoudi, and Andreas Rieck. 2001. "Iran." In Dieter Nohlen, Florian Grotz, and Christof Hartmann, eds., *Elections in Asia and the Pacific: A Data Handbook, Volume 1*, 57–85. Oxford: Oxford University Press.

Kaufman, Robert. 1986. "Liberalization and Democratization in South America: Perspectives from the 1970s." In Guillermo O'Donnell, Philippe C. Schmitter, and Laurence Whitehead, eds., *Transitions from Authoritarian Rule: Comparative Perspectives*, 85–107. Baltimore: Johns Hopkins University Press.

Kazemi, Farhad. 2003. "The Precarious Revolution: Unchanging Institutions and the Fate of Reform in Iran." *Journal of International Affairs*, 57 (1) (Fall): 81–95.

Keefer, Philip. 2002. *Database of Political Institutions: Changes and Variable Definitions*. New York: The World Bank.

Kerkvliet, Benedict. 1977. *The Huk Rebellion: A Study of Peasant Revolt in the Philippines*. Berkeley: University of California Press.

Keshavarzian, Arang and Mohammad Maljoo. 2005. "Paradox and Possibility in Iran's Presidential Election." *Middle East Report On-Line* (12 June).

Khawaga, Dina al-. 1997. "Le Parti National Démocrate et les Élections de 1995." In Sandrine Gamblin, ed., *Contours et Détours du Politique en Égypte: Les Elections Législatives de 1995*, 83–99. Cairo: CEDEJ.

Khong Kim Hoong. 1987. "The Early Political Movements Before Independence." In Zakaria Haji Ahmad, ed., *Government and Politics of Malaysia*, 11–39. New York: Oxford University Press.

———. 1991a. "Malaysia 1990: The Election Show-down." *Southeast Asian Affairs*, 161–179.

———. 1991b. *Malaysia's General Election 1990: Continuity, Change, and Ethnic Politics*. Singapore: Institute of Southeast Asian Studies.

Khoo Boo Teik. 1997a. "Democracy and Authoritarianism in Malaysia Since 1957." In Anek Laothamatas, ed., *Democratization in Southeast and East Asia*, 46–76. Singapore: Institute of Southeast Asian Studies.

———. 1997b. "Malaysia: Challenges and Upsets in Politics and Other Contestations." *Southeast Asian Affairs*: 163–184.

———. 2000. "Unfinished Crises: Malaysian Politics in 1999." *Southeast Asian Affairs*: 165–183.

Khosrokhavar, Farhad. 2004. "The New Conservatives Take a Turn." *Middle East Report Online* 233 (Winter).

Kienle, Eberhard. 2001. *A Grand Delusion: Democracy and Economic Reform in Egypt*. New York: I.B. Tauris.

Kirchheimer, Otto. 1966. "The Transformation of the Western European Party Systems." In Joseph LaPalombara and Myron Weiner, eds., *Political Parties and Political Development*, 177–200. Princeton, N.J.: Princeton University Press.

Kitschelt, Herbert. 1999. "Accounting for Outcomes of Post-Communist Regimes Change: Causal Depth or Shallowness in Rival Explanations." Paper presented at the annual meeting of the American Political Science Association, Atlanta, Ga., 2–5 September.

———. 2000. "Linkages between Citizens and Politicians in Democratic Polities." *Comparative Political Studies*, 33 (6–7), August/September: 845–879.

Knight, Alan. 1992a. "Mexico's Elite Settlement: Conjuncture and Consequences." In John Higley and Richard Gunther, eds., *Elites and Democratic Consolidation in Latin America and Southern Europe*, 113–145. New York: Cambridge University Press.

Knight, Jack. 1992b. *Institutions and Social Conflict*. New York: Cambridge University Press.

Kohli, Atul. 1990. *Democracy and Discontent: India's Growing Crisis of Governability*. New York: Cambridge University Press.

———. 1994. "Centralization and Powerlessness: India's Democracy in Comparative Perspective." In Joel Migdal, Atul Kohli, and Vivienne Shue, eds., *State Power and Social Forces: Domination and Transformation in the Third World*, 89–107. New York: Cambridge University Press.

Krasner, Stephen D. 1984. "Approaches to the State: Alternative Conceptions and Historical Dynamics." *Comparative Politics* 16 (2), January: 223–246.

———. 2004. "Sharing Sovereignty: New Institutions for Collapsed and Failing States." *International Security*, 29 (2), 2004: 85–120.

Lande, Carl H. 1965. *Leaders, Factions, and Parties: The Structure of Philippine Politics*. New Haven: Yale University Press.

Langston, Joy. 2006. "Elite Ruptures: When Do Ruling Parties Split?" In Andreas Schedler, ed., *Electoral Authoritarianism: The Dynamics of Unfree Competition:* 57–75. Boulder, Colo.: Lynne Rienner.

Laothamatas, Anek, ed., 1997. *Democratization in Southeast and East Asia*. Singapore: Institute of Southeast Asian Studies.

LaPalombara, Joseph, and Myron Weiner, eds. 1966. *Political Parties and Political Development*. Princeton, N.J.: Princeton University Press.

Leifer, Michael. 1976. "Malaysia After Tan Razak: Tensions in a Multi-Racial State." *Round Table* (262): 153–160.

Lemarchand, Rene, and Keith Legg. 1972. "Political Clientelism and Development: A Preliminary Analysis." *Comparative Politics* 4 (2) (January): 149–178.

Levitsky, Steven, and Lucan A. Way. 2002. "The Rise of Competitive Authoritarianism." *Journal of Democracy 13* (2) (April): 51–65.

Liak Teng Kiat. 1996. "Malaysia: Mahathir's Last Hurrah?" *Southeast Asian Affairs*, 217–237.

Library of Congress. 1991. *A Country Study: Philippines*. Washington, D.C: United States Government Publications Office.

Lichbach Mark Irving, and Alan S. Zuckerman, eds. 1997. *Comparative Politics: Rationality, Culture and Structure*. New York: Cambridge University Press.

Lieberman, Evan S. 2001. "Causal Inference in Historical Institutional Analysis: A Specification of Periodization Strategies." *Comparative Political Studies 34* (9) (November): 1011–1035.

Lilla, Mark. 2002. "The New Age of Tyranny." *New York Review of Books, 49* (16) (24 October): 28–29.

Linz, Juan J. 1964. "An Authoritarian Regime: The Case of Spain." In Erik Allardt and Yrgo Littunen, eds., *Cleavages, Ideologies, and Party Systems: Contributions to Comparative Political Sociology*. Transactions of the Westermarck Society 10, 291–342.

———. 1973. "The Future of an Authoritarian Situation or the Institutionalization of an Authoritarian Regime: The Case of Brazil." In Alfred Stepan, ed., *Authoritarian Brazil: Origins, Policies, and Future*, 233–254. New Haven, Conn.: Yale University Press.

———. 1975. "Totalitarian and Authoritarian Regimes." In Fred I. Greenstein and Nelson W. Polsby, eds., *Handbook of Political Science, Vol. 3 Macropolitical Theory*, 175–357. Reading, Mass.: Addison-Wesley.

———. 1978. *The Breakdown of Democratic Regimes: Crisis, Breakdown, Reequilibration*. Baltimore: Johns Hopkins University Press.

———. 1993. "The Perils of Presidentialism." In Larry Diamond and Marc Plattner, eds., *The Global Resurgence of Democracy*, 108–126. Baltimore: Johns Hopkins University Press.

Linz, Juan J. and Alfred C. Stepan. 1996. *Problems of Democratic Transition and Consolidation: Southern Europe, South America, and Post-Communist Europe.* Baltimore: Johns Hopkins University Press.

Lipset, Seymour Martin. 1959. "Some Social Requisites of Democracy: Economic-Development and Political Legitimacy." *American Political Science Review* 53 (1) (March): 69–105.

Lipset, Seymour Martin and Stein Rokkan. 1967. *Party Systems and Voter Alignments: Cross-National Perspectives.* New York: Free Press.

Lust-Okar, Ellen. 2005. *Structuring Contestation in the Arab World: Incumbents, Opponents, and Institutions.* New York: Cambridge University Press.

Lust-Okar, Ellen and Amaney Jamal. 2002. "Rulers and Rules: Reassessing the Influence of Regime Type on Electoral Law Formation." *Comparative Political Studies* 35 (3) (April): 337–366.

MacAndrews, Colin. 1977. "The Politics of Planning: Malaysia and the New Third Malaysia Plan (1976–1980)." *Asian Survey* 17 (3) (March): 293–308.

Mahoney, James and Richard Snyder. 1999. "Rethinking Agency and Structure in the Study of Regime Change." *Studies in Comparative International Development* 34 (2) (Summer): 3–32.

Mahoney, James. 2000. "Strategies of Causal Inference in Small-N Analysis." *Sociological Methods and Research* 28 (4) (May): 387–424.

———. 2002. *The Legacies of Liberalism: Path Dependence and Political Regimes in Central America.* Baltimore: Johns Hopkins University Press.

Mahoney, James, and Dietrich Rueschemeyer, eds. 2003. *Comparative Historical Analysis in the Social Sciences.* New York: Cambridge University Press.

Mainwaring, Scott and Anibal Perez-Linan. 2003. "Level of Development and Democracy: Latin American Exceptionalism." *Comparative Political Studies* 11 (9) (November): 1031–1067.

Mainwaring, Scott and Timothy Scully, eds. 1995a. *Building Democratic Institutions: Party Systems in Latin America.* Stanford: Stanford University Press.

———. 1995b. "Introduction: Party Systems in Latin America." In Scott Mainwaring and Timothy Scully, eds., *Building Democratic Institutions: Party Systems in Latin America*, 1–34. Stanford: Stanford University Press.

Makram-Ebeid, Mona. 1996. "Egypt's Elections: One Step Forward, Two Steps Back?" *Middle East Policy* 4 (3): 119–136.

Maloney, Susan. 2000. "Elections in Iran: A New Majlis and a Mandate for Reform." *Middle East Policy* 7 (3): 59–66.

March, James G., ed., 1965. *Handbook of Organizations.* Chicago: Rand McNally.

March, James G. and Jonah P. Olsen. 1984. "New Institutionalism: Organizational Factors in Political Life." *American Political Science Review* 78 (3), September: 734–749.

Marsh, Ian, Jean Blondel, and Takashi Inoguchi, eds. 1999. *Democracy, Governance, and Economic Performance: East and Southeast Asia.* New York: United Nations University Press.

Marx, Karl. 2004 [1852]. *The Eighteenth Brumaire of Louis Bonaparte.* New York: International Publishers.

McCoy, Alfred W. 1988. "Quezon's Commonwealth: The Emergence of Philippine Authoritarianism." In Ruby R. Paredes, ed., *Philippine Colonial Democracy*, 114–160. New Haven: Yale University Southeast Asia Studies.

McFaul, Michael A., and Abbas Milani. 2005. "Cracks in the Land of the Aya-tollahs." *International Herald Tribune* (17 June): 6.

Means, Gordon Paul. 1976. *Malaysian Politics*. London: Hodder and Stoughton.

Medina, Luis Fernando and Susan Stokes. 2002. "Clientelism as Political Monopoly." Paper presented at the annual meeting of the American Political Science Association, 29 August–1 September, Boston, Mass.

Menashri, David. 1980. *Iran: A Decade of War and Revolution*. New York: Holmes and Meier.

————. 1990. *The Iranian Revolution and the Muslim World*. Boulder, Colo.: Westview Press.

————. 2001. *Post-Revolutionary Politics in Iran: Religion, Society, and Power*. London: Frank Cass.

MERIP Special Correspondent. 1999. "Report from Iran." *Middle East Report Online*, 15 July.

Metz, Helen Chapin and Library of Congress. 1989. *Iran: A Country Study*. Washington, D.C.: United States Government Publications Office.

Migdal, Joel S. 1988. *Strong Societies and Weak States: State-Society Relations and State Capabilities in the Third World*. Princeton, N.J.: Princeton University Press.

Milne, Robert S., and Diane K. Mauzy. 1980. *Politics and Government in Malaysia*. Vancouver: University of British Columbia Press.

————. 1983. "The Mahathir Administration in Malaysia: Discipline Through Islam." *Pacific Affairs* 56 (4) (Winter): 617–648.

————. 1999. *Malaysian Politics under Mahathir*. London: Routledge.

Milner, Helen. 1988. "Trading Places: Industries for Free-Trade." *World Politics*, 40 (3): 350–376.

Moore, Barrington Jr. 1966. *Social Origins of Dictatorship and Democracy: Lord and Peasant in the Making of the Modern World*. Boston, Mass.: Beacon Press.

Moore, Clement Henry. 1974. "Authoritarian Politics in Unincorporated Society: The Case of Nasser's Egypt." *Comparative Politics* 6 (2) (January): 193–218.

Moore, Pete W. 2004. *Doing Business in the Middle East: Politics and Economic Crisis in Jordan and Kuwait*. New York: Cambridge University Press.

Moslem, Mehdi. 2002. *Factional Politics in Post-Khomeini Iran*. Syracuse, N.Y.: Syracuse University Press.

Mudara, Ali. 2001. "Iran's Reform Dilemma: Within and Against the State." *Middle East Report Online* (12 September).

Munck, Gerardo L., and Jay Verkuilen. 2002. "Conceptualizing and Measuring Democracy: Evaluating Alternative Indices." *Comparative Political Studies* 35 (1), February: 5–24.

Munro, Ross H. 1984. "Dateline Manila: Moscow's Next Win?" *Foreign Policy* 56 (Fall): 173–190.

Mustafa, Hala, ed. 1997. *The Parliamentary Elections in Egypt 1995*. Cairo: Al-Ahram Center for Political and Strategic Studies.

_____. 1997a. *Al-Intikhabat Al-Barlamaniyya fi Misr 1995.* Cairo: Al-Ahram Center for Political and Strategic Studies.

_____. 1997b. "Intikhabat 1995 fi siyaq al-tatawwur al-siyasi fi Misr." In Hala Mustafa, ed. *Al-Intikhabat Al-Barlamaniyya fi Misr 1995,* 15–34. Cairo: Al-Ahram Center for Political and Strategic Studies.

_____. 1997c. "Mu'ashshirat wa nita'ij intikhabat 1995." In Hala Mustafa, ed. *Al-Intikhabat Al-Barlamaniyya fi Misr 1995,* 35–51. Cairo: Al-Ahram Center for Political and Strategic Studies.

Mustafa, Hala, ed. 2001a. *Intikhabat Majlis Al-Sh'ab 2000.* Cairo: Al-Ahram Center for Political and Strategic Studies.

_____. 2001b. "Intikhabat 2000: Mu'ashshirat Amma." In Hala Mustafa, ed. *Intikhabat Majlis Al-Sh'ab 2000,* 7–14. Cairo: Al-Ahram Center for Political and Strategic Studies.

National Citizens Movement for Free Elections. 1986. *The NAMFREL Report on the February 7, 1986 Philippine Presidential Elections.* Manila: National Citizens Movement for Free Elections.

National Media Production Center. 1980. *The Marcos Revolution: A Progress Report on the New Society of the Philippines.* Manila: National Media Production Center.

Nohlen, Dieter, Michael Krennerich, and Bernhard Thibaut, eds. 1999. *Elections in Africa: A Data Handbook.* Oxford: Oxford University Press.

North, Douglass C. 1990. *Institutions, Institutional Change, and Economic Performance.* Cambridge: Cambridge University Press.

O'Donnell, Guillermo A. 1973. *Modernization and Bureaucratic-Authoritarianism: Studies in South American Politics.* Berkeley: Institute of International Studies, University of California.

O'Donnell, Guillermo A. and Philippe C. Schmitter. 1986. *Transitions from Authoritarian Rule: Tentative Conclusions about Uncertain Democracies.* Baltimore: Johns Hopkins University Press.

Ongkili, James P. 1985. *Nation-Building in Malaysia, 1946–1974.* Singapore: Oxford University Press.

Ottaway, Marina. 2003. *Democracy Challenged: The Rise of Semi-Authoritarianism.* Washington, D.C.: Carnegie Endowment for International Peace, 2003.

Ottaway, Marina and Olcott Martha Brill. 1999. "The Challenge of Semi-Authoritarianism." *Carnegie Paper No.7.* Washington, D.C.: Carnegie Endowment for International Peace (October).

Ouda, Jihad, Negad El-Borai, and Hafez Abu Se'ada. *A Door Onto the Desert: The Egyptian Parliamentary Elections of 2000, Course, Dilemmas, and Recommendations for the Future.* Cairo: United Group.

Overholt, William. 1986. "The Rise and Fall of Ferdinand Marcos." *Asian Survey* 26 (11), November: 1137–1163.

Paguia, Alan F. 2003. *Estrada V. Arroyo: Rule of Law or Rule of Force?* Manila: Icon Press Incorporated.

Paredes, Ruby R., ed. 1988. *Philippine Colonial Democracy.* New Haven, Conn.: Yale University Southeast Asia Studies.

———. 1988a. "Introduction: The Paradox of Philippine Colonial Democracy."
In Ruby R. Paredes, ed., *Philippine Colonial Democracy*, 1–12. New Haven,
Conn.: Yale University Southeast Asia Studies.

——— 1988b. "The Origins of National Politics: Taft and the Partido Federal."
In Ruby R. Paredes, ed., *Philippine Colonial Democracy*, 41–69. New Haven,
Conn.: Yale University Southeast Asia Studies.

Parsa, Misagh. 2000. *States, Ideologies, and Social Revolutions: A Comparative
Analysis of Iran, Nicaragua, and the Philippines*. New York: Cambridge University Press.

Pempel, T. J. 1990a. "Introduction. Uncommon Democracies: The One-Party
Dominant Regimes." In T. J. Pempel, ed., *Uncommon Democracies: The One-
Party Dominant Regimes*, 1–32. Ithaca, N.Y.: Cornell University Press.

———. 1990b. "Conclusion: One-Party Dominance and the Creation of
Regimes." In T. J. Pempel, ed., *Uncommon Democracies: The One-Party Dominant Regimes*, 333–360. Ithaca, N.Y.: Cornell University Press.

———, ed. 1990. *Uncommon Democracies: The One-Party Dominant Regimes*.
Ithaca, N.Y.: Cornell University Press.

Pierson, Paul. 2003. "Big, Slow-Moving, and...Invisible: Macrosocial Processes in the Study of Comparative Politics." In James Mahoney and Dietrich
Rueschemeyer, eds., *Comparative Historical Analysis in the Social Sciences*,
177–207. New York: Cambridge University Press.

Pripstein-Posusney, Marsha. 1998. "Behind the Ballot Box: Electoral Engineering
in the Arab World." *Middle East Report* 209 (Winter): 12–15.

———. 2002. "Multi-Party Elections in the Arab World: Institutional Engineering and Oppositional Strategies. *Studies in Comparative International Development* 36 (4) (Winter): 34–62.

Przeworski, Adam. 1986. "Some Problems in the Study of the Transition to
Democracy." In Guillermo O'Donnell, Philippe Schmitter, and Laurence Whitehead, eds., *Transitions from Authoritarian Rule: Comparative Perspectives*, 47–
63. Baltimore: Johns Hopkins University Press.

———. 1991. *Democracy and the Market: Political and Economic Reforms in
Eastern Europe and Latin America*. New York: Cambridge University Press.

Przeworski, Adam and Henry Teune. 1970. *The Logic of Comparative Social
Inquiry*. New York: Wiley-Interscience.

Przeworski, Adam and Jennifer Gandhi. 2001. "Dictatorial Institutions and the
Survival of Dictators." Paper presented at the Annual Meeting of the American
Political Science Association, 30 August–2 September. San Francisco, Calif.

Pye, Lucian W. 1990. "Political Science and the Crisis of Authoritarianism." *American Political Science Review* 84 (1) (March): 3–19.

Rabei, Amro Hashem. 2001. "Al-musharaka al-siyasiyya: Mu'ashshirat kaifiyya
wa kammiyya." In Hala Mustafa, ed. *Intikhabat Majlis Al-Sh'ab 2000*, 163–
208. Cairo: Al-Ahram Center for Political and Strategic Studies.

Rajaee, Bahram. 2004. "Deciphering Iran: The Political Evolution of the Islamic
Republic and U.S. Foreign Policy After September 11." *Comparative Studies of
South Asia, Africa, and the Middle East* 24 (1): 159–172.

Rajaee, Farhang. 1999. "A Thermidor of Islamic Yuppies? Conflict and Compromise in Iran's Politics." *Middle Eastern Journal* 53 (2) (Spring): 217–232.

Ramanathan Sankaran and Mohammad Hamdan Adnan. 1988. *Malaysia's 1986 General Election: The Urban-Rural Dichotomy*. Singapore: Institute of Southeast Asian Studies.

Remmer, Karen L. 1991. "New Wine or Old Bottlenecks?" *Comparative Politics* 23 (4) (July): 479–495.

———. 1999. "Regime Sustainability in the Latin Caribbean, 1944–1994." *Journal of Developing Areas* 33 (3) (Spring): 331–354.

Reshad, Abdel Ghefar. 2000. "Intikhabat majlis al-sh'ab 2000: Tahlil al-itar al-'amm." In Mustafa Alawi, ed. 2000. *Intikhabat Majlis al-Sh'ab 2000*, 31–291. Cairo: Konrad Adenauer Stiftung.

Rezaie, Ali. 2003. "Last Efforts of Iran's Reformists." *Middle East Report* 226, (Spring): 40–46.

Richards, Alan and John Waterbury. 1996. *A Political Economy of the Middle East*. Boulder, Colo.: Westview Press.

Rida, Mohammed Abu. 2001. "The Political and Social Makeup of the 2000 People's Assembly." *Al-Dimuqratiyya*, 1.

Ries, Matthias. 1999. "Egypt." In Dieter Nohlen, Michael Krennerich, and Bernhard Thibaut, eds., *Elections in Africa: A Data Handbook*, 329–350. Oxford: Oxford University Press.

Roberts, Clayton. 1996. *The Logic of Historical Explanation*. University Park: Pennsylvania State University Press.

Rocamora, Joel. 1998. "Philippine Political Parties: Continuity and Change." Unpublished Paper. Quezon City, 27 February.

Rosenberg, David A. 1979. "Liberty Versus Loyalty: The Transformation of Philippine News Media Under Martial Law." In David Rosenberg, ed., *Marcos and Martial Law in the Philippines*, 145–179. Ithaca, N.Y.: Cornell University Press.

Rosenberg, David, ed. 1979. *Marcos and Martial Law in the Philippines*. Ithaca, N.Y.: Cornell University Press.

Rouleau, Eric. 1981. "The War and the Struggle for the State." *MERIP Reports* 98 (July–August): 3–8.

Rueschemeyer, Dietrich, Evelyne Huber Stephens, and John D. Stephens. 1992. *Capitalist Development and Democracy*. Chicago: University of Chicago Press.

Rustow, Dankwart A. 1967. *A World of Nations: Problems of Political Modernization*. Washington, D.C.: Brookings Institution.

Rustow, Dankwart A. 1970. "Transitions to Democracy: Toward a Dynamic Model." *Comparative Politics* 2 (3) (April): 337–363.

Saghafi, Morad. 1996. "The Return of Iranian Immigrants: A Suspended Experience." *Goft-o-goo* 1: 77–87.

———. 2002. "The Eighth Presidential Election: Another Election Without a Choice?" In Haleh Esfandiari and Andrea Bertone, eds., *An Assessment of the Iranian Presidential Elections*, 15–26. Washington, D.C.: Woodrow Wilson International Center for Scholars.

———. 2004. "The New Landscape of Iranian Politics." *Middle East Report Online* 233 (Winter).

Sahimi, Mohammad. 2003. "Iran's Nuclear Program. Part I: Its History." *Payvand*. http://www.payvand.com/news/03/oct/1015.html. Accessed 19 February 2007.

Salame, Ghassan, ed. 1994. *Democracy Without Democrats? The Renewal of Politics in the Muslim World*. London: I.B. Tauris Publishers.

Sartori, Giovanni. 1976. *Parties and Party Systems: A Framework for Analysis*. New York: Cambridge University Press.

Schedler, Andreas. 2000. "The Democratic Revelation." *Journal of Democracy*, 11 (4) (October): 5–19.

————. 2002. "The Menu of Manipulation." *Journal of Democracy*, 13 (2) (April): 36–50.

————, ed. 2006. *Electoral Authoritarianism: The Dynamics of Unfree Competition*. Boulder, Colo.: Lynne Rienner.

Scheiner, Ethan. 2006. *Democracy Without Competition in Japan: Opposition Failure in a One-Party Dominant State*. New York: Cambridge University Press.

Schemm, Paul. 2003. "Egypt Struggles to Control Anti-War Protests." *Middle East Report Online* (31 March).

Schickler, Eric. 2001. *Disjointed Pluralism: Institutional Innovation and the Development of the U.S. Congress*. Princeton, N.J.: Princeton University Press.

Schirazi, Asghar. 1997. *The Constitution of Iran: Politics and the State in the Islamic Republic*. New York: I.B. Tauris.

Schlesinger, Joseph A. 1975. "The Primary Goals of Political Parties: A Clarification of Positive Theory." *American Political Science Review* 69 (3) (September): 840–849.

Schmitter, Philippe and Terry Lynn Karl. 1991. "What Democracy Is . . . And Is Not." *Journal of Democracy* 2 (3) (Summer): 75–88.

Schumpeter, Joseph Alois. 1947. *Capitalism, Socialism, and Democracy*. New York: Harper & Brothers.

Searle, Peter. 1999. *The Riddle of Malaysian Capitalism: Rent-Seekers or Real Capitalists?* Honolulu: Asian Studies Association of Australia in Association with Allen & Unwin and University of Hawaii Press.

Semati, Hadi. 2004. "Democracy in Retrograde: The Iraq War has Slowed Calls for Reform in Iran." *Los Angeles Times* 24 (September): B11.

Shamsul Amri Baharuddin. 1988. "'The Battle Royal': The UMNO Elections of 1987." *Southeast Asian Affairs*, 170–188.

Shefter, Martin. 1994. *Political Parties and the State: The American Historical Experience*. Princeton, N.J.: Princeton University Press.

Shin, Doh Chull. 1994. "On the Third Wave of Democratization: A Synthesis and Evaluation of Recent Theory and Research." *World Politics* 47 (1), October: 135–170.

Shoubaki, Amr al-. 2001. "Al-Intikhabat wa d'af al-mua'ssasa al-hizbiyya." *Al-Dimuqratiyya* 1 (1) (Winter): 104–114.

Siavoshi, Sussan. 1992. "Factionalism and Iranian Politics: The Post-Khomeini Experience." *Journal of the Society for Iranian Studies* 25 (3–4): 27–49.

Skocpol, Theda. 1979. *States and Social Revolutions: A Comparative Analysis of France, Russia, and China*. Cambridge: Cambridge University Press.

Slater, Daniel. 2003. "Iron Cage in an Iron Fist: Authoritarian Institutions and the Personalization of Power in Malaysia." *Comparative Politics* 36 (1) (October): 81–102.

Smith, Benjamin. 2005. "Life of the Party: The Origins of Regime Breakdown and Persistence under Single-Party Rule." *World Politics* 57 (3), April: 421–451.
———. 2007. *Hard Times in the Land of Plenty: Oil, Opposition, and Late Development*. Ithaca, N.Y.: Cornell University Press.
Smith, Simon C. 1994. "The Rise, Decline and Survival of the Malay Rulers during the Colonial Period, 1874–1957." *Journal of Imperial and Commonwealth History* 22 (1) (January): 84–108.
Snyder, Richard. 1992. "Explaining Transitions from Neopatrimonial Dictatorships." *Comparative Politics* 24 (4) (July): 379–399.
———. 2006. "Beyond Electoral Authoritarianism." In Andreas Schedler, ed., *Electoral Authoritarianism: The Dynamics of Unfree Competition*, 219–231. Boulder, Colo.: Lynne Rienner.
Snyder, Richard and James Mahoney. 1999. "The Missing Variable – Institutions and the Study of Regime Change." *Comparative Politics* 32 (1) (October): 103–122.
Sohrabi, Naghmeh and Arang Keshavarzian. 2001. "On the Eve of Iran's Presidential Elections." *Middle East Report Online* 212.
Solinger, Dorothy J. 2001. "Ending One-Party Dominance: Korea, Taiwan, Mexico." *Journal of Democracy*, 12 (1) (January): 30–42.
Stacher, Joshua A. 2001. "A Democracy with Fangs and Claws and Its Effects On Egyptian Political Culture." *Arab Studies Quarterly* 23 (3) (Summer): 83–99.
———. 2004. "Parties Over: The Demise of Egypt's Opposition Parties." *British Journal of Middle East Studies* 31 (2) (November): 215–233.
Steinberg, David Joel. 1994. *The Philippines: A Singular and a Plural Place*. Boulder, Colo.: Westview Press.
Stinchcombe, Arthur. 1965. "Social Structure and Organizations." In James G. March, ed., *Handbook of Organizations*, 142–193. Chicago: Rand McNally.
Stockwell, A. J. 1977. "The Formation and First Years of the United Malays National Organization (U.M.N.O.)." *Modern Asian Studies* 11 (4): 481–513.
Stubbs, Richard. 1979. "The United Malays National Organization, the Malayan Chinese Association, and the Early Years of the Malayan Emergency, 1948–1955." *Journal of Southeast Asian Studies* 10 (1) (March): 77–88.
Sullivan, Denis. 1992. "Extra-State Actors and Privatization in Egypt." In Ilya Harik and Denis J. Sullivan, eds., *Privatization and Liberalization in the Middle East*, 24–45. Bloomington: Indiana University Press.
Tajbakhsh, Kian. 2000. "Political Decentralization and the Creation of Local Government in Iran: Consolidation or Transformation of the Theocratic State?" *Social Research* 67 (2) (Summer): 377–404.
Tan, Kevin. 2001. "Malaysia." In Dieter Nohlen, Florian Grotz, and Christof Hartmann, eds., *Elections in Asia and the Pacific: A Data Handbook: Volume 2*, 143–183. Oxford: Oxford University Press.
Tancangco, Luzviminda G. 1988. "The Electoral System and Political Parties in the Philippines." In R. De Guzman and M. Reforma, eds., *Government and Politics in the Philippines*, 77–112. Singapore: Oxford University Press.
Tarrow, Sidney. 1999. "Expanding Paired Comparison: A Modest Proposal." *American Political Science Association: Comparative Politics Newsletter* 10 (2): 9–12.

Thelen, Kathleen. 1992. *Historical Institutionalism in Comparative Analysis.* Cambridge: Cambridge University Press.

Thompson, Mark R. 1995. *The Anti-Marcos Struggle: Personalistic Rule and Democratic Transition in the Philippines.* New Haven, Conn.: Yale University Press.

———. 1996. "Off the Endangered List: Philippine Democratization in Comparative Perspective." *Comparative Politics* 28 (2) (January): 179–205.

———. 1998. "The Marcos Regime in the Philippines." In H. E. Chehabi and Juan J. Linz, eds., *Sultanistic Regimes*, 206–229. Baltimore: Johns Hopkins University Press.

Tilly, Charles. 1975a. "Reflections on the History of European State-Making." In Charles Tilly, ed., *The Formation of National States in Western Europe*: 3–83. Princeton, N.J.: Princeton University Press.

Tilly, Charles, ed. 1975b. *The Formation of National States in Western Europe.* Princeton, N.J.: Princeton University Press.

Tilman, Robert O. and Jo H. Tilman. 1977. "Malaysia and Singapore, 1976: A Year of Challenge, a Year of Change." *Asian Survey* 17 (2) (February): 143–154.

Tocqueville, Alexis de. 1955. *The Old Regime and the French Revolution.* Garden City, N.Y.: Doubleday.

Tucker, Judith. 1978. "While Sadat Shuffles: Economic Decay, Political Ferment in Egypt." *MERIP Reports, 8* (2): 3–9, 26.

Vatikiotis, P. J. 1991. *The History of Modern Egypt: From Muhammad Ali to Mubarak.* Baltimore: Johns Hopkins University Press.

Vaziri, Haleh. 1999. "Deja Vu All Over Again?" *Middle East Report Online* (20 July).

von Vorys, Karl. 1975. *Democracy without Consensus: Communalism and Political Stability in Malaysia.* Princeton, N.J.: Princeton University Press.

Waldner, David. 1999. *State Building and Late Development.* Ithaca, N.Y.: Cornell University Press.

———. 2002a. "From Intra-Type Variations to the Origins of Types: Recovering the Macro-Analytics of State Building." Paper presented at the Conference on Asian Political Economy in an Era of Globalization, Dartmouth College, 10–11 May.

———. 2002b. "Rural Incorporation and Regime Outcomes." Paper presented at the annual meeting of the Middle East Studies Association, Washington, D.C., 23–26 November.

———. 2004. "Democracy and Dictatorship in the Post-Colonial World." Paper presented at the annual meeting of the American Political Science Association, Chicago, Ill., 2–5 September.

Wallerstein, Immanuel. 1961. *Africa, The Politics of Independence: An Interpretation of Modern African History.* New York: Vintage Books.

Ware, Alan. 1996. *Political Parties and Party Systems.* Oxford: Oxford University Press.

Waterbury, John. 1983. *The Egypt of Nasser and Sadat: The Political Economy of Two Regimes.* Princeton, N.J.: Princeton University Press.

Way, Lucan A. 2002. "Pluralism by Default in Moldova." *Journal of Democracy* *13* (4) (October): 127–141.

Weiner, Myron, and Joseph LaPalombara, eds. 1966. *Political Parties and Political Development.* Princeton, N.J.: Princeton University Press.

Wood, Elisabeth Jean. 2001. "An Insurgent Path to Democracy: Popular Mobilization, Economic Interests, and Regime Transition in South Africa and El Salvador." *Comparative Political Studies* 34 (8) (October): 862–888.

World Bank. 2002. *World Development Indicators.* Washington, D.C.: World Bank.

Wurfel, David. 1988. *Filipino Politics: Development and Decay.* Ithaca, N.Y.: Cornell University Press.

Yashar, Deborah J. 1997. *Demanding Democracy: Reform and Reaction in Costa Rica and Guatemala, 1870s–1950s.* Stanford, Calif.: Stanford University Press.

Yeo Kim Wah. 1980. "Grooming of an Elite: Malay Administrators in the Federated Malay States, 1903–1941." *Journal of Southeast Asian Studies* 11 (2), September: 287–319.

Zakaria Haji Ahmad, ed., 1987. *Government and Politics of Malaysia.* New York: Oxford University Press.

Zakaria, Fareed. 1997. "The Rise of Illiberal Democracy." *Foreign Affairs* 76 (6), (November/December): 22–43.

Zaki, Moheb. 1995. *Civil Society & Democratization in Egypt, 1981–1994.* Cairo: Konrad Adenauer Stiftung.

Zolberg, Aristide R. 1966. *Creating Political Order: The Party-States of West Africa.* Chicago: Rand McNally.

Media Sources

Al-Ahali (Egypt)
Al-Ahram (Egypt)
Al-Ahram Weekly Online
Agence France-Presse
Associated Press
BBC Monitoring Service
Cairo Times
Country Watch Country Reports
Economist
Financial Times
Foreign Broadcast Information Service (FBIS-APA Series)
Foreign Broadcast Information Service (FBIS-NES Series)
Foreign Broadcast Information Service (FBIS-SAS Series)
Japan Economic Newswire
Middle East Economic Digest
National Public Radio
New Straits Times (Malaysia)
New York Times
Newshour with Jim Lehrer

Newsweek International
Reuters News
Sidney Morning Herald
Wall Street Journal
Washington Post

Index

Note: *Italicized page numbers refer to tables and figures*